ABRAHAM LINCOLN.

From a photograph by Alexander Hesler, Chicago, 1858.

ABRAHAM LINCOLN

The True Story of a Great Life

BY
WILLIAM H. HERNDON AND JESSE W. WEIK

WITH AN INTRODUCTION
BY HORACE WHITE

ILLUSTRATED

IN TWO VOLUMES
VOL. I

NEW YORK
D. APPLETON AND COMPANY
1900

TO

THE MEN AND WOMEN OF AMERICA

WHO HAVE GROWN UP SINCE HIS TRAGIC DEATH, AND

WHO HAVE YET TO LEARN THE STORY OF HIS LIFE,

THIS RECORD OF

ABRAHAM LINCOLN

IS FAITHFULLY INSCRIBED

ORIGINAL PREFACE TO HERNDON'S LINCOLN.

A QUARTER of a century has well-nigh rolled by since the tragic death of Abraham Lincoln. The prejudice and bitterness with which he was assailed have disappeared from the minds of men, and the world is now beginning to view him as a great historical character. Those who knew and walked with him are gradually passing away, and ere long the last man who ever heard his voice or grasped his hand will have gone from earth. With a view to throwing a light on some attributes of Lincoln's character heretofore obscure, and thus contributing to the great fund of history which goes down to posterity, these volumes are given to the world.

If Mr. Lincoln is destined to fill that exalted station in history or attain that high rank in the estimation of the coming generations which has been predicted of him, it is alike just to his memory and the proper legacy of mankind that the whole truth concerning him should be known. If the story of his life is truthfully and courageously told—nothing colored or suppressed; nothing false either written or suggested—the reader will see and feel the presence of the living man. He will, in fact, live with him and be moved to think and act with him. If, on the other hand, the story is colored or the facts in any degree suppressed, the reader will be not only misled, but imposed upon as well. At last the truth will come, and no man need hope to evade it.

" There is but one true history in the world," said one of Lincoln's closest friends to whom I confided the project of writing a history of his life several years ago, "and that is the Bible. It is often said of the old characters portrayed there that they were bad men. They are contrasted with other characters in history, and much to the detriment of the old worthies. The reason is, that the Biblical historian told the whole truth—the inner life. The heart and secret acts are brought to light and faithfully photographed. In other histories virtues are perpetuated and vices concealed. If the life of King David had been written by an ordinary historian the affair of Uriah would at most have been a quashed indictment with a denial of all the substantial facts. You should not forget there is a skeleton in every house. The finest character dug out thoroughly, photographed honestly, and judged by that standard of morality or excellence which we exact for other men is never perfect. Some men are cold, some lewd, some dishonest, some cruel, and many a combination of all. The trail of the serpent is over them all! Excellence consists, not in the absence of these attributes, but in the degree in which they are redeemed by the virtues and graces of life. Lincoln's character will, I am certain, bear close scrutiny. I am

not afraid of you in this direction. Don't let anything deter you from digging to the bottom ; yet
don't forget that if Lincoln had some faults, Washington had more—few men have less. In drawing
the portrait tell the world what the skeleton was
with Lincoln. What gave him that peculiar melancholy? What cancer had he inside?"

Some persons will doubtless object to the narration of certain facts which appear here for the first
time, and which they contend should have been
consigned to the tomb. Their pretense is that no
good can come from such ghastly exposures. To
such over-sensitive souls, if any such exist, my
answer is that these facts are indispensable to a full
knowledge of Mr. Lincoln in all the walks of life.
In order properly to comprehend him and the stirring, bloody times in which he lived, and in which
he played such an important part, we must have all
the facts—we must be prepared to take him as he
was.

In determining Lincoln's title to greatness we
must not only keep in mind the times in which
he lived, but we must, to a certain extent, measure him with other men. Many of our great men
and our statesmen, it is true, have been self-made,
rising gradually through struggles to the topmost
round of the ladder; but Lincoln rose from a lower
depth than any of them. His origin was in that
unknown and sunless bog in which history never
made a foot-print. I should be remiss in my duty
if I did not throw the light on this part of the
picture, so that the world may realize what mar-

vellous contrast one phase of his life presents to another.

The purpose of these volumes is to narrate facts, avoiding as much as possible any expression of opinion, and leaving the reader to form his own conclusions. Use has been made of the views and recollections of other persons, but only those known to be truthful and trustworthy. A thread of the narrative of Lincoln's life runs through the work, but an especial feature is an analysis of the man and a portrayal of his attributes and characteristics. The attempt to delineate his qualities, his nature and its manifestations, may occasion frequent repetitions of fact, but if truthfully done this can only augment the store of matter from which posterity is to learn what manner of man he was.

The object of this work is to deal with Mr. Lincoln individually and domestically; as lawyer, as citizen, as statesman. Especial attention is given to the history of his youth and early manhood; and while dwelling on this portion of his life the liberty is taken to insert many things which would be omitted or suppressed in other places, where the cast-iron rules that govern magazine-writing are allowed to prevail. Thus much is stated in advance, so that no one need be disappointed in the scope and extent of the work. The endeavor is to keep Lincoln in sight all the time; to cling close to his side all the way through—leaving to others the more comprehensive task of writing a history of his times. I have no theory of his life to establish or destroy. Mr. Lincoln was my warm, devoted friend.

I always loved him, and I revere his name to this day. My purpose to tell the truth about him need occasion no apprehension ; for I know that " God's naked truth," as Carlyle puts it, can never injure the fame of Abraham Lincoln. It will stand that or any other test, and at last untarnished will reach the loftiest niche in American history.

My long personal association with Mr. Lincoln gave me special facilities in the direction of obtaining materials for these volumes. Such were our relations during all that portion of his life when he was rising to distinction, that I had only to exercise a moderate vigilance in order to gather and preserve the real data of his personal career. Being strongly drawn to the man, and believing in his destiny, I was not unobservant or careless in this respect. It thus happened that I became the personal depositary of the larger part of the most valuable *Lincolniana* in existence. Out of this store the major portion of the materials of the following volumes has been drawn. I take this, my first general opportunity, to return thanks to the scores of friends in Kentucky, Indiana, Illinois, and elsewhere for the information they have so generously furnished and the favors they have so kindly extended me. Their names are too numerous for separate mention, but the recompense of each one will be the consciousness of having contributed a share towards a true history of the " first American."

Over twenty years ago I began this book; but an active life at the bar has caused me to postpone

the work of composition, until, now, being somewhat advanced in years, I find myself unable to
carry out the undertaking.   Within the past three
years I have been assisted in the preparation of the
book by Mr. Jesse W. Weik, of Greencastle, Ind.,
whose industry, patience, and literary zeal have not
only lessened my labors, but have secured for him
the approbation of Lincoln's friends and admirers.
Mr. Weik has by his personal investigation greatly
enlarged our common treasure of facts and information.   He has for several years been indefatigable
in exploring the course of Lincoln's life.   In no
particular has he been satisfied with anything taken
at second hand.   He has visited—as I also did in
1865—Lincoln's birthplace in Kentucky, his early
homes in Indiana and Illinois, and together, so to
speak, he and I have followed our hero continuously and attentively till he left Springfield in 1861
to be inaugurated President.   We have retained
the original MSS. in all cases, and they have never
been out of our hands.   In relating facts therefore,
we refer to them in most cases, rather than to the
statements of other biographers.

This brief preliminary statement is made so that
posterity, in so far as posterity may be interested in
the subject, may know that the vital matter of this
narrative has been deduced directly from the consciousness, reminiscences, and collected data of

WILLIAM H. HERNDON.

SPRINGFIELD, ILL.,
      November 1, 1888.

CONTENTS.

                                                                    PAGES
INTRODUCTION . . . . xix–xxviii

CHAPTER I.

Date and place of Lincoln's birth.—The interview with
J. L. Scripps.—Lincoln's reference to his mother.—The
Bible record.—The journal of William Calk.—The death of
Abraham Lincoln, the President's grandfather.—Mordecai's
revenge.—Thomas Lincoln, his marriage and married life.—
Nancy Hanks, the President's mother.—Her sadness, her
disposition and mental nature.—The camp-meeting at Eliza-
bethtown. 1–12

CHAPTER II.

Sarah Lincoln.—She attends school with her brother
Abraham.—The tribute by Helm to Abe, the little boy.—
Boyhood exploits with John Duncan and Austin Gollaher.—
Dissatisfaction of Thomas Lincoln with Kentucky.—The
removal to Indiana.—The "half-faced camp."—Thomas
and Betsy Sparrow follow.—How Thomas Lincoln and the
Sparrows farmed.—Life in the Lincoln cabin.—Abe and
David Turnham go to mill.—Appearance of the "milk
sick" in the Pigeon Creek settlement.—Death of the Spar-
rows.—Death of Nancy Lincoln.—The widowerhood of
Thomas Lincoln.—He marries Sarah Bush Johnston.—The
Lincoln and Johnston children.—'Tilda Johnston's indiscre-
tion.—Attending school.—Abe's gallantry toward Kate
Roby.—"Blue-Nose" Crawford and the book.—Schoolboy
poetry.—Abe's habits of study.—Testimony of his stepmother. 13–41

CHAPTER III.

PAGES

Abe reads his first law-book.—The fight between John Johnston and William Grigsby.—Recollections of Elizabeth Crawford.—Marriage of Sarah Lincoln and Aaron Grigsby. —The wedding song.—More poetry.—Abe attends court at Booneville.—The accident at Gordon's mill.—Borrowing law-books of Judge Pitcher.—Compositions on Temperance and Government.—The journey with Allen Gentry to New Orleans.—Return to Indiana.—Customs and superstition of the pioneers.—Reappearance of the "milk sick."—Removal to Illinois.—Abe and his pet dog.   42–59

CHAPTER IV.

The settlement in Illinois.—Splitting rails with John Hanks.—Building the boat for Offut.—The return to Illinois.—New Salem described.—Clerking on the election board.—The lizard story.—Salesman in Offut's store.—The wrestle with Jack Armstrong.—Studying in the store.—Disappearance of Offut.—The *Talisman.*—Oliphant's poetry.— The reception at Springfield.—The Captain's wife.—Return trip of the *Talisman.*—Rowan Herndon and Lincoln pilot her through.—The navigability of the Sangamon fully demonstrated.—The vessel reaches Beardstown.   .   .   .   60–82

CHAPTER V.

The Black Hawk war.—Lincoln elected captain—Under arrest.—Protecting the Indian.—Recollections of a comrade.—Lincoln re-enlists as a private.—Return to New Salem.—Candidate for the Legislature.—The handbill.— First political speech.—The canvass.—Defeat.—Partnership in the store with Berry.—The trade with William Greene.— Failure of the business.—Law studies.—Pettifogging.— Stories and poetry.—Referee in rural sports.—Deputy surveyor under John Calhoun.—Studying with Mentor Graham. —Postmaster at New Salem.—The incident with Chandler.—Feats of strength.—Second race for the Legislature.— Election.   83–118

CHAPTER VI.

PAGES

Lincoln falls in love with Anne Rutledge.—The old story.—Description of the girl.—The affair with John McNeil.—Departure of McNeil for New York.—Anne learns of the change of name.—Her faith under fire.—Lincoln appears on the scene.—Courting in dead earnest.—Lincoln's proposal accepted.—The ghost of another love.—Death of Anne.—Effect on Lincoln's mind.—His suffering.—Kindness of Bowlin Greene.—"Oh, why should the spirit of mortal be proud?"—Letter to Dr. Drake.—Return of McNamar. 119–133

CHAPTER VII.

An amusing courtship.—Lincoln meets Mary S. Owens.—Her nature, education, and mind.—Lincoln's boast.—He pays his addresses.—The lady's letters to Herndon.—Lincoln's letters.—His avowals of affection.—The letter to Mrs. Browning.—Miss Owens' estimate of Lincoln. . . 134–152

CHAPTER VIII.

Lincoln a member of the Legislature at Vandalia.—First meeting with Douglas.—The society of Vandalia.—Pioneer legislation.—Deputy surveyor under Thomas M. Neal.—Candidate for the Legislature again.—Another handbill.—Favors "Woman's Rights."—The letter to Col. Robert Allen.—The canvass.—The answer to George Forquer.—The election, Lincoln leading the ticket.—The "Long Nine."—Reckless legislation.—The "DeWitt Clinton" of Illinois.—Internal improvements.—The removal of the capital to Springfield.—The Committee on Finance.—The New England importation.—The Lincoln-Stone protest.—Return of the "Long Nine" to Springfield.—Lincoln removes to Springfield.—Licensed to practise law.—In partnership with John T. Stuart.—Early practice.—Generosity of Joshua F. Speed.—The bar of Springfield.—Speed's store.—Political discussions.—More poetry.—Lincoln addresses the "Young Men's Lyceum."—The debate in the

PAGES

Presbyterian Church.—Elected to the Legislature again.—
Answering Col. Dick Taylor on the stump.—Rescue of
Baker.—Last canvass for the Legislature.—The Thomas
"skinning."—The Presidential canvass of 1840.   .   . 153–190

CHAPTER IX.

Lincoln still unmarried.—The Todd family.—Mary Todd.
—Introduced to Lincoln.—The courtship.—The flirtation
with Douglas.—The advice of Speed.—How Lincoln broke
the engagement.—Preparations for marriage.—A disap-
pointed bride.—A crazy groom.—Speed takes Lincoln to
Kentucky.—Restored spirits.—Return of Lincoln to Illinois.
—Letters to Speed.—The party at Simeon Francis's house.
—The reconciliation.—The marriage.—The duel with James
Shields.—The "Rebecca" letters.—"Cathleen" invokes
the muse.—Whiteside's account of the duel.—Merryman's
account.—Lincoln's address before the Washingtonian Soci-
ety.—Meeting with Martin Van Buren.—Partnership with
Stephen T. Logan.—Partnership with William H. Herndon.
—Congressional aspirations.—Nomination and election of
John J. Hardin.—The Presidential campaign of 1844.—Lin-
coln takes the stump in Southern Indiana.—Lincoln nomi-
nated for Congress.—The canvass against Peter Cartwright.
—Lincoln elected.—In Congress.—The "Spot Resolutions."
—Opposes the Mexican war.—Letters to Herndon.—
Speeches in Congress.—Stumping through New England.—
A Congressman's troubles.—A characteristic letter.—End of
Congressional term.   191–280

CHAPTER X.

Lincoln takes part in the campaign in Massachusetts in
1848.—The account of Edward L. Pierce.—Report of Boston *Advertiser.*—Speeches in Boston, Dorchester, Chelsea,
Dedham, and Cambridge.—Lincoln's impression on the
Whigs.—Meets Governor Seward.—Editorial in Lowell
Journal and Courier.—Reminiscence of ex-Governor Gardner.—Recollections of George H. Monroe.   .   .   . 281–294

CHAPTER XI.

PAGES

Early married life.—Boarding at the "Globe Tavern."—
A plucky little wife.—Niagara Falls.—The patent for lifting
vessels over shoals.—Candidate for Commissioner of the
Land Office.—The appointment of Butterfield.—The offer
of Territorial posts by President Taylor.—A journey to
Washington and incidents.—Return to Illinois.—Settling
down to practice law.—Life on the circuit.—Story-telling.—
Habits as lawyer and methods of study.—Law-office of Lincoln and Herndon.—Recollections of Littlefield.—Studying
Euclid.—Taste for literature.—Lincoln's first appearance in
the Supreme Court of Illinois.—Professional honor and personal honesty.—The juror in the divorce case.   .   . 295-331

LIST OF ILLUSTRATIONS.

VOL. I.

FACING
PAGE

Abraham Lincoln, from a photograph by Alexander Hesler, Chicago, 1858. . . . . . . *Frontispiece*

W. H. Herndon 1

The Lincoln family record 5

Sarah Bush Lincoln 28

Lines written by Lincoln on the leaf of his school-book in his fourteenth year 37

House near Farmington, Coles County, Illinois, in which Thomas Lincoln died 61

Mary S. Owens 138

Springfield Court-House. Stuart and Lincoln's office, in 1839 . 172

Items from Lincoln's fee-book, in his handwriting . . . 177

First Presbyterian Church, Springfield 183

Joshua Fry Speed and wife 195

The Edwards residence, Springfield, in which Lincoln and Mary Todd were married, and in which the latter died . . . 215

General James Shields 237

U. S. Court Building, Springfield, 1850–1860. Lincoln and Logan's office 250

Lincoln and Herndon's law-office in 1860 257

Mary Todd Lincoln, Rev. Peter Cartwright, Stephen T. Logan . 271

The Globe Tavern, Springfield 295

INTRODUCTION.

I WAS called upon during the lifetime of Mr. Herndon to write for the second edition of this work a chapter on the Lincoln-Douglas campaign of 1858. After this had been done and the book had been revised for the press, I was requested by the publishers to add something in the nature of a character sketch of Mr. Lincoln as I knew him before his fame had spread much beyond the confines of Illinois, and to tell what were those qualities that made him so attractive then. Of course, they were the same qualities which made him attractive afterward on a wider scale. The popular judgment of him is, in the main, correct and unshakable. I say in the main, because there is in this judgment a tendency to apotheosis which, while pardonable, is not historical, and will not last.

At the time when he was preparing himself unconsciously to be the nation's leader in a great crisis the only means of gaining public attention was by public speech. The press did not exist for him, or for the people among whom he lived. The ambitious young men of the day must make their mark by oratory, or not at all. There was no division of labor between the speaker and the editor. If a man was to gain any popularity he must gain it by talking into the faces of the people. He must have a ready tongue, and must be prepared to meet all comers and to accept all challenges. Stump-speaking, wrestling, story-telling, and horse-racing were the only amusements of the people. In the first three of these Mr. Lincoln excelled. He grew up in this atmosphere, as did all his rivals. It was a school to develop all the debating powers that the community possessed, and to bring them to a high degree of perfection. Polish was not necessary to success, but plainness of diction was. The successful speaker was he who could make himself best understood by the common people, and in turn could best understand them.

Among the earliest accounts that we get of Mr. Lincoln we find him talking to other boys from some kind of a platform. He had a natural gift, and he exercised it as opportunity came to him. When he arrived at man's estate these opportunities came as often as could be desired. Other young men gifted in the same way were growing up around him. Douglas, Baker, Trumbull, Hardin, Browning, Yates, Archibald Williams, Josiah Lamborn, and Lisle Smith were among them. All these had the same kind of training for public preferment that Lincoln had; some of them had more book learning, but not much more. We have his own word for it that he was as ambitious of such preferment as Douglas was; and this was putting it in the superlative degree.

The popular conception of Mr. Lincoln as one not seeking public honors, but not avoiding public duties, is a *post bellum* growth, very wide of the mark. He was entirely human in this regard, but his desire for political preferment was hedged about by a sense of obligation to the truth which nothing could shake. This fidelity to truth was ingrained and unchangeable. In all the speeches I ever heard him make—and they were many—he never even insinuated an untruth, nor did he ever fail when stating his opponent's positions to state them fully and fairly. He often stated his opponent's position better than his opponent did or could. To say what was false, or even to leave his hearers under a wrong impression, was impossible to him. Within this high inclosure he was as ambitious of earthly honors as any man of his time. Furthermore, he was an adept at log-rolling or any political game that did not involve falsity. I was Secretary of the Republican State Committee of Illinois during some years when he was in active campaign work. He was often present at meetings of the committee, although not a member, and took part in the committee work. His judgment was very much deferred to in such matters. He was one of the shrewdest politicians of the State. Nobody had had more experience in that way, nobody knew better than he what was passing in the minds of the people. Nobody knew better how to turn things to advantage politically, and nobody was readier to take such advantage, provided it did not involve dishonorable means. He could not cheat people out of their votes any more than out of their money. The Abraham Lincoln that some people have pictured to themselves, sitting in his dingy law office, working over his cases till the voice of duty roused him, never existed. If this had been his type he never would have been called at all. It was precisely because he was up and stirring, and in hot, incessant competition with his fellows for earthly honors, that the public eye became fixed upon him and the public ear attuned to his words. Fortunate was it for all of us that he was no shrinking patriot, that he was moved as other men are moved, so that his fellows might take heed of him and know him as one of themselves, and as fit to be their leader in a crisis.

Let me repeat and emphasize what I have here said. Mr. Lincoln never gave his assent, so far as my knowledge goes, to any plan or project for getting votes that would not have borne the full light of day. At the same time, he had no objection to the getting of votes by the pledge of offices, nor was he too particular what kind of men got the offices. His preference was always for good men; but he could not resist pressure where persons were concerned, even though his conscience told him that he was doing wrong.

We have seen what kind of debating school Mr. Lincoln grew up in. It was the best possible school for him, and it was an advantage to him that he had able men for his competitors. Among them was Stephen A. Douglas, the most versatile, indomitable, and unscrupulous of all of them. He was Lincoln's rival, as is shown in these pages, for almost everything, from the hand of Mary Todd to the presidency of the United States. He had the strength and presence of a lion, with all the cunning of a fox. He possessed every quality which wins popular favor and high station except veracity, and I know of nothing in the pages of history more cheering to pious souls than the eventual triumph of Honest Abe over the Little Giant.

It was by restless competition and rough-and-tumble with Douglas and others that Mr. Lincoln acquired that rare power of expression, by mouth and pen, which drew to himself the attention of the State and afterward of the nation and the world. He rarely used ornament in his speeches. Although gifted with the power of humor to an extraordinary degree, he seldom employed it in his later years except in private circles. Thus it came about that this growing master of logic, this profound and earnest debater of the most serious questions of the day, was the most popular of tavern loungers, and could draw more people together and hold them longer by mere drollery and *cameraderie* than any other man I ever knew. Mr. Lincoln's nature was one of almost child-like sweetness. He did not " put you at your ease " when you came into his presence. You felt at your ease without being put there. He never assumed superiority over anybody in the ordinary intercourse of life.

A good test of this trait in his character was furnished in my own experience. When I was first thrown into his society I was just out of college, and was as callow and as self-confident as boys usually are at that time of life. Mr. Lincoln was at the maturity of his powers. I was often with him when he had no other companion. In our intercourse he always paid marked deference to my opinions, and if we differed he would argue the point with me as earnestly as though I had been the opposing counsel in a lawsuit. And this he would do with anybody, young or old, ignorant or learned. I never heard him express contempt for any man's honest errors, although he would sometimes make a droll remark or tell a funny story about them. Deference to other people's opinions was habitual to him. There was no calculation, no politics in it. It was part and parcel of his sense of equal rights. His democracy was of the unconscious kind—he did not know anything different from it. Coupled with this was a habit of unselfishness and kindly temper most engaging to all who knew him or had any dealings with him. At the same time he knew when he was imposed upon, and it was unsafe for anybody to presume upon his good nature or to take him for a flat.

But more than intellectual gifts, more than good-fellowship, did the sense of justice give him his hold on others. That was a magnetic field whose influences could not be escaped. He carried it as unconsciously as he carried his hair. The Athenians would never have ostracized him—indeed, they would never have called him the Just. They would have taken him as they took the bees on Hymettus—as one naturally searching after sweet things.

To say that Mr. Lincoln was a man who had the courage of his convictions would be rather an under-statement. This was part and parcel of his sense of justice. He wore it as he wore his clothes, except that it fitted him much better than his garments usually did. At the time I first knew him it was irksome to very many of his friends to be told that there ought to be an efficient fugitive slave law. But it was his conviction as a lawyer that there ought to be one, and he never failed to say so when interrogated, or when occasion required that that subject should be touched upon. And it is a fact that abolitionists like Lovejoy and Codding would take this from Lincoln without murmuring, when they would not take it from anybody else. He never would echo the popular cry, "No more slave States!" Whenever this subject was discussed he would say that if a Territory having the requisite population and belonging to us should apply for admission to the Union without fraud or constraint, yet with slavery, he could not see any other disposition to be made of her than to admit her. And when he had said this, even to an audience of radical antislavery men, there would be no protestations. Those who were not convinced would observe a respectful silence.

Mr. Lincoln's facial expression when in repose

and when animated presented most remarkable
contrasts. I have before me a photograph of him
taken at Pittsfield, Illinois, during the campaign
of 1858. It looks as I have seen him a hundred
times, his lantern jaws and large mouth and
solid nose firmly set, his sunken eyes looking
at nothing yet not unexpressive, his wrinkled and
retreating forehead cut off by a mass of tousled
hair, with a shade of melancholy drawn like a veil
over his whole face. Nothing more unlike this
can be imagined than the same Lincoln when taking part in a conversation, or addressing an audience, or telling a story. The dull, listless features dropped like a mask. The melancholy shadow disappeared in a twinkling. The eye began
to sparkle, the mouth to smile, the whole countenance was wreathed with animation, so that a
stranger would have said: "Why, this man, so
angular and somber a moment ago, is really handsome."

What more can be said of the qualities that first
made Mr. Lincoln attractive to his contempora-
ries? These were debating power, honesty of
purpose, a child-like temper, purity of life, and
courage of conviction. All these traits will be
seen in the following pages, rising, unfolding, ex-
panding in a regular, orderly, human way as the
young Lincoln grew to mature years.

What Mr. Lincoln was after he became President can be best understood by knowing what he
was before. The world owes more to William
H. Herndon for this particular knowledge than to

all other persons taken together. It is no exaggeration to say that his death, which took place at his farm near Springfield, Illinois, March 18, 1891, removed from earth the person who, of all others, had most thoroughly searched the sources of Mr. Lincoln's biography and had most attentively, intelligently, and also lovingly studied his character. He was generous in imparting his information to others. Almost every life of Lincoln published since the tragedy at Ford's Theatre has been enriched by his labors. He was nine years the junior of Mr. Lincoln. Their partnership began in 1843, and it continued until it was dissolved by the death of the senior member. Between them there was never an unkind word or thought. When Mr. Lincoln became President, Mr. Herndon could have had his fortunes materially advanced under the new Administration by saying a word. He was a poor man then and always, but he chose to remain in his more humble station and to earn his bread by his daily labor.

Some six years ago Mr. Herndon conceived the project of writing a series of magazine articles intended to portray the youth and early manhood of Lincoln. Being somewhat infirm, he called Mr. Weik to his assistance, as he has explained in his preface. The magazine articles expanded insensibly to the present volumes. Lincolniana is increasing and is destined to increase. It has been enriched within recent years by the indispensable but too massive work of Nicolay and Hay, by the masterly essay of Schurz, and by the posthumous lecture of Greeley, which latter, being in reality if not in terms a hearty, ungrudging confession that he had underestimated Lincoln in his lifetime, is doubly welcome. As a portraiture of the man Lincoln—and this is what we look for above all things in a biography—I venture to think that Mr. Herndon's work will never be surpassed.

HORACE WHITE.

NEW YORK, *February, 1892.*

Your Friend
W. H. Herndon

THE LIFE OF LINCOLN.

CHAPTER I.

BEYOND the fact that he was born on the 12th day of February, 1809, in Hardin county, Kentucky, Mr. Lincoln usually had but little to say of himself, the lives of his parents, or the history of the family before their removal to Indiana. If he mentioned the subject at all, it was with great reluctance and significant reserve. There was something about his origin he never cared to dwell upon. His nomination for the Presidency in 1860, however, made the publication of his life a necessity, and attracted to Springfield an army of campaign biographers and newspaper men. They met him in his office, stopped him in his walks, and followed him to his house. Artists came to paint his picture, and sculptors to make his bust. His autographs were in demand, and people came long distances to shake him by the hand. This sudden elevation to national prominence found Mr. Lincoln unprepared in a great measure for the unaccustomed demonstrations that awaited him. While he was easy of approach and equally courteous to all, yet, as he said to me one evening after a long day of hand-shaking, he could not understand why people should make so much over him.

Among the earliest newspaper men to arrive in Springfield after the Chicago convention was the late J. L. Scripps of the Chicago *Tribune*, who proposed to prepare a history of his life. Mr. Lincoln deprecated the idea of writing even a campaign biography. " Why, Scripps," said he, " it is a great piece of folly to attempt to make anything out of me or my early life. It can all be condensed into a single sentence, and that sentence you will find in Gray's Elegy,

' The short and simple annals of the poor.'

That's my life, and that's all you or anyone else can make out of it."

He did, however, communicate some facts and meagre incidents of his early days, and, with the matter thus obtained, Mr. Scripps prepared his book. Soon after the death of Lincoln I received a letter from Scripps, in which, among other things, he recalled the meeting with Lincoln, and the view he took of the biography matter.

" Lincoln seemed to be painfully impressed," he wrote, " with the extreme poverty of his early surroundings, and the utter absence of all romantic and heroic elements. He communicated some facts to me concerning his ancestry, which he did not wish to have published then, and which I have never spoken of or alluded to before."

What the facts referred to by Mr. Scripps were

we do not know; for he died several years ago without, so far as is known, revealing them to anyone.

On the subject of his ancestry and origin I only remember one time when Mr. Lincoln ever referred to it. It was about 1850, when he and I were driving in his one-horse buggy to the court in Menard county, Illinois. The suit we were going to try was one in which we were likely, either directly or collaterally, to touch upon the subject of hereditary traits. During the ride he spoke, for the first time in my hearing, of his mother, dwelling on her characteristics, and mentioning or enumerating what qualities he inherited from her. He said, among other things, that she was the daughter of Lucy Hanks and a well-bred but obscure Virginia farmer or planter; and he argued that from this last source came his power of analysis, his logic, his mental activity, his ambition, and all the qualities that distinguished him from the other members and descendants of the Hanks family.

In only two instances did Mr. Lincoln over his own hand leave any record of his history or family descent. One of these was the modest bit of autobiography furnished to Jesse W. Fell, in 1859, in which, after stating that his parents were born in Virginia of "undistinguished or second families," he makes the brief mention of his mother, saying that she came "of a family of the name of Hanks."* The other record was the register of marriages, births, and deaths which he made in his father's Bible. The

---

* If anyone will take the pains to read the Fell autobiography they will be struck with Lincoln's meagre reference to his mother. He even fails to give her maiden or Christian name, and devotes but three lines to her family. A history of the Lincolns occupies almost an entire page.

latter now lies before me. That portion of the page which probably contained the record of the marriage of his parents, Thomas Lincoln and Nancy Hanks, has been lost; but fortunately the records of Washington county, Kentucky, and the certificate of the minister who performed the marriage ceremony—the Rev. Jesse Head—fix the fact and date of the latter on the 12th day of June, 1806.

On the 10th day of February in the following year a daughter Sarah * was born, and two years later, on the 12th of February, the subject of these memoirs came into the world. After him came the last child, a boy—named Thomas after his father—who lived but a few days. No mention of his existence is found in the Bible record.

Abraham Lincoln, the grandfather of the President, emigrated to Jefferson county, Kentucky, from Virginia, about 1780, and from that time forward the former State became an important one in the history of the family, for in it was destined to be born its most illustrious member. About five years before this, a handful of Virginians had started across the

---

* Most biographers of Lincoln, in speaking of Mr. Lincoln's sister, call her Nancy, some—notably Nicolay and Hay—insisting that she was known by that name among her family and friends. In this they are in error. I have interviewed the different members of the Hanks and Lincoln families who survived the President, and her name was invariably given as Sarah. The mistake, I think, arises from the fact that, in the Bible record referred to, all that portion relating to the birth of " Sarah, daughter of Thomas and Nancy Lincoln," down to the word Nancy has been torn away, and the latter name has therefore been taken erroneously for that of the daughter. Reading the entry of Abraham's birth below satisfies one that it must refer to the mother.

LINCOLN FAMILY RECORD,

Nancy Lincoln, was born Feb
10th 1807 -
Thomas Lincoln, son of Thos. &
Nancy Lincoln was born Oct.
13th 1809 -
Sarah Bush, first married to
Daniel Johnston, and afterwards
married with Thos. Lincoln,
was born Decbr 13th 1788 -
Jno D. Johnston, son of Daniel &
Sarah Johnston, was born May
8th, married to Nancy Burr
13th 1834 -

Thomas Lincoln married to second
Johnston Decbr 2nd 1819 -
Sarah Lincoln, daughter of Thos.
Lincoln, was married to
Aug 8 -

Abraham Lincoln, son of Thos.
Lincoln was married to Mary
Todd Novr 4th 1842 -
John D. Johnston was married to his
second wife, Nancy Jane Mc
March 5, 1851

John D. Johnston son
of

mountains for Kentucky, and in the company, besides their historian, William Calk,—whose diary recently came to light,—was one Abraham Hanks. They were evidently a crowd of jolly young men bent on adventure and fun, but their sport was attended with frequent disasters. Their journey began at " Mr. Priges' tavern on the Rapidan.'' When only a few days out " Hanks' Dog's leg got broke." Later in the course of the journey, Hanks and another companion became separated from the rest of the party and were lost in the mountains for two days ; in crossing a stream "Abraham's saddle turned over and his load all fell in Indian creek"; finally they meet their brethren from whom they have been separated and then pursue their way without further interruption. Returning emigrants whom they meet, according to the journal of Calk, " tell such News of the indians " that certain members of the company are " afrade to go aney further." The following day more or less demoralization takes place among the members of this pioneer party when the announcement is made, as their chronicler so faithfully records it, that " Philip Drake Bakes bread without washing his hands." This was an unpardonable sin, and at it they revolted. A day later the record shows that " Abram turns Back." Beyond this we shall never know what became of Abraham Hanks, for no further mention of him is made in this or any other history. He may have returned to Virginia and become, for aught we know, one of the President's ancestors on the maternal side of the house ; but if so his illustrious descendant was never able to establish the fact or trace his lineage satisfactorily beyond the first generation which preceded him. He never mentioned who his maternal grandfather was, if indeed he knew.

His paternal grandfather, Abraham Lincoln,* the pioneer from Virginia, met his death within two years after his settlement in Kentucky at the hands of the Indians; "not in battle," as his distinguished grandson tells us, "but by stealth, when he was laboring to open a farm in the forest." The story of his death in sight of his youngest son Thomas, then only six years old, is by no means a new one to the world. In fact I have often heard the President describe the tragedy as he had inherited the story from his father. The dead pioneer had three sons, Mordecai, Josiah, and Thomas, in the order named. When the father fell, Mordecai, having hastily sent Josiah to the neighboring fort after assistance, ran into the cabin, and pointing his rifle through a crack between the logs, prepared for defense. Presently an Indian came stealing up to the dead father's body. Beside the latter sat the little boy Thomas. Mordecai took deliberate aim at a silver crescent which hung suspended from the Indian's breast, and brought him to the ground. Josiah returned from the fort with the desired relief, and

---

* "They [the Lincolns] were also called Linkhorns. The old settlers had a way of pronouncing names not as they were spelled, but rather, it seemed, as they pleased. Thus they called Medcalf 'Medcap,' and Kaster they pronounced 'Custard.' "—MS. letter, Charles Friend, March 19, 1866.

the savages were easily dispersed, leaving behind one dead and one wounded.

The tragic death of his father filled Mordecai with an intense hatred of the Indians—a feeling from which he never recovered. It was ever with him like an avenging spirit. From Jefferson county he removed to Grayson, where he spent the remainder of his days. A correspondent * from there wrote me in 1865 : " Old Mordecai was easily stirred up by the sight of an Indian. One time, hearing of a few Indians passing through the county, he mounted his horse, and taking his rifle on his shoulder, followed on after them and was gone two days. When he returned he said he left one lying in a sink hole. The Indians, he said, had killed his father, and he was determined before he died to have satisfaction." The youngest boy, Thomas, retained a vivid recollection of his father's death, which, together with other reminiscences of his boyhood, he was fond of relating later in life to his children to relieve the tedium of long winter evenings. Mordecai and Josiah,† both remaining in Kentucky, became the heads of good-sized families, and although never known or

* W. T. Claggett, unpublished MS.

† " I knew Mordecai and Josiah Lincoln intimately. They were excellent men, plain, moderately educated, candid in their manners and intercourse, and looked upon as honorable as any men I have ever heard of. Mordecai was the oldest son, and his father having been killed by the Indians before the law of primogeniture was repealed, he inherited a very competent estate. The others were poor. Mordecai was celebrated for his bravery, and had been in the early campaigns of the West."–Henry Pirtle, letter, June 17, 1865, MS.

heard of outside the limits of the neighborhoods in which they lived, were intelligent, well-to-do men. In Thomas, roving and shiftless, to whom was "reserved the honor of an illustrious paternity," are we alone interested. He was, we are told, five feet ten inches high, weighed one hundred and ninety-five pounds, had a well-rounded face, dark hazel eyes, coarse black hair, and was slightly stoop-shouldered. His build was so compact that Dennis Hanks used to say he could not find the point of separation between his ribs. He was proverbially slow of movement, mentally and physically; was careless, inert, and dull; was sinewy, and gifted with great strength; was inoffensively quiet and peaceable, but when roused to resistance a danger-ous antagonist. He had a liking for jokes and stories, which was one of the few traits he trans-mitted to his illustrious son; was fond of the chase, and had no marked aversion for the bottle, though in the latter case he indulged no more freely than the average Kentuckian of his day. At the time of his marriage to Nancy Hanks he could neither read nor write; but his wife, who was gifted with more education, and was otherwise his mental supe-rior, taught him, it is said, to write his name and to read—at least, he was able in later years to spell his way slowly through the Bible. In his relig-ious belief he first affiliated with the Free-Will Baptists. After his removal to Indiana he changed his adherence to the Presbyterians—or Predestina-rians, as they were then called—and later united with the Christian—vulgarly called Campbellite—

Church, in which latter faith he is supposed to have died. He was a carpenter by trade, and essayed farming too ; but in this, as in almost every other undertaking, he was singularly unsuccessful. He was placed in possession of several tracts of land at different times in his life, but was never able to pay for a single one of them. The farm on which he died was one his son purchased, providing a life estate therein for him and his wife. He never fell in with the routine of labor ; was what some people would call unfortunate or unlucky in all his business ventures—if in reality he ever made one—and died near the village of Farmington in Coles county, Illinois, on the 17th day of January, 1851. His son, on account of sickness in his own family, was unable to be present at his father's bedside, or witness his death. To those who notified him of his probable demise he wrote : " I sincerely hope that father may yet recover his health ; but at all events tell him to remember to call upon and confide in our great and good and merciful Maker, who will not turn away from him in any extremity. He notes the fall of a sparrow, and numbers the hairs of our heads ; and He will not forget the dying man who puts his trust in him. Say to him that if we could meet now it is doubtful whether it would not be more painful than pleasant ; but that if it be his lot to go now he will soon have a joyous meeting with the many loved ones gone before, and where the rest of us, through the help of God, hope ere long to join them." *

---

* MS. letter to John Johnston, Jan. 12, 1851.

Nancy Hanks, the mother of the President, at a very early age was taken from her mother Lucy— afterwards married to Henry Sparrow—and sent to live with her aunt and uncle, Thomas and Betsy Sparrow. Under this same roof the irrepressible and cheerful waif, Dennis Hanks *—whose name will be frequently seen in these pages—also found a shelter. At the time of her marriage to Thomas Lincoln, Nancy was in her twenty-third year. She was above the ordinary height in stature, weighed about 130 pounds, was slenderly built, and had much the appearance of one inclined to consumption. Her skin was dark; hair dark brown; eyes gray and small; forehead prominent; face sharp and angular, with a marked expression of melancholy which fixed itself in the memory of everyone who ever saw or knew her. Though her life was seemingly beclouded by a spirit of sadness, she was in disposition amiable and generally cheerful. Mr. Lincoln himself said to me in 1851, on receiving the news of his father's death, that whatever might be said of his parents, and however unpromising the early surroundings of his mother may have been, she was highly intellectual by nature, had a strong memory, acute judgment, and was cool and heroic. From a mental standpoint she no doubt rose above her surroundings, and had she lived, the stimulus of

---

* Dennis Hanks, still living at the age of ninety years in Illinois, was the son of another Nancy Hanks—the aunt of the President's mother. He furnished Mr. Weik and me with much interesting information, especially facts and incidents relating to early life in Indiana.

her nature would have accelerated her son's success, and she would have been a much more ambitious prompter than his father ever was.

As a family the Hankses were peculiar to the civilization of early Kentucky. Illiterate and superstitious, they corresponded to that nomadic class still to be met with throughout the South, and known as " poor whites." They are happily and vividly depicted in the description of a camp-meeting held at Elizabethtown, Kentucky, in 1806, which was furnished me in August, 1865, by an eye-witness.* "The Hanks girls," narrates the latter, "were great at camp-meetings. I remember one in 1806. I will give you a scene, and if you will then read the books written on the subject you may find some apology for the superstition that was said to be in Abe Lincoln's character. It was at a camp-meeting, as before said, when a general shout was about to commence. Preparations were being made ; a young lady invited me to stand on a bench by her side where we could see all over the altar. To the right a strong, athletic young man, about twenty-five years old, was being put in trim for the occasion, which was done by divesting him of all apparel except shirt and pants. On the left a young lady was being put in trim in much the same manner, so that her clothes would not be in the way, and so that, when her combs flew out, her hair would go into graceful braids. She, too, was young—not more than twenty perhaps. The per-

---

* J. B. Helm, MS.

formance commenced about the same time by the
young man on the right and the young lady on the
left. Slowly and gracefully they worked their way
towards the centre, singing, shouting, hugging and
kissing, generally their own sex, until at last nearer
and nearer they came. The centre of the altar was
reached, and the two closed, with their arms around
each other, the man singing and shouting at the
top of his voice,

> " ' I have my Jesus in my arms
>   Sweet as honey, strong as bacon ham.'

" Just at this moment the young lady holding to
my arm whispered, ' They are to be married next
week ; her name is Hanks.' There were very few
who did not believe this true religion, inspired by
the Holy Spirit, and the man who could not believe
it, did well to keep it to himself. The Hankses were
the finest singers and shouters in our country."

Here my informant stops, and on account of his
death several years ago I failed to learn whether
the young lady shouter who figured in the foregoing
scene was the President's mother or not. The fact
that Nancy Hanks did marry that year gives color
to the belief that it was she. As to the probability
of the young man being Thomas Lincoln it is difficult to say ; such a performance as the one described must have required a little more emotion
and enthusiasm than the tardy and inert carpenter
was in the habit of manifesting.

CHAPTER II.

SARAH, the sister of Abraham Lincoln, though in some respects like her brother, lacked his stature. She was thick-set, had dark-brown hair, deep-gray eyes, and an even disposition. In contact with others she was kind and considerate. Her nature was one of amiability, and God had endowed her with that invincible combination—modesty and good sense. Strange to say, Mr. Lincoln never said much about his sister in after years, and we are really indebted to the Hankses—Dennis and John—for the little we have learned about this rather unfortunate young woman. She was married to Aaron Grigsby, in Spencer county, Indiana, in the month of August, 1826, and died January 20, 1828. Her brother accompanied her to school while they lived in Kentucky, but as he was only seven, and as she had not yet finished her ninth year when their father removed with them to Indiana, it is to be presumed that neither made much progress in the matter of school education. Still it is authoritatively stated that they attended two schools during this short period. One of these was kept by Zachariah Riney, the other by Caleb Hazel. It is difficult at this late day to learn much of the boy Abraham's life during those seven years of resi-

dence in Kentucky. One man, * who was a clerk in
the principal store in the village where the Lincolns
purchased their family supplies, remembers him as
a "small boy who came sometimes to the store with
his mother. He would take his seat on a keg of
nails, and I would give him a lump of sugar. He
would sit there and eat it like any other boy ; but
these little acts of kindness," observes my informant, in an enthusiastic statement made in 1865, "so
impressed his mind that I made a steadfast friend
in a man whose power and influence have since
been felt throughout the world." A school-mate †
of Lincoln's at Hazel's school, speaking of the master, says: "He perhaps could teach spelling and
reading and indifferent writing, and possibly could
cipher to the rule of three ; but he had no other
qualification of a teacher, unless we accept large size
and bodily strength. Abe was a mere spindle
of a boy, had his due proportion of harmless mischief, but as we lived in a country abounding in
hazel switches, in the virtue of which the master
had great faith, Abe of course received his due
allowance."

This part of the boy's history is painfully vague
and dim, and even after arriving at man's estate
Mr. Lincoln was significantly reserved when reference was made to it. It is barely mentioned in the
autobiography furnished to Fell in 1859. John
Duncan,‡ afterwards a preacher of some promi-

---

* John B. Helm, June 20, 1865.
† Samuel Haycraft, December 6, 1866.
‡ Letter, February 21, 1867.

nence in Kentucky, relates how he and Abe on one occasion ran a ground-hog into a crevice between two rocks, and after working vainly almost two hours to get him out, "Abe ran off about a quarter of a mile to a blacksmith shop, and returned with an iron hook fastened to the end of a pole," and with this rude contrivance they virtually "hooked" the animal out of his retreat. Austin Gollaher of Hodgensville, claims to have saved Lincoln from drowning one day as they were trying to "coon it" across Knob creek on a log. The boys were in pursuit of birds, when young Lincoln fell into the water, and his vigilant companion, who still survives to narrate the thrilling story, fished him out with a sycamore branch.

Meanwhile Thomas Lincoln was becoming daily more dissatisfied with his situation and surroundings. He had purchased, since his marriage, on the easy terms then prevalent, two farms or tracts of land in succession ; no terms were easy enough for him, and the land, when the time for the payment of the purchase-money rolled around, reverted to its former owner. Kentucky, at that day, afforded few if any privileges, and possessed fewer advantages to allure the poor man ; and no doubt so it seemed to Thomas Lincoln. The land he occupied was sterile and broken. A mere barren glade, and destitute of timber, it required a persistent effort to coax a living out of it ; and to one of his easy-going disposition, life there was a never-ending struggle. Stories of vast stretches of rich and unoccupied lands in Indiana reaching his ears, and despairing of

the prospect of any betterment in his condition so
long as he remained in Kentucky, he resolved, at
last, to leave the State and seek a more inviting
lodgment beyond the Ohio. The assertion made
by some of Mr. Lincoln's biographers, and so often
repeated by sentimental writers, that his father left
Kentucky to avoid the sight of or contact with
slavery, lacks confirmation. In all Hardin county
—at that time a large area of territory—there
were not over fifty slaves; and it is doubtful if he
saw enough of slavery to fill him with the righteous
opposition to the institution with which he has so
frequently been credited. Moreover, he never in
later years manifested any especial aversion to
it.

Having determined on emigrating to Indiana, he
began preparations for removal in the fall of 1816
by building for his use a flat-boat. Loading it with
his tools and other personal effects, including in the
invoice, as we are told, four hundred gallons of
whiskey, he launched his "crazy craft" on a tribu-
tary of Salt creek known as the Rolling Fork.
Along with the current he floated down to the Ohio
river, but his rudely-made vessel, either from the
want of experience in its navigator, or because of
its ill adaptation to withstand the force and caprices
of the currents in the great river, capsized one day,
and boat and cargo went to the bottom. The luck-
less boatman set to work however, and by dint of
great patience and labor succeeded in recovering
the tools and the bulk of the whiskey. Righting
his boat, he continued down the river, landing at a

point called Thompson's Ferry, in Perry county, on the Indiana side. Here he disposed of his vessel, and placing his goods in the care of a settler named Posey, he struck out through the interior in search of a location for his new home. Sixteen miles back from the river he found one that pleased his fancy, and he marked it off for himself. His next move in the order of business was a journey to Vincennes to purchase the tract at the Land Office—under the "two-dollar-an-acre law," as Dennis Hanks puts it —and a return to the land to identify it by blazing the trees and piling up brush on the corners to establish the proper boundary lines. Having secured a place for his home he trudged back to Kentucky—walking all the way—for his family. Two horses brought them and all their household effects to the Indiana shore. Posey kindly gave or hired them the use of a wagon, into which they packed not only their furniture and carpenter tools, but the liquor, which it is presumed had lain undisturbed in the former's cellar. Slowly and carefully picking their way through the dense woods, they at last reached their destination on the banks of Little Pigeon creek. There were some detentions on the way, but no serious mishaps.

The head of the household now set resolutely to work to build a shelter for his family.

The structure, when completed, was fourteen feet square, and was built of small unhewn logs. In the language of the day, it was called a "half-faced camp," being enclosed on all sides but one. It had neither floor, door, nor windows. In this forbidding hovel these doughty emigrants braved the exposure of the varying seasons for an entire year. At the end of that time Thomas and Betsy Sparrow followed, bringing with them Dennis Hanks; and to them Thomas Lincoln surrendered the "half-faced camp," while he moved into a more pretentious structure—a cabin enclosed on all sides. The country was thickly covered with forests of walnut, beech, oak, elm, maple, and an undergrowth of dog-wood, sumac, and wild grape-vine. In places where the growth was not so thick grass came up abundantly, and hogs found plenty of food in the unlimited quantity of mast the woods afforded. The country abounded in bear, deer, turkey, and other wild game, which not only satisfied the pioneer's love for sport, but furnished his table with its supply of meat.

Thomas Lincoln, with the aid of the Hankses and Sparrows, was for a time an attentive farmer. The implements of agriculture then in use were as rude as they were rare, and yet there is nothing to show that in spite of the slow methods then in vogue he did not make commendable speed. "We raised corn mostly"—relates Dennis—"and some wheat—enough for a cake Sunday morning. Hog and venison hams were a legal tender, and coon skins also. We raised sheep and cattle, but they did not bring much. Cows and calves were only worth six to eight dollars; corn ten cents, and wheat twenty-five cents, a bushel." So with all his application and frugality the head of this ill-assorted household made but little headway in the accumulation of the world's goods. We are told that he was indeed a poor man, and that during his entire stay in Indiana his land barely yielded him sufficient return to keep his larder supplied with the commonest necessaries of life. His skill as a hunter—though never brought into play unless at the angered demand of a stomach hungry for meat—in no slight degree made up for the lack of good management in the cultivation of his land. His son Abraham * never evinced the same fondness for hunting, although his cousin Dennis with much pride tells us how he could kill a wild turkey on the wing. "At that time," relates one of the latter's playmates,† descanting on the abundance of wild game, "there were a great many deer-licks; and Abe and myself would go to these licks sometimes and watch of nights to kill deer, though Abe was not so fond of a gun or the sport as I was."‡

---

* "Abe was a good boy—an affectionate one—a boy who loved his parents well and was obedient to their every wish. Although anything but an impudent or rude boy he was sometimes uncomfortably inquisitive. When strangers would ride along or pass by his father's fence he always—either through boyish pride or to tease his father—would be sure to ask the first question. His father would sometimes knock him over. When thus punished he never bellowed, but dropped a kind of silent, unwelcome tear as evidence of his sensitiveness or other feelings."—Dennis Hanks, MS., June 13, 1865.

† David Turnham, MS. letter, June 10, 1866.

‡ Mr. Lincoln used to relate the following "coon" story : His father had at home a little yellow house-dog, which invariably gave the alarm if the boys undertook to slip away unobserved after night had set in—as they oftentimes did—to go coon hunting. One evening

The cabin to which the Lincoln family removed after leaving the little half-faced camp to the Sparrows was in some respects a pretentious structure. It was of hewed logs, and was eighteen feet square. It was high enough to admit of a loft, where Abe slept, and to which he ascended each night by means of pegs driven in the wall. The rude furniture was in keeping with the surroundings. Three-legged stools answered for chairs. The bedstead, made of poles fastened in the cracks of the logs on one side, and supported by a crotched stick driven in the ground floor on the other, was covered with skins, leaves, and old clothes. A table of the same finish as the stools, a few pewter dishes, a Dutch oven, and a skillet completed the household outfit. In this uninviting frontier structure the future President was destined to pass the greater part of his boyhood. Withal his spirits were light, and it can-

---

Abe and his step-brother, John Johnston, with the usual complement of boys required in a sucessful coon hunt, took the insignificant little cur with them. They located the coveted coon, killed him, and then in a sportive vein sewed the hide on the diminutive yellow dog. The latter struggled vigorously during the operation of sewing on, and being released from the hands of his captors made a bee-line for home. Other large and more important canines, on the way, scenting coon, tracked the little animal home, and possibly mistaking him for real coon, speedily demolished him. The next morning old Thomas Lincoln discovered lying in his yard the lifeless remains of yellow "Joe," with strong proof of coon-skin accompaniment. "Father was much incensed at his death," observed Mr. Lincoln, in relating the story, "but as John and I, scantily protected from the morning wind, stood shivering in the doorway, we felt assured little yellow Joe would never be able again to sound the call for another coon hunt."

not be denied that he must have enjoyed unrestrained pleasure in his surroundings. It is related that one day the only thing that graced the dinner-table was a dish of roasted potatoes. The elder Lincoln, true to the custom of the day, returned thanks for the blessing. The boy, realizing the scant proportions of the meal, looked up into his father's face and irreverently observed, " Dad, I call these "—meaning the potatoes—" mighty poor blessings." Among other children of a similar age he seemed unconsciously to take the lead, and it is no stretch of the truth to say that they, in turn, looked up to him. He may have been a little precocious—children sometimes are—but in view of the summary treatment received at the hands of his father it cannot truthfully be said he was a " spoiled child." One morning when his mother was at work he ran into the cabin from the outside to enquire, with a quizzical grin, " Who was the father of Zebedee's children ? " As many another mother before and since has done, she brushed the mischievous young inquirer aside to attend to some more important detail of household concern.*

The dull routine of chores and household errands in the boy's every-day life was brightened now and then by a visit to the mill. I often in later years heard Mr. Lincoln say that going to mill gave him the greatest pleasure of his boyhood days.

"We had to go seven miles to mill," relates David Turnham, the friend of his youth, "and then

---

4   * Harriet Chapman, MS. letter.

it was a hand-mill that would only grind from fifteen to twenty bushels of corn in a day. There was but little wheat grown at that time, and when we did have wheat we had to grind it in the mill described and use it without bolting, as there were no bolts in the country. Abe and I had to do the milling, frequently going twice to get one grist."

In his eleventh year he began that marvellous and rapid growth in stature for which he was so widely noted in the Pigeon creek settlement. "As he shot up," says Turnham, " he seemed to change in appearance and action. Although quick-witted and ready with an answer, he began to exhibit deep thoughtfulness, and was so often lost in studied reflection we could not help noticing the strange turn in his actions. He disclosed rare timidity and sensitiveness, especially in the presence of men and women, and although cheerful enough in the presence of the boys, he did not appear to seek our company as earnestly as before." * It was only the development we find in the history of every boy. Nature was a little abrupt in the case of Abraham Lincoln; she tossed him from the nimbleness of boyhood to the gravity of manhood in a single night.

In the fall of 1818, the scantily settled region in the vicinity of Pigeon creek—where the Lincolns were then living—suffered a visitation of that dread disease common in the West in early days, and known in the vernacular of the frontier as "the

* D. Turnham, MS. letter.

milk-sick." It hovered like a spectre over the Pigeon creek settlement for over ten years, and its fatal visitation and inroads among the Lincolns, Hankses, and Sparrows finally drove that contingent into Illinois. To this day the medical profession has never agreed upon any definite cause for the malady, nor have they in all their scientific wrangling determined exactly what the disease itself is. A physician, who has in his practice met a number of cases, describes the symptoms to be " a whitish coat on the tongue, burning sensation of the stomach, severe vomiting, obstinate constipation of the bowels, coolness of the extremities, great restlessness and jactitation, pulse rather small, somewhat more frequent than natural, and slightly chorded. In the course of the disease the coat on the tongue becomes brownish and dark, the countenance dejected, and the prostration of the patient is great. A fatal termination may take place in sixty hours, or life may be prolonged for a period of fourteen days. These are the symptoms of the disease in an acute form. Sometimes it runs into the chronic form, or it may assume that form from the commencement, and after months or years the patient may finally die or recover only a partial degree of health."

When the disease broke out in the Pigeon creek region it not only took off the people, but it made sad havoc among the cattle. One man testifies that he "lost four milch cows and eleven calves in one week." This, in addition to the risk of losing his own life, was enough, he declared, to ruin him, and prompted him to leave for "points further west."

Early in October of the year 1818, Thomas and Betsy Sparrow fell ill of the disease and died within a few days of each other. Thomas Lincoln performed the services of undertaker. With his whipsaw he cut out the lumber, and with commendable promptness he nailed together the rude coffins to enclose the forms of the dead. The bodies were borne to a scantily cleared knoll in the midst of the forest, and there, without ceremony, quietly let down into the grave. Meanwhile Abe's mother had also fallen a victim to the insidious disease. Her sufferings, however, were destined to be of brief duration. Within a week she too rested from her labors. "She struggled on, day by day," says one of the household, "a good Christian woman, and died on the seventh day after she was taken sick. Abe and his sister Sarah waited on their mother, and did the little jobs and errands required of them. There was no physician nearer than thirty-five miles. The mother knew she was going to die, and called the children to her bedside. She was very weak, and the children leaned over while she gave her last message. Placing her feeble hand on little Abe's head she told him to be kind and good to his father and sister; to both she said, 'Be good to one another,' expressing a hope that they might live, as they had been taught by her, to love their kindred and worship God." Amid the miserable surroundings of a home in the wilderness Nancy Hanks passed across the dark river. Though of lowly birth, the victim of poverty and hard usage, she takes a place in history as the mother of a son who liberated a race of men. At her side stands another Mother whose son performed a similar service for all mankind eighteen hundred years before.

After the death of their mother little Abe and his sister Sarah began a dreary life—indeed, one more cheerless and less inviting seldom falls to the lot of any child. In a log-cabin without a floor, scantily protected from the severities of the weather, deprived of the comfort of a mother's love, they passed through a winter the most dismal either one ever experienced. Within a few months, and before the close of the winter, David Elkin, an itinerant preacher whom Mrs. Lincoln had known in Kentucky, happened into the settlement, and in response to the invitation from the family and friends, delivered a funeral sermon over her grave. No one is able now to remember the language of Parson Elkin's discourse, but it is recalled that he commemorated the virtues and good phases of character, and passed in silence the few shortcomings and frailties of the poor woman sleeping under the winter's snow. She had done her work in this world. Stoop-shouldered, thin-breasted, sad, —at times miserable,—groping through the perplexities of life, without prospect of any betterment in her condition, she passed from earth, little dreaming of the grand future that lay in store for the ragged, hapless little boy who stood at her bedside in the last days of her life.

Thomas Lincoln's widowerhood was brief. He

had scarcely mourned the death of his first wife a year until he reäppeared in Kentucky at Elizabethtown in search of another. His admiration had centred for a second time on Sally Bush, the widow of Daniel Johnston, the jailer of Hardin county, who had died several years before of a disease known as the " cold plague." The tradition still kept alive in the Kentucky neighborhood is that Lincoln had been a suitor for the hand of the lady before his marriage to Nancy Hanks, but that she had rejected him for the hand of the more fortunate Johnston. However that may have been, it is certain that he began his campaign in earnest this time, and after a brief siege won her heart. " He made a very short courtship," wrote Samuel Haycraft * to me in a letter, December 7, 1866. " He came to see her on the first day of December, 1819, and in a straightforward manner told her that they had known each other from childhood. '*Miss* Johnston,' said he, ' I have no wife and you no husband. I came a-purpose to marry you. I knowed you from a gal and you knowed me from a boy. I've no time to lose ; and if you're willin' let it be done straight off.' She replied that she could not marry him right off, as she had some little debts which she wanted to pay first. He replied, 'Give me a list of them.' He got the list and paid them that evening. Next morning I issued the license, and they were married within sixty yards of my house."

Lincoln's brother-in-law, Ralph Krume, and his

---

* Clerk of the Court.   MS.

four horses and spacious wagon were again brought into requisition. With commendable generosity he transported the newly married pair and their household effects to their home in Indiana. The new Mrs. Lincoln was accompanied by her three children, John, Sarah, and Matilda. Her social status is fixed by the comparison of a neighbor, who observed that "life among the Hankses, the Lincolns, and the Enlows was a long ways below life among the Bushes."

In the eyes of her spouse she could not be regarded as a poor widow. She was the owner of a goodly stock of furniture and household goods; bringing with her among other things a walnut bureau valued at fifty dollars. What effect the new family, their collection of furniture, cooking utensils, and comfortable bedding must have had on the astonished and motherless pair who from the door of Thomas Lincoln's forlorn cabin watched the well-filled wagon as it came creaking through the woods can better be imagined than described. Surely Sarah and Abe, as the stores of supplies were rolled in through the doorless doorways, must have believed that a golden future awaited them. The presence and smile of a motherly face in the cheerless cabin radiated sunshine into every neglected corner. If the Lincoln mansion did not in every respect correspond to the representations made by its owner to the new Mrs. Lincoln before marriage, the latter gave no expression of disappointment or even surprise. With true womanly courage and zeal she set resolutely to work to make right that which seemed wrong.   Her husband was made to put a floor in the cabin, as well as to supply doors and windows.   The cracks between the logs were plastered up.   A clothes-press filled the space between the chimney jamb and the wall, and the mat of corn husks and leaves on which the children had slept in the corner gave way to the comfortable luxuriance of a feather bed.   She washed the two orphans, and fitted them out in clothes taken from the stores of her own.   The work of renovation in and around the cabin continued until even Thomas Lincoln himself, under the general stimulus of the new wife's presence, caught the inspiration, and developed signs of intense activity.   The advent of Sarah Bush was certainly a red-letter day for the Lincolns.   She was not only industrious and thrifty, but gentle and affectionate ; and her newly adopted children for the first time, perhaps, realized the benign influence of a mother's love.   Of young Abe she was especially fond, and we have her testimony that her kindness and care for him were warmly and bountifully returned.   Her granddaughter furnished me * in after years with this description of her :

   " My grandmother is a very tall woman, straight as an Indian, of fair complexion, and was, when I first remember her, very handsome, sprightly, talkative, and proud. She wore her hair curled till gray ; is kind-hearted and very charitable, and also very industrious."   In September, 1865, I visited the old

---

* Harriet Chapman.   MS.

SARAH BUSH LINCOLN.

After photograph taken in 1865.

lady * and spent an entire day with her. She was then living on the farm her stepson had purchased and given her, eight miles south of the town of Charleston, in Illinois. She died on the 10th of April, 1869.

The two sets of children in the Lincoln household—to their credit be it said—lived together in perfect accord. Abe was in his tenth year, and his stepmother, awake to the importance of an education, made a way for him to attend school. To her he seemed full of promise; and although not so quick of comprehension as other boys, yet she believed in encouraging his every effort. He had had a few weeks of schooling under Riney and Hazel in Kentucky, but it is hardly probable that he could read ; he certainly could not write. As illustrating his moral make-up, I diverge from the chronological order of the narrative long enough to relate an incident which occurred some years later. In the Lincoln family, Matilda Johnston, or 'Tilda,

---

* During my interview with this old lady I was much and deeply impressed with the sincerity of her affection for her illustrious stepson. She declined to say much in answer to my questions about Nancy Hanks, her predecessor in the Lincoln household, but spoke feelingly of the latter's daughter and son. Describing Mr. Lincoln's last visit to her in February, 1861, she broke into tears and wept bitterly. " I did not want Abe to run for President," she sobbed, " and did not want to see him elected. I was afraid that something would happen to him, and when he came down to see me, after he was elected President, I still felt, and my heart told me, that something would befall him, and that I should never see him again. Abe and his father are in heaven now, I am sure, and I expect soon to go there and meet them."

as her mother called her, was the youngest child. After Abe had reached the estate of manhood, she was still in her 'teens. It was Abe's habit each morning one fall, to leave the house early, his axe on his shoulder, to clear a piece of forest which lay some distance from home. He frequently carried his dinner with him, and remained all day. Several times the young and frolicsome 'Tilda sought to accompany him, but was each time restrained by her mother, who firmly forbade a repetition of the attempt. One morning the girl escaped maternal vigilance, and slyly followed after the young woodman, who had gone some distance from the house, and was already hidden from view behind the dense growth of trees and underbrush. Following a deer-path, he went singing along, little dreaming of the girl in close pursuit. The latter gained on him, and when within a few feet, darted forward and with a cat-like leap landed squarely on his back. With one hand on each shoulder, she planted her knee in the middle of his back, and dexterously brought the powerful frame of the rail-splitter to the ground. It was a trick familiar to every schoolboy. Abe, taken by surprise, was unable at first to turn around or learn who his assailant was. In the fall to the ground, the sharp edge of the axe imbedded itself in the young lady's ankle, inflicting a wound from which there came a generous effusion of blood. With sundry pieces of cloth torn from Abe's shirt and the young lady's dress, the flow of blood was stanched, and the wound rudely bound up. The girl's cries having lessened somewhat, her tall companion, looking at her in blank astonishment, knowing what an infraction the whole thing was of her mother's oft-repeated instructions, asked; "'Tilda, what are you going to tell mother about getting hurt?"

"Tell her I did it with the axe," she sobbed. "That will be the truth, won't it?" To which last inquiry Abe manfully responded,

"Yes, that's the truth, but it's not all the truth. Tell the whole truth, 'Tilda, and trust your good mother for the rest."

This incident was, many years afterward, related to me by 'Tilda, who was then the mother of a devoted and interesting family herself.

Hazel Dorsey was Abe's first teacher in Indiana. He held forth a mile and a half from the Lincoln farm. The school-house was built of round logs, and was just high enough for a man to stand erect under the loft. The floor was of split logs, or what were called puncheons. The chimney was made of poles and clay; and the windows were made by cutting out parts of two logs, placing pieces of split boards a proper distance apart, and over the aperture thus formed pasting pieces of greased paper to admit light. At school Abe evinced ability enough to gain him a prominent place in the respect of the teacher and the affections of his fellow-scholars.* Elements of leader-

---

* "He always appeared to be very quiet during playtime; never was rude; seemed to have a liking for solitude; was the one chosen in almost every case to adjust difficulties between boys of his age

ship in him seem to have manifested themselves already. Nathaniel Grigsby—whose brother, Aaron, afterwards married Abe's sister, Sarah—attended the same school. He certifies to Abe's proficiency and worth in glowing terms.

" He was always at school early," writes Grigsby, "and attended to his studies. He was always at the head of his class, and passed us rapidly in his studies. He lost no time at home, and when he was not at work was at his books. He kept up his studies on Sunday, and carried his books with him to work, so that he might read when he rested from labor." Now and then, the family exchequer running low, it would be found necessary for the young rail-splitter to stop school, and either work with his father on the farm, or render like service for the neighbors. These periods of work occurred so often and continued so long, that all his school days added together would not make a year in the aggregate. When he attended school, his sister Sarah usually accompanied him. "Sally was a quick-minded young woman," is the testimony of a school-mate. "She was more industrious than Abe, in my opinion. I can hear her good-humored laugh now. Like her brother, she could greet you kindly and put you at ease. She was really an intelligent woman." *

---

and size, and when appealed to, his decision was an end of the trouble. He was also rather noted for keeping his clothes clean longer than any of the others, and although considered a boy of courage, had few, if any, difficulties."—E. R. Burba, letter, March 31, 1866.

* Nat Grigsby, Sept. 12, 1865, MS.

Abe's love for books, and his determined effort to obtain an education in spite of so many obstacles, induced the belief in his father's mind, that book-learning was absorbing a greater proportion of his energy and industry than the demands of the farm. The old gentleman had but little faith in the value of books or papers,* and hence the frequent drafts he made on the son to aid in the drudgery of daily toil. He undertook to teach him his own trade †— he was a carpenter and joiner—but Abe manifested such a striking want of interest that the effort to make a carpenter of him was soon abandoned.

At Dorsey's school Abe was ten years old; at the next one, Andrew Crawford's, he was about fourteen; and at Swaney's he was in his seventeenth year. The last school required a walk of over four miles, and on account of the distance his attendance was not only irregular but brief. Schoolmaster Crawford introduced a new feature in his school, and we can imagine its effect on his pupils, whose training had been limited to the

---

* " I induced my husband to permit Abe to read and study at home as well as at school. At first he was not easily reconciled to it, but finally he too seemed willing to encourage him to a certain extent. Abe was a dutiful son to me always, and we took particular care when he was reading not to disturb him—would let him read on and on till he quit of his own accord."—Mrs. Thomas Lincoln, Sept. 8, 1865.

† A little walnut cabinet, two feet high, and containing two rows of neat drawers, now in the possession of Captain J. W. Wartmann, clerk of the United States Court in Evansville, Ind., is carefully preserved as a specimen of the joint work of Lincoln and his father at this time.

social requirements of the backwoods settlement. It was instruction in manners. One scholar was required to go outside, and re-enter the room as a lady or gentleman would enter a drawing-room or parlor. Another scholar would receive the first party at the door, and escort him or her about the room, making polite introductions to each person in the room. How the gaunt and clumsy Abe went through this performance we shall probably never know. If his awkward movements gave rise to any amusement, his school-mates never revealed it.

The books used at school were Webster's Spelling Book and the American Speller. All the scholars learned to cipher, and afterwards used Pike's Arithmetic. Mr. Lincoln told me in later years that Murray's English Reader was the best school-book ever put into the hands of an American youth. I conclude, therefore, he must have used that also. At Crawford's school Abe was credited with the authorship of several literary efforts—short dissertations in which he strove to correct some time-honored and wanton sport of the schoolboy. While in Indiana I met several persons who recalled a commendable and somewhat pretentious protest he wrote against cruelty to animals. The wholesome effects of a temperate life and the horrors of war were also subjects which claimed the services of his pen then, as they in later years demanded the devoted attention of his mind and heart.

He was now over six feet high and was growing at a tremendous rate, for he added two inches more before the close of his seventeenth year, thus reaching the limit of his stature. He weighed in the region of a hundred and sixty pounds; was wiry, vigorous, and strong. His feet and hands were large, arms and legs long and in striking contrast with his slender trunk and small head. " His skin was shrivelled and yellow," declares one of the girls* who attended Crawford's school. " His shoes, when he had any, were low. He wore buckskin breeches, linsey-woolsey shirt, and a cap made of the skin of a squirrel or coon. His breeches were baggy and lacked by several inches meeting the tops of his shoes, thereby exposing his shin-bone, sharp, blue, and narrow." In one branch of school learning he was a great success; that was spelling. We are indebted to Kate Roby, a pretty miss of fifteen, for an incident which illustrates alike his proficiency in orthography and his natural inclination to help another out of the mire. The word "defied" had been given out by Schoolmaster Crawford, but had been misspelled several times when it came Miss Roby's turn. "Abe stood on the opposite side of the room" (related Miss Roby † to me in 1865) " and was watching me. I began d-e-f—and then I stopped, hesitating whether to proceed with an 'i' or a ' y.' Looking up I beheld Abe, a grin covering his face, and pointing with his index finger to his eye. I took the hint, spelled the word with an 'i,' and it went through all right."

---

* Kate Gentry.
† Miss Roby afterward married Allen Gentry.

There was more or less of an attachment between Miss Roby and Abe, although the lady took pains to assure me that they were never in love. She described with self-evident pleasure, however, the delightful experience of an evening's stroll down to the river with him, where they were wont to sit on the bank and watch the moon as it slowly rose over the neighboring hills. Dangling their youthful feet in the water, they gazed on the pale orb of night, as many a fond pair before them had done and will continue to do until the end of the world. One evening, when thus engaged, their conversation and thoughts turned on the movement of the planets. "I did not suppose that Abe, who had seen so little of the world, would know anything about it, but he proved to my satisfaction that the moon did not go down at all; that it only seemed to; that the earth, revolving from west to east, carried us under, as it were. 'We do the sinking,' he explained; 'while to us the moon is comparatively still. The moon's sinking is only an illusion.' I at once dubbed him a fool, but later developments convinced me that I was the fool, not he. He was well acquainted with the general laws of astronomy and the movements of the heavenly bodies, but where he could have learned so much, or how to put it so plainly, I never could understand."

Absalom Roby is authority for the statement that even at that early day Abe was a patient reader of a Louisville newspaper, which some one at Gentryville kindly furnished him. Among the books he read were the Bible, "Æsop's Fables,"

Abraham Lincoln
his hand and pen.
he will be good but
god knows When

" Robinson Crusoe," Bunyan's " Pilgrim's Progress," a " History of the United States," and Weems' " Life of Washington." A little circumstance attended the reading of the last-named book, which only within recent years found its way into public print. The book was borrowed from a close-fisted neighbor, Josiah Crawford, and one night, while lying on a little shelf near a crack between two logs in the Lincoln cabin during a storm, the covers were damaged by rain. Crawford—not the schoolmaster, but old " Blue Nose," as Abe and others called him—assessed the damage to his book at seventy-five cents, and the unfortunate borrower was required to pull fodder for three days at twenty-five cents a day in settlement of the account. While at school it is doubtful if he was able to own an arithmetic. His stepmother was unable to remember his ever having owned one. She gave me, however, a few leaves from a book made and bound by Abe, in which he had entered, in a large, bold hand, the tables of weights and measures, and the " sums " to be worked out in illustration of each table. Where the arithmetic was obtained I could not learn. On one of the pages which the old lady gave me, and just underneath the table which tells how many pints there are in a bushel, the facetious young student had scrawled these four lines of schoolboy doggerel :

> " Abraham Lincoln,
>   His hand and pen,
>   He will be good,
>   But God knows when."

5

On another page were found, in his own hand, a few lines which it is also said he composed. Nothing indicates that they were borrowed, and I have always, therefore, believed that they were original with him. Although a little irregular in metre, the sentiment would, I think, do credit to an older head.

> " Time, what an empty vapor 'tis,
>   And days how swift they are :
> Swift as an Indian arrow—
>   Fly on like a shooting star.
> The present moment just is here,
>   Then slides away in haste,
> That we can never say they're ours,
>   But only say they're past."

His penmanship, after some practice, became so regular in form that it excited the admiration of other and younger boys. One of the latter, Joseph C. Richardson, said that "Abe Lincoln was the best penman in the neighborhood." At Richardson's request he made some copies for practice. During my visit to Indiana I met Richardson, who showed these two lines, which Abe had prepared for him :

> " Good boys who to their books apply
>   Will all be great men by and by."

To comprehend Mr. Lincoln fully we must know in substance not only the facts of his origin, but also the manner of his development. It will always be a matter of wonder to the American people, I have no doubt—as it has been to me— that from such restricted and unpromising opportunities in early life, Mr. Lincoln grew into the great man he was. The foundation for his education was laid in Indiana and in the little town of New Salem in Illinois, and in both places he gave evidence of a nature and characteristics that distinguished him from every associate and surrounding he had. He was not peculiar or eccentric, and yet a shrewd observer would have seen that he was decidedly unique and original. Although imbued with a marked dislike for manual labor, it cannot be truthfully said of him that he was indolent. From a mental standpoint he was one of the most energetic young men of his day. He dwelt altogether in the land of thought. His deep meditation and abstraction easily induced the belief among his horny-handed companions that he was lazy. In fact, a neighbor, John Romine, makes that charge. " He worked for me," testifies the latter, " but was always reading and thinking. I used to get mad at him for it. I say he was awfully lazy. He would laugh and talk—crack his jokes and tell stories all the time; didn't love work half as much as his pay. He said to me one day that his father taught him to work, but he never taught him to love it." Verily there was but one Abraham Lincoln!

His chief delight during the day, if unmolested, was to lie down under the shade of some inviting tree to read and study. At night, lying on his stomach in front of the open fireplace, with a piece of charcoal he would cipher on a broad wooden shovel. When the latter was covered over on both sides he would take his father's drawing knife or

plane and shave it off clean, ready for a fresh supply
of inscriptions the next day. He often moved about
the cabin with a piece of chalk, writing and cipher-
ing on boards and the flat sides of hewn logs. When
every bare wooden surface had been filled with his
letters and ciphers he would erase them and begin
anew. Thus it was always; and the boy whom
dull old Thomas Lincoln and rustic John Romine
conceived to be lazy was in reality the most tireless
worker in all the region around Gentryville. His stepmother told me he devoured everything in the book
line within his reach. If in his reading he came
across anything that pleased his fancy, he entered
it down in a copy-book—a sort of repository, in which
he was wont to store everything worthy of preserva-
tion. "Frequently," related his stepmother, " he
had no paper to write his pieces down on. Then he
would put them with chalk on a board or plank,
sometimes only making a few signs of what he
intended to write. When he got paper he would
copy them, always bringing them to me and reading
them. He would ask my opinion of what he had
read, and often explained things to me in his plain
and simple language." How he contrived at the
age of fourteen to absorb information is thus told
by John Hanks: "When Abe and I returned to
the house from work he would go to the cupboard,
snatch a piece of corn bread, sit down, take a book,
cock his legs up as high as his head, and read. We
grubbed, plowed, mowed, and worked together barefooted in the field. Whenever Abe had a chance
in the field while at work, or at the house, he

would stop and read." He kept the Bible and "Æsop's Fables" always within reach, and read them over and over again. These two volumes furnished him with the many figures of speech and parables which he used with such happy effect in his later and public utterances.

Amid such restricted and unromantic environments the boy developed into the man. The intellectual fire burned slowly, but with a steady and intense glow. Although denied the requisite training of the school-room, he was none the less competent to cope with those who had undergone that discipline. No one had a more retentive memory. If he read or heard a good thing it never escaped him. His powers of concentration were intense, and in the ability through analysis to strip bare a proposition he was unexcelled. His thoughtful and investigating mind dug down after ideas, and never stopped till bottom facts were reached. With such a mental equipment the day was destined to come when the world would need the services of his intellect and heart. That he was equal to the great task when the demand came is but another striking proof of the grandeur of his character.

CHAPTER III.

THE first law book Lincoln ever read was "The Statutes of Indiana." He obtained the volume from his friend David Turnham, who testifies that he fairly devoured the book in his eager efforts to abstract the store of knowledge that lay between the lids. No doubt, as Turnham insists, the study of the statutes at this early day led Abe to think of the law as his calling in maturer years. At any rate he now began to evince no little zeal in the matter of public speaking—in compliance with the old notion, no doubt, that a lawyer can never succeed unless he has the elements of the orator or advocate in his construction—and even when at work in the field he could not resist the temptation to mount the nearest stump and practise on his fellow laborers. The latter would flock around him, and active operations would cease whenever he began. A cluster of tall and stately trees often made him a most dignified and appeciative audience during the delivery of these maiden forensic efforts. He was old enough to attend musters, log-rollings, and horse-races, and was rapidly becoming a favored as well as favorite character. "The first time I ever remember of seeing Abe Lincoln," is the testimony of one of his neighbors,* "was when I was a small boy and had gone with my father to attend some kind of an election. One of our neighbors, James Larkins, was there. Larkins was a great hand to brag on anything he owned. This time it was his horse. He stepped up before Abe, who was in the crowd, and commenced talking to him, boasting all the while of his animal.

"'I have got the best horse in the country'" he shouted to his young listener. "'I ran him three miles in exactly nine minutes, and he never fetched a long breath.'"

"'I presume,' said Abe, rather dryly, 'he fetched a good many short ones though.'"

With all his peaceful propensities Abe was not averse to a contest of strength, either for sport or in settlement—as in one memorable case—of grievances. Personal encounters were of frequent occurrence in Gentryville in those days, and the prestige of having thrashed an opponent gave the victor marked social distinction. Green B. Taylor, with whom Abe worked the greater part of one winter on a farm, furnished me with an account of the noted fight between John Johnston, Abe's step-brother, and William Grigsby, in which stirring drama Abe himself played an important rôle before the curtain was rung down. Taylor's father was the second for Johnston, and William Whitten officiated in a similar capacity for Grigsby. "They had a terrible fight," relates Taylor, "and it soon became

---

* John W. Lamar, MS. letter, June 29, 1866.

apparent that Grigsby was too much for Lincoln's man, Johnston. After they had fought a long time without interference, it having been agreed not to break the ring, Abe burst through, caught Grigsby, threw him off and some feet away. There he stood, proud as Lucifer, and swinging a bottle of liquor over his head swore he was ' the big buck of the lick.' ' If any one doubts it,' he shouted, ' he has only to come on and whet his horns.' " A general engagement followed this challenge, but at the end of hostilities the field was cleared and the wounded retired amid the exultant shouts of their victors.

Much of the latter end of Abe's boyhood would have been lost in the midst of tradition but for the store of information and recollections I was fortunate enough to secure from an interesting old lady whom I met in Indiana in 1865. She was the wife of Josiah Crawford *—" Blue Nose," as Abe had named him—and possessed rare accomplishments for a woman reared in the backwoods of Indiana. She was not only impressed with Abe's early efforts, but expressed great admiration for his sister Sarah, whom she often had with her at her own hospitable home and whom she described as a modest, indus-

---

* In one of her conversations with me Mrs. Crawford told me of the exhibitions with which at school they often entertained the few persons who attended the closing day. Sometimes, in warm weather, the scholars made a platform of clean boards covered overhead with green boughs. Generally, however, these exhibitions took place in the school-room. The exercises consisted of the varieties offered at this day at the average seminary or school—declamations and dialogues or debates. The declamations were obtained principally from a book called " The Kentucky Preceptor," which volume

trious, and sensible sister of a humorous and equally sensible brother. From Mrs. Crawford I obtained the few specimens of Abe's early literary efforts and much of the matter that follows in this chapter. The introduction here of the literary feature as affording us a glimpse of Lincoln's boyhood days may to a certain extent grate harshly on over-refined ears ; but still no apology is necessary, for, as intimated at the outset, I intend to keep close to Lincoln all the way through. Some writers would probably omit these songs and backwoods recitals as savoring too strongly of the Bacchanalian nature, but that would be a narrow view to take of history. If we expect to know Lincoln thoroughly we must be prepared to take him as he really was.

In 1826 Abe's sister Sarah was married to Aaron Grigsby, and at the wedding the Lincoln family sang a song composed in honor of the event by Abe himself. It is a tiresome doggerel and full of painful rhymes. I reproduce it here from the manuscript furnished me by Mrs. Crawford. The author and composer called it " Adam and Eve's Wedding Song."

Mrs. Crawford gave me as a souvenir of my visit. Lincoln had often used it himself, she said. The questions for discussion were characteristic of the day and age. The relative merits of the " Bee and the Ant," the difference in strength between " Wind and Water," taxed their knowledge of physical phenomena ; and the all-important question " Which has the most right to complain, the Indian or the Negro ? " called out their conceptions of a great moral or national wrong. In the discussion of all these grave subjects Lincoln took a deep interest.

" When Adam was created
    He dwelt in Eden's shade,
As Moses has recorded,
    And soon a bride was made.

Ten thousand times ten thousand
    Of creatures swarmed around
Before a bride was formed,
    And yet no mate was found.

The Lord then was not willing
    That man should be alone,
But caused a sleep upon him,
    And from him took a bone.

And closed the flesh instead thereof,
    And then he took the same
And of it made a woman,
    And brought her to the man.

Then Adam he rejoiced
    To see his loving bride
A part of his own body,
    The product of his side.

The woman was not taken
    From Adam's feet we see,
So he must not abuse her,
    The meaning seems to be.

The woman was not taken
    From Adam's head, we know,
To show she must not rule him—
    'Tis evidently so.

The woman she was taken
    From under Adam's arm,
So she must be protected
    From injuries and harm."

Poor Sarah, at whose wedding this song was sung,
never lived to see the glory nor share in the honor
that afterwards fell to the lot of her tall and angular
brother. Within two years after her marriage she
died in childbirth.

Although devoid of any natural ability as a singer Abe nevertheless made many efforts and had great appreciation of certain songs. In after years he told me he doubted if he really knew what the harmony of sound was. The songs in vogue then were principally of the sacred order. They were from Watts' and Dupuy's hymn-books. David Turnham furnished me with a list, marking as especial favorites the following: "Am I a Soldier of the Cross"; "How Tedious and Tasteless the Hours"; "There is a Fountain Filled with Blood," and, "Alas, and did my Saviour Bleed?" One song pleased Abe not a little. "I used to sing it for old Thomas Lincoln," relates Turnham, "at Abe's request. The old gentleman liked it and made me sing it often. I can only remember one couplet:

> "'There was a Romish lady
> She was brought up in Popery.'"

Dennis Hanks insists that Abe used to try his hand and voice at "Poor old Ned," but never with any degree of success. "Rich, racy verses" were sung by the big boys in the country villages of that day with as keen a relish as they are to-day. There is no reason and less evidence for the belief that Abe did not partake of this forbidden fruit along with other boys of the same age and condition in life. Among what Dennis called "field songs" are a few lines from this one:

> "The turbaned Turk that scorns the world
> And struts about with his whiskers curled,
> For no other man but himself to see."

Of another ballad we have this couplet:

> " Hail Columbia, happy land,
>   If you aint drunk then I'll be damned."

We can imagine the merry Dennis, hilarious with the exhilaration of deep potations at the village grocery, singing this " field song " as he and Abe wended their way homeward. A stanza from a campaign song which Abe was in the habit of rendering, according to Mrs. Crawford, attests his earliest political predilections:

> " Let auld acquaintance be forgot
>   And never brought to mind,
> May Jackson be our president,
>   And Adams left behind."

A mournful and distressing ballad, " John Anderson's Lamentation," as rendered by Abe, was written out for me by Mrs. Crawford, but the first lines,

> " Oh, sinners, poor sinners, take warning by me,
>   The fruits of transgression behold now and see,"

will suffice to indicate how mournful the rest of it was.

The centre of wit and wisdom in the village of Gentryville was at the store. This place was in charge of one Jones, who soon after embarking in business seemed to take quite a fancy to Abe. He took the only newspaper—sent from Louisville— and at his place of business gathered Abe, Dennis Hanks, Baldwin the blacksmith, and other kindred spirits to discuss such topics as are the exclusive property of the store lounger. Abe's original and ridiculous stories not only amused the crowd, but the display of his unique faculties made him many friends. One who saw him at this time says:

"Lincoln would frequently make political speeches to the boys; he was always calm, logical, and clear. His jokes and stories were so odd, original, and witty all the people in town would gather around him. He would keep them till midnight. Abe was a good talker, a good reasoner, and a kind of newsboy." He attended all the trials before the "squire," as that important functionary was called, and frequently wandered off to Boonville, a town on the river, distant fifteen miles, and the county seat of Warrick County, to hear and see how the courts were conducted there. On one occasion, at the latter place, he remained during the trial of a murderer and attentively absorbed the proceedings. A lawyer named Breckenridge represented the defense, and his speech so pleased and thrilled his young listener that the latter could not refrain from approaching the eloquent advocate at the close of his address and congratulating him on his signal success. How Breckenridge accepted the felicitations of the awkward, hapless youth we shall probably never know. The story is told that during Lincoln's term as President, he was favored one day at the White House with a visit by this same Breckenridge, then a resident of Texas, who had called to pay his respects. In a conversation about early days in Indiana, the President, recalling Breckenridge's argument in the murder trial, remarked, " If I could, as I then thought, have made as good a speech as that, my soul would have been satisfied; for it was up to that time the best speech I had ever heard.

No feature of his backwoods life pleased Abe so well as going to mill. It released him from a day's work in the woods, besides affording him a much desired opportunity to watch the movement of the mill's primitive and cumbersome machinery. It was on many of these trips that David Turnham accompanied him. In later years Mr. Lincoln related the following reminiscence of his experience as a miller in Indiana: One day, taking a bag of corn, he mounted the old flea-bitten gray mare and rode leisurely to Gordon's mill. Arriving somewhat late, his turn did not come till almost sundown. In obedience to the custom requiring each man to furnish his own power he hitched the old mare to the arm, and as the animal moved round, the machinery responded with equal speed. Abe was mounted on the arm, and at frequent intervals made use of his whip to urge the animal on to better speed. With a careless "Get up, you old hussy," he applied the lash at each revolution of the arm. In the midst of the exclamation, or just as half of it had escaped through his teeth, the old jade, resenting the continued use of the goad, elevated her shoeless hoof and striking the young engineer in the forehead, sent him sprawling to the earth. Miller Gordon hurried in, picked up the bleeding, senseless boy, whom he took for dead, and at once sent for his father. Old Thomas Lincoln came— came as soon as embodied listlessness could move—

loaded the lifeless boy in a wagon and drove home. Abe lay unconscious all night, but towards break of day the attendants noticed signs of returning consciousness. The blood beginning to flow normally, his tongue struggled to loosen itself, his frame jerked for an instant, and he awoke, blurting out the words "you old hussy," or the latter half of the sentence interrupted by the mare's heel at the mill.

Mr. Lincoln considered this one of the remarkable incidents of his life. He often referred to it, and we had many discussions in our law office over the psychological phenomena involved in the operation. Without expressing my own views I may say that his idea was that the latter half of the expression," Get up, you old hussy," was cut off by a suspension of the normal flow of his mental energy, and that as soon as life's forces returned he unconsciously ended the sentence ; or, as he in a plainer figure put it : " Just before I struck the old mare my will through the mind had set the muscles of my tongue to utter the expression, and when her heels came in contact with my head the whole thing stopped half-cocked, as it were, and was only fired off when mental energy or force returned."

By the time he had reached his seventeenth year he had attained the physical proportions of a full-grown man. He was employed to assist James Taylor in the management of a ferry-boat across the Ohio river near the mouth of Anderson's creek, but was not allowed a man's wages for the work. He received thirty-seven cents a day for what he afterwards told me was the roughest work a young man could be made to do. In the midst of whatever work he was engaged on he still found time to utilize his pen. He prepared a composition on the American Government, calling attention to the necessity of preserving the Constitution and perpetuating the Union, which with characteristic modesty he turned over to his friend and patron, William Woods, for safe-keeping and perusal. Through the instrumentality of Woods it attracted the attention of many persons, among them one Pitcher,* a lawyer at Rockport, who with faintly concealed enthusiasm declared " the world couldn't beat it." An article on Temperance was shown under similar circumstance to Aaron Farmer, a Baptist preacher of local renown, and by him furnished to an Ohio newspaper for publication. The thing, however, which gave him such prominence— a prominence too which could have been attained in no other way—was his remarkable physical strength, for he was becoming not only one of the longest,

---

*This gentleman, Judge John Pitcher, ninety-three years old, is still living in Mount Vernon, Indiana. He says that young Lincoln often called at his office and borrowed books to read at home during leisure hours. On one occasion he expressed a desire to study law with Pitcher, but explained that his parents were so poor that he could not be spared from the farm on which they lived. " He related to me in my office one day," says Pitcher, " an account of his payment to Crawford of the damage done to the latter's book—Weems' ' Life of Washington.' Lincoln said, " You see, I am tall and long-armed, and I went to work in earnest. At the end of the two days there was not a corn-blade left on a stalk in the field. I wanted to pay full damage for all the wetting the book got, and I made a clean sweep."

but one of the strongest men around Gentryville.
He enjoyed the brief distinction his exhibitions of
strength gave him more than the admiration of his
friends for his literary or forensic efforts. Some
of the feats attributed to him almost surpass belief.
One witness declares he was equal to three men,
having on a certain occasion carried a load of six
hundred pounds   At another time he walked away
with a pair of logs which three robust men were
skeptical of their ability to carry. " He could
strike with a maul a heavier blow—could sink an
axe deeper into wood than any man I ever saw," is
the testimony of another witness.

After he had passed his nineteenth year and was
nearing his majority he began to chafe and grow
restless under the restraints of home rule.   Seeing
no prospect of betterment in his condition, so long
as his fortune was interwoven with that of his father,
he at last endeavored to strike out into the broad
world for himself.   Having great faith in the judgment and influence of his fast friend Wood, he
solicited from him a recommendation to the officers
of some one of the boats plying up and down the
river, hoping thereby to obtain employment more
congenial than the dull, fatiguing work of the farm.
To this project the judicious Wood was much
opposed, and therefore suggested to the would-be
boatman the moral duty that rested on him to
remain with his father till the law released him from
that obligation.   With deep regret he retraced his
steps to the paternal mansion, seriously determined

6

not to evade the claim from which in a few weary months he would be finally released. Meanwhile occurred his first opportunity to see the world. In March, 1828, James Gentry, for whom he had been at work, had fitted out a boat with a stock of grain and meat for a trading expedition to New Orleans, and placed his son Allen in charge of the cargo for the voyage. Abe's desire to make a river trip was at last satisfied, and he accompanied the proprietor's son, serving as "bow hand." His pay was eight dollars a month and board. In due course of time the navigators returned from their expedition with the evidence of profitable results to gladden the heart of the owner. The only occurrence of interest they could relate of the voyage was the encounter with a party of marauding negroes at the plantation of Madame Duchesne, a few miles below Baton Rouge. Abe and Gentry, having tied up for the night, were fast asleep on their boat when aroused by the arrival of a crowd of negroes bent on plunder. They set to work with clubs, and not only drove off the intruders, but pursued them inland, then hastily returning to their quarters they cut loose their craft and floated down-stream till daylight.

Before passing on further it may not be amiss to glance for a moment at the social side of life as it existed in Gentryville in Abe's day. "We thought nothing," said an old lady whom I interviewed when in Indiana, "of going eight or ten miles to church. The ladies did not stop for the want of a shawl, cloak, or riding-dress in winter time, but would put on their husbands' old overcoats and wrap up their little ones and take one or two of them on their beasts. Their husbands would walk, and thus they would go to church, frequently remaining till the second day before they returned home."

The old men starting from the fields and out of the woods would carry their guns on their shoulders and go also. They dressed in deer-skin pants, moccasins, and coarse hunting shirts—the latter usually fastened with a rope or leather strap. Arriving at the house where services were to be held they would recite to each other thrilling stories of their hunting exploits, and smoke their pipes with the old ladies. They were treated, and treated each other, with the utmost kindness. A bottle of liquor, a pitcher of water, sugar, and glasses were set out for them ; also a basket of apples or turnips, with, now and then, a pie or cakes. Thus they regaled themselves till the preacher found himself in a condition to begin. The latter, having also partaken freely of the refreshments provided, would " take his stand, draw his coat, open his shirt collar, read his text, and preach and pound till the sweat, produced alike by his exertions and the exhilarating effects of the toddy, rolled from his face in great drops. Shaking hands and singing ended the service."

The houses were scattered far apart, but the people travelled great distances to participate in the frolic and coarse fun of a log-rolling and sometimes a wedding. Unless in mid-winter the young ladies carried their shoes in their hands, and only put them on when the scene of the festivities was reached. The ladies of maturer years drank whiskey toddy, while the men took the whiskey straight. They all danced merrily, many of them barefooted, to the tune of a cracked fiddle the night through. We can imagine the gleeful and more hilarious swaggering home at daybreak to the tune of Dennis Hanks' festive lines :

> " Hail Columbia, happy land,
>   If you ain't drunk then I'll be damned."

Although gay, prosperous, and light-hearted, these people were brimming over with superstition. It was at once their food and drink. They believed in the baneful influence of witches, pinned their faith to the curative power of wizards in dealing with sick animals, and shot the image of a witch with a silver ball to break the spell she was supposed to have over human beings. They followed with religious minuteness the directions of the water-wizard, with his magic divining rod, and the faith doctor who wrought miraculous cures by strange sounds and signals to some mysterious agency. The flight of a bird in at the window, the breath of a horse on a child's head, the crossing by a dog of a hunter's path, all betokened evil luck in store for some one. The moon exercised greater influence on the actions of the people and the growth of vegetation than the sun and all the planetary system combined. Fence rails could only be cut in the light of the moon, and potatoes planted in the dark of the moon. Trees and plants which bore their wielded the gad and urged the patient oxen forward. As these humble emigrants entered the new State little did the curious people in the towns through which they passed dream that the obscure and penniless driver who yelled his commands to the oxen would yet become Chief Magistrate of the greatest nation of modern times.*

---

* Mr. Lincoln once described this journey to me. He said the ground had not yet yielded up the frosts of winter; that during the day the roads would thaw out on the surface and at night freeze over again, thus making travelling, especially with oxen, painfully slow and tiresome. There were, of course, no bridges, and the party were consequently driven to ford the streams, unless by a circuitous route they could avoid them. In the early part of the day the latter were also frozen slightly, and the oxen would break through a square yard of thin ice at every step. Among other things which the party brought with them was a pet dog, which trotted along after the wagon. One day the little fellow fell behind and failed to catch up till after they had crossed the stream. Missing him they looked back, and there, on the opposite bank, he stood, whining and jumping about in great distress. The water was running over the broken edges of the ice, and the poor animal was afraid to cross. It would not pay to turn the oxen and wagon back and ford the stream again in order to recover a dog, and so the majority, in their anxiety to move forward, decided to go on without him. " But I could not endure the idea of abandoning even a dog," related Lincoln. " Pulling off shoes and socks I waded across the stream and triumphantly returned with the shivering animal under my arm. His frantic leaps of joy and other evidences of a dog's gratitude amply repaid me for all the exposure I had undergone."

CHAPTER IV.

AFTER a fortnight of rough and fatiguing travel the colony of Indiana emigrants reached a point in Illinois five miles north-west of the town of Decatur in Macon county. John Hanks, son of that Joseph Hanks in whose shop at Elizabethtown Thomas Lincoln had learned what he knew of the carpenter's art, met and sheltered them until they were safely housed on a piece of land which he had selected for them five miles further westward. He had preceded them over a year, and had in the meantime hewed out a few timbers to be used in the construction of their cabin. The place he had selected was on a bluff overlooking the Sangamon river,—for these early settlers must always be in sight of a running stream,—well supplied with timber. It was a charming and picturesque site, and all hands set resolutely to work to prepare the new abode. One felled the trees; one hewed the timbers for the cabin; while another cleared the ground of its accumulated growth of underbrush. All was bustle and activity. Even old Thomas Lincoln, infused with the spirit of the hour, was spurred to unwonted exertion. What part of the work fell to his lot our only chronicler, John Hanks, fails to note; but it is conjectured from the old gentleman's

House near Farmington, Coles County, Illinois, in which Thomas Lincoln died.

experience in the art of building that his services corresponded to those of the more modern supervising architect. With the aid of the oxen and a plow John and Abe broke up fifteen acres of sod, and "Abe and myself," observes Hanks in a matter-of-fact way, "split rails enough to fence the place in." As they swung their axes, or with wedge and maul split out the rails, how strange to them the thought would have seemed that those self-same rails were destined to make one of them immortal. If such a vision flashed before the mind of either he made no sign of it, but each kept steadily on in his simple, unromantic task.

Abe had now attained his majority and began to throw from his shoulders the vexations of parental restraint. He had done his duty to his father, and felt able to begin life on his own account. As he steps out into the broad and inviting world we take him up for consideration as a man. At the same time we dispense with further notice of his father, Thomas Lincoln. In the son are we alone interested. The remaining years of his life marked no change in the old gentleman's nature. He still listened to the glowing descriptions of prosperity in the adjoining counties, and before his death moved three times in search of better times and a healthy location. In 1851 we find him living on forty acres of land on Goose Nest prairie, in Coles county, Illinois. The land bore the usual incumbrance—a mortgage for two hundred dollars, which his son afterwards paid. On the 17th of January, after suffering for many weeks from a disorder of the kidneys, he passed away at the ripe old age—as his son tells us—of "seventy-three years and eleven days."

For a long time after beginning life on his own account Abe remained in sight of the parental abode. He worked at odd jobs in the neighborhood, or wherever the demand for his services called him. As late as 1831 he was still in the same parts, and John Hanks is authority for the statement that he "made three thousand rails for Major Warnick" walking daily three miles to his work. During the intervals of leisure he read the few books obtainable, and continued the practice of extemporaneous speaking to the usual audience of undemonstrative stumps and voiceless trees. His first attempt at public speaking after landing in Illinois is thus described to me by John Hanks, whose language I incorporate : "After Abe got to Decatur, or rather to Macon county, a man by the name of Posey came into our neighborhood and made a speech. It was a bad one, and I said Abe could beat it. I turned down a box and Abe made his speech. The other man was a candidate—Abe wasn't. Abe beat him to death, his subject being the navigation of the Sangamon river. The man, after Abe's speech was through, took him aside and asked him where he had learned so much and how he could do so well. Abe replied, stating his manner and method of reading, and what he had read. The man encouraged him to persevere."

For the first time we are now favored with the appearance on the scene of a very important personage—one destined to exert no little influence in shaping Lincoln's fortunes. It is Denton Offut, a brisk and venturesome business man, whose operations extended up and down the Sangamon river for many miles. Having heard glowing reports of John Hanks' successful experience as a boatman in Kentucky he had come down the river to engage the latter's services to take a boat-load of stock and provisions to New Orleans. " He wanted me to go badly," observes Hanks, " but I waited awhile before answering. I hunted up Abe, and I introduced him and John Johnston, his step-brother, to Offut. After some talk we at last made an engagement with Offut at fifty cents a day and sixty dollars to make the trip to New Orleans. Abe and I came down the Sangamon river in a canoe in March, 1831 ; landed at what is now called Jamestown, five miles east of Springfield, then known as Judy's Ferry." Here Johnston joined them, and, leaving their canoe in charge of one Uriah Mann, they walked to Springfield, where after some inquiry they found the genial and enterprising Offut regaling himself with the good cheer dispensed at " The Buckhorn " inn. This hostelry, kept by Andrew Elliot, was the leading place of its kind in the then unpretentious village of Springfield. The figure of a buck's head painted on a sign swinging in front of the house gave rise to its name. Offut had agreed with Hanks to have a boat ready for him and his two companions at the mouth of Spring creek on their arrival, but too many deep potations with the new-comers who daily thronged about the " Buckhorn " had interfered with the execution of his plans, and the boat still remained in the womb of the future. Offut met the three expectant navigators on their arrival, and deep were his regrets over his failure to provide the boat. The interview resulted in the trio engaging to make the boat themselves. From what was known as "Congress land" they obtained an abundance of timber, and by the aid of the machinery at Kirkpatrick's mill they soon had the requisite material for their vessel. While the work of construction was going on a shanty was built in which they were lodged. Lincoln was elected cook, a distinction he never underestimated for a moment. Within four weeks the boat was ready to launch. Offut was sent for, and was present when she slid into the water. It was the occasion of much political chat and buncombe, in which the Whig party and Jackson alike were, strangely enough, lauded to the skies. It is difficult to account for the unanimous approval of such strikingly antagonistic ideas, unless it be admitted that Offut must have brought with him some substantial reminder of the hospitality on draught at the "Buckhorn" inn. Many disputes arose, we are told, in which Lincoln took part and found a good field for practice and debate.

A travelling juggler halted long enough in Sangamontown, where the boat was launched, to give an exhibition of his art and dexterity in the loft of Jacob Carman's house. In Lincoln's low-crowned, broad-brimmed hat the magician cooked eggs. As explanatory of the delay in passing up his hat Lincoln drolly observed," It was out of respect for the eggs, not care for my hat."

Having loaded the vessel with pork in barrels, corn, and hogs, these sturdy boatmen swung out into the stream. On April 19 they reached the town of New Salem, a place destined to be an important spot in the career of Lincoln. There they met with their first serious delay. The boat stranded on Rutledge's mill-dam and hung helplessly over it a day and a night. "We unloaded the boat," narrated one of the crew to explain how they obtained relief from their embarrassing situation; "that is, we transferred the goods from our boat to a borrowed one. We then rolled the barrels forward; Lincoln bored a hole in the end [projecting] over the dam; the water which had leaked in ran out and we slid over." Offut was profoundly impressed with this exhibition of Lincoln's ingenuity. In his enthusiasm he declared to the crowd who covered the hill and who had been watching Lincoln's operation that he would build a steamboat to plow up and down the Sangamon, and that Lincoln should be her Captain. She would have rollers for shoals and dams, runners for ice, and with Lincoln in charge, " By thunder, she'd have to go ! "

After release from their embarrassing, not to say perilous, position the boat and her crew floated away from New Salem and passed on to a point known as Blue Banks, where as the historian of the voyage says : " We had to load some hogs bought of Squire Godbey. We tried to drive them aboard, but could not. They would run back past us. Lincoln then suggested that we sew their eyes shut. Thinking to try it, we caught them, Abe holding their heads and I their tails while Offut sewed up their eyes. Still they wouldn't drive. At last, becoming tired, we carried them to the boat. Abe received them and cut open their eyes, Johnston and I handing them to him." After thus disposing of the hog problem they again swung loose and floated down-stream. From the Sangamon they passed to the Illinois. At Beardstown their unique craft, with its "sails made of planks and cloth," excited the amusement and laughter of those who saw them from the shore. Once on the bosom of the broad Mississippi they glided past Alton, St. Louis, and Cairo in rapid succession, tied up for a day at Memphis, and made brief stops at Vicksburg and Natchez. Early in May they reached New Orleans, where they lingered a month, disposing of their cargo and viewing the sights which the Crescent City afforded.

In New Orleans, for the first time Lincoln beheld the true horrors of human slavery. He saw "negroes in chains—whipped and scourged." Against this inhumanity his sense of right and justice rebelled, and his mind and conscience were awakened to a realization of what he had often heard and read. No doubt, as one of his companions has said, "Slavery ran the iron into him then and there." One morning in their rambles over the city the trio passed a slave auction. A vigorous and comely mulatto girl was being sold. She underwent a thorough examination at the hands of the bidders; they pinched her flesh and made her trot up and down the room like a horse, to show how she moved, and in order, as the auctioneer said, that "bidders might satisfy themselves" whether the article they were offering to buy was sound or not. The whole thing was so revolting that Lincoln moved away from the scene with a deep feeling of "unconquerable hate." Bidding his companions follow him he said, "By God, boys, let's get away from this. If ever I get a chance to hit that thing [meaning slavery], I'll hit it hard." This incident was furnished me in 1865, by John Hanks. I have also heard Mr. Lincoln refer to it himself.

In June the entire party, including Offut, boarded a steamboat going up the river. At St. Louis they disembarked, Offut remaining behind while Lincoln, Hanks, and Johnston started across Illinois on foot. At Edwardsville they separated, Hanks going to Springfield, while Lincoln and his step-brother followed the road to Coles county, to which point old Thomas Lincoln had meanwhile removed. Here Abe did not tarry long, probably not over a month, but long enough to dispose most effectually of one Daniel Needham, a famous wrestler who had challenged the returned boatman to a test of strength. The contest took place at a locality known as "Wabash Point." Abe threw his antagonist twice with comparative ease, and thereby demonstrated such marked strength and agility as to render him forever popular with the boys of that neighborhood.

In August the waters of the Sangamon river

washed Lincoln in to New Salem. This once
sprightly and thriving village is no longer in existence. Not a building, scarcely a stone, is left to
mark the place where it once stood. To reach it
now the traveller must ascend a bluff a hundred
feet above the general level of the surrounding
country. The brow of the ridge, two hundred and
fifty feet broad where it overlooks the river, widens
gradually as it extends westwardly to the forest
and ultimately to broad pastures. Skirting the base
of the bluff is the Sangamon river, which, coming
around a sudden bend from the south-east, strikes
the rocky hill and is turned abruptly north. Here
is an old mill, driven by water-power, and reaching
across the river is the mill-dam on which Offut's
vessel hung stranded in April, 1831. As the river
rolled her turbid waters over the dam, plunging
them into the whirl and eddy beneath, the roar
of waters, like low, continuous, distant thunder,
could be distinctly heard through the village day
and night.

The country in almost every direction is diversi-
fied by alternate stretches of hills and level lands,
with streams between each struggling to reach the
river. The hills are bearded with timber—oak,
hickory, walnut, ash, and elm. Below them are
stretches of rich alluvial bottom land, and the eye
ranges over a vast expanse of foliage, the monotony
of which is relieved by the alternating swells and
depressions of the landscape. Between peak and
peak, through its bed of limestone, sand, and clay,
sometimes kissing the feet of one bluff and then

hugging the other, rolls the Sangamon river. The village of New Salem, which once stood on the ridge, was laid out in 1828 ; it became a trading place, and in 1836 contained twenty houses and a hundred inhabitants. In the days of land offices and stage-coaches it was a sprightly village with a busy market. Its people were progressive and industrious. Propitious winds filled the sails of its commerce, prosperity smiled graciously on its every enterprise, and the outside world encouraged its social pretensions. It had its day of glory, but, singularly enough, cotemporaneous with the departure of Lincoln from its midst it went into a rapid decline. A few crumbling stones here and there are all that attest its former existence. " How it vanished," observes one writer, " like a mist in the morning, to what distant places its inhabitants dispersed, and what became of the abodes they left behind, shall be questions for the local historian."

Lincoln's return to New Salem in August, 1831, was, within a few days, contemporaneous with the reappearance of Offut, who made the gratifying announcement that he had purchased a stock of goods which were to follow him from Beardstown. He had again retained the services of Lincoln to assist him when his merchandise should come to hand. The tall stranger—destined to be a stranger in New Salem no longer—pending the arrival of his employer's goods, lounged about the village with nothing to do. Leisure never sat heavily on him. To him there was nothing uncongenial in it, and he might very properly have been dubbed at the time

7

a " loafer." He assured those with whom he came in contact that he was a piece of floating driftwood; that after the winter of deep snow, he had come down the river with the freshet; borne along by the swelling waters, and aimlessly floating about, he had accidentally lodged at New Salem. Looking back over his history we are forced to conclude that Providence or chance, or whatever power is responsible for it, could not have assigned him to a more favorable refuge.

His introduction to the citizens of New Salem, as Mentor Graham* the school-teacher tells us, was in the capacity of clerk of an election board. Graham furnishes ample testimony of the facility, fairness, and honesty which characterized the new clerk's work, and both teacher and clerk were soon bound together by the warmest of ties. During the day, when votes were coming in slowly, Lincoln began to entertain the crowd at the polls with a few attempts at story-telling. My cousin, J. R. Herndon, was present and enjoyed this feature of the election with the keenest relish. He never forgot some of Lincoln's yarns, and was fond of repeating them in after years. The recital of a few stories by Lincoln easily established him in the good graces of all New Salem. Perhaps he did not know it at the time, but he had used the weapon nearest at hand and had won.†

---

* Nicolay and Hay in the *Century* make the mistake of spelling this man's name " Menton " Graham. In all the letters and papers from him he signs himself " Mentor " in every case.—J. W. W.

† " In the afternoon, as things were dragging a little, Lincoln the

A few days after the election Lincoln found employment with one Dr. Nelson, who after the style of dignitaries of later days started with his family and effects in his " private " conveyance—which in this instance was a flat-boat—for Texas. Lincoln was hired to pilot the vessel through to the Illinois river. Arriving at Beardstown the pilot was discharged, and returned on foot across the sand and

---

new man, began to spin out a stock of Indiana yarns. One that amused me more than any other he called the lizard story. 'The meeting-house,' he said, 'was in the woods and quite a distance from any other house. It was only used once a month. The preacher—an old line Baptist—was dressed in coarse linen pantaloons, and shirt of the same material. The pants, manufactured after the old fashion, with baggy legs and a flap in front, were made to attach to his frame without the aid of suspenders. A single button held his shirt in position, and that was at the collar. He rose up in the pulpit and with a loud voice announced his text thus : ' I am the Christ, whom I shall represent to-day.' About this time a little blue lizard ran up underneath his roomy pantaloons. The old preacher, not wishing to interrupt the steady flow of his sermon, slapped away on his legs, expecting to arrest the intruder ; but his efforts were unavailing, and the little fellow kept on ascending higher and higher. Continuing the sermon, the preacher slyly loosened the central button which graced the waist-band of his pantaloons and with a kick off came that easy-fitting garment. But meanwhile Mr. Lizard had passed the equatorial line of waist-band and was calmly exploring that part of the preacher's anatomy which lay underneath the back of his shirt. Things were now growing interesting, but the sermon was still grinding on. The next movement on the preacher's part was for the collar button, and with one sweep of his arm off came the tow linen shirt. The congregation sat for an instant as if dazed ; at length one old lady in the rear of the room rose up and glancing at the excited object in the pulpit, shouted at the top of her voice : 'If you represent Christ then I'm done with the Bible.' "—J. R. Herndon, MS., July 2, 1865.

hills to New Salem.   In the meantime Offut's long
expected goods had arrived, and Lincoln was placed
in charge.   Offut relied in no slight degree on the
business capacity of his clerk.   In his effusive way
he praised him beyond reason.   He boasted of his
skill as a business man and his wonderful intellectual acquirements.   As for physical strength and
fearlessness of danger, he challenged New Salem
and the entire world to produce his equal.   In
keeping with his widely known spirit of enterprise
Offut rented the Rutledge and Cameron mill, which
stood at the foot of the hill, and thus added another
iron to keep company with the half-dozen already
in the fire.   As a further test of his business ability
Lincoln was placed in charge of this also.   William
G. Greene was hired to assist him, and between the
two a life-long friendship sprang up.   They slept in
the store, and so strong was the intimacy between
them that "when one turned over the other had to
do likewise."   At the head of these varied enterprises was Offut, the most progressive man by all
odds in the village.   He was certainly an odd
character, if we accept the judgment of his cotem-
poraries.   By some he is given the character of
a clear-headed, brisk man of affairs.   By others
he is variously described as "wild, noisy, and
reckless," or "windy, rattle-brained, unsteady, and
improvident."   Despite the unenviable traits as-
cribed to him he was good at heart and a generous
friend of Lincoln.   His boast that the latter could
outrun, whip, or throw down any man in Sangamon
county was soon tested, as we shall presently see,

for, as another has truthfully expressed it, "honors such as Offut accorded to Abe were to be won before they were worn at New Salem." In the neighborhood of the village, or rather a few miles to the south-west, lay a strip of timber called Clary's Grove. The boys who lived there were a terror to the entire region—seemingly a necessary product of frontier civilization. They were friendly and good-natured ; they could trench a pond, dig a bog, build a house ; they could pray and fight, make a village or create a state. They would do almost anything for sport or fun, love or necessity. Though rude and rough, though life's forces ran over the edge of the bowl, foaming and sparkling in pure deviltry for deviltry's sake, yet place before them a poor man who needed their aid, a lame or sick man, a defenceless woman, a widow, or an orphaned child, they melted into sympathy and charity at once. They gave all they had, and willingly toiled or played cards for more. Though there never was under the sun a more generous parcel of rowdies, a stranger's introduction was likely to be the most unpleasant part of his acquaintance with them. They conceded leadership to one Jack Armstrong, a hardy, strong, and well-developed specimen of physical manhood, and under him they were in the habit of "cleaning out" New Salem whenever his order went forth to do so. Offut and "Bill" Clary —the latter skeptical of Lincoln's strength and agility—ended a heated discussion in the store one day over the new clerk's ability to meet the tactics of Clary's Grove, by a bet of ten dollars that Jack

Armstrong was, in the language of the day, "a better man than Lincoln." The new clerk strongly opposed this sort of an introduction, but after much entreaty from Offut, at last consented to make his bow to the social lions of the town in this unusual way. He was now six feet four inches high, and weighed, as his friend and confidant, William Greene, tells us with impressive precision, "two hundred and fourteen pounds." The contest was to be a friendly one and fairly conducted. All New Salem adjourned to the scene of the wrestle. Money, whiskey, knives, and all manner of property were staked on the result. It is unnecessary to go into the details of the encounter. Everyone knows how it ended; how at last the tall and angular rail-splitter, enraged at the suspicion of foul tactics, and profiting by his height and the length of his arms, fairly lifted the great bully by the throat and shook him like a rag; how by this act he established himself solidly in the esteem of all New Salem, and secured the respectful admiration and friendship of the very man whom he had so thoroughly vanquished.* From this time forward Jack Armstrong, his wife

---

* Mr. Lincoln's remarkable strength resulted not so much from muscular power as from the toughness of his sinews. He could not only lift from the ground enormous weight, but could throw a cannon-ball or a maul farther than anyone else in New Salem. I heard him explain once how he was enabled thus to excel others. He did not attribute it to a greater proportion of physical strength, but contended that because of the unusual length of his arms the ball or projectile had a greater swing and therefore acquired more force and momentum than in the hands of an average man.

Hannah, and all the other Armstrongs became his warm and trusted friends. None stood readier than they to rally to his support, none more willing to lend a helping hand. Lincoln appreciated their friendship and support, and in after years proved his gratitude by saving one member of the family from the gallows.

The business done over Offut's counter gave his clerk frequent intervals of rest, so that, if so inclined, an abundance of time for study was always at his disposal. Lincoln had long before realized the deficiencies of his education, and resolved, now that the conditions were favorable, to atone for early neglect by a course of study. Nothing was more apparent to him than his limited knowledge of language, and the proper way of expressing his ideas. Moreover, it may be said that he appreciated his inefficiency in a rhetorical sense, and therefore determined to overcome all these obstacles by mastering the intricacies of grammatical construction. Acting on the advice of Mentor Graham he hunted up one Vaner, who was the reputed owner of Kirkham's Grammar, and after a walk of several miles returned to the store with the coveted volume under his arm. With zealous perseverance he at once applied himself to the book. Sometimes he would stretch out at full length on the counter, his head propped up on a stack of calico prints, studying it; or he would steal away to the shade of some inviting tree, and there spend hours at a time in a determined effort to fix in his mind the arbitrary rule that " adverbs qualify verbs, adjectives, and other adverbs." From the vapidity of grammar it was now and then a great relaxation to turn to the more agreeable subject of mathematics ; and he might often have been seen lying face downwards, stretched out over six feet of grass, figuring out on scraps of paper some problem given for solution by a quizzical store lounger, or endeavoring to prove that, " multiplying the denominator of a fraction divides it, while dividing the denominator multiplies it." Rather a poor prospect one is forced to admit for a successful man of business.

At this point in my narrative I am pained to drop from further notice our buoyant and effusive friend Offut. His business ventures failing to yield the extensive returns he predicted, and too many of his obligations maturing at the same time, he was forced to pay the penalty of commercial delinquency and went to the wall. He soon disappeared from the village, and the inhabitants thereof never knew whither he went. In the significant language of Lincoln he "petered out." As late as 1873 I received a letter from Dr. James Hall, a physician living at St. Dennis, near Baltimore, Maryland, who, referring to the disappearance of Offut, relates the following reminiscence : " Of what consequence to know or learn more of Offut I cannot imagine ; but be assured he turned up after leaving New Salem. On meeting the name it seemed familiar, but I could not locate him. Finally I fished up from memory that some twenty-five years ago one " Denton Offut" appeared in Baltimore, hailing from Kentucky, advertising himself in the city papers as a veterinary surgeon and horse tamer, professing to have a secret to whisper in the horse's ear, or a secret manner of whispering in his ear, which he could communicate to others, and by which the most refractory and vicious horse could be quieted and controlled. For this secret he charged five dollars, binding the recipient by oath not to divulge it. I know several persons, young fancy horsemen, who paid for the trick. Offut advertised himself not only through the press, but by his strange attire. He appeared in the streets on horseback and on foot, in plain citizens' dress of black, but with a broad sash across his right shoulder, of various colored ribbons, crossed on his left hip under a large rosette of the same material, the whole rendering his appearance most ludicrously conspicuous. Having occasion to purchase a horse I encountered him at several of our stables and was strongly urged to avail myself of his secret. So much for Offut; but were he living in '61, I doubt not Mr. Lincoln would have heard of him."

The early spring of 1832 brought to Springfield and New Salem a most joyful announcement. It was the news of the coming of a steamboat down the Sangamon river—proof incontestable that the stream was navigable. The enterprise was undertaken and carried through by Captain Vincent Bogue, of Springfield, who had gone to Cincinnati to procure a vessel and thus settle the much-mooted question of the river's navigability. When, therefore, he notified the people of his town that the steamboat *Talisman* would put out from Cincinnati for Springfield, we can well imagine what great excitement and unbounded enthusiasm followed the announcement. Springfield, New Salem, and all the other towns along the now interesting Sangamon* were to be connected by water with the outside world. Public meetings, with the accompaniment of long subscription lists, were held ; the merchants of Springfield advertised the arrival of goods " direct from the East per steamer *Talisman ;*" the mails were promised as often as once a week from the same direction ; all the land adjoining each enterprising and aspiring village along the river was subdivided into town lots—in fact, the whole region began to feel the stimulating effects of what, in later days, would have been called a "boom." I remember the occasion well, for two reasons. It was my first sight of a steamboat, and also the first time I ever saw Mr. Lincoln—although I never became acquainted with him till his second race for the Legislature in 1834. In response to the suggestion of Captain Bogue, made from Cincinnati, a number of citizens—among the number Lincoln— had gone down the river to Beardstown to meet the vessel as she emerged from the Illinois. These were armed with axes having long handles, to cut away, as Bogue had recommended, " branches of trees hanging over from the banks." After having passed New Salem, I and other boys on horseback followed the boat, riding along the river's bank as far as

---

* The final syllable of this name was then pronounced to rhyme with " raw." In later days the letter " n" was added—probably for euphony's sake.

Bogue's mill, where she tied up. There we went aboard, and lost in boyish wonder, feasted our eyes on the splendor of her interior decorations. The *Sangamon Journal* of that period contains numerous poetical efforts celebrating the *Talisman's* arrival. A few lines under date of April 5, 1832, unsigned, but supposed to have been the product of a local poet—one Oliphant*—were sung to the tune of "Clar de Kitchen." I cannot refrain from inflicting a stanza or two of this ode on the reader :

> " O, Captain Bogue he gave the load,
> And Captain Bogue he showed the road;
> And we came up with a right good will,
> And tied our boat up to his mill.
>
> Now we are up the Sangamo,
> And here we'll have a grand hurra,
> So fill your glasses to the brim,
> Of whiskey, brandy, wine, and gin.
>
> Illinois suckers, young and raw,
> Were strung along the Sangamo,
> To see a boat come up by steam
> They surely thought it was a dream."

On its arrival at Springfield, or as near Springfield as the river ran, the crew of the boat were given a reception and dance in the court-house. The cream of the town's society attended to pay their respects to the newly arrived guests. The captain in charge of the boat—not Captain Bogue, but a vainly dressed fellow from the East—was accompanied by a woman, more gaudily attired than himself, whom

---

* E. P. Oliphant, a lawyer.

he introduced as his wife. Of course the most considerate attention was shown them both, until later in the evening, when it became apparent that the gallant officer and his fair partner had imbibed too freely—for in those days we had plenty of good cheer—and were becoming unpleasantly demonstrative in their actions. This breach of good manners openly offended the high-toned nature of Springfield's fair ladies ; but not more than the lamentable fact, which they learned on the following day, that the captain's partner was not his wife after all, but a woman of doubtful reputation whom he had brought with him from some place further east. But to return to the *Talisman*. That now interesting vessel lay for a week longer at Bogue's mill, when the receding waters admonished her officers that unless they purposed spending the remainder of the year there they must head her down-stream, In this emergency recourse was had to my cousin Rowan Herndon, who had had no little experience as a boatman, and who recommended the employment of Lincoln as a skilful assistant. These two inland navigators undertook therefore the contract of piloting the vessel—which had now become elephantine in proportions—through the uncertain channel of the Sangamon to the Illinois river. The average speed was four miles a day. At New Salem safe passage over the mill-dam was deemed impossible unless the same could be lowered or a portion removed.* To this, Cameron and Rut-

---

* The affair at New Salem is thus described by Oliphant in the poem before referred to :

ledge, owners of the mill, entered their most stren-
uous protest. The boat's officers responded that
under the Federal Constitution and laws no one had
the right to dam up or in any way obstruct a navigable stream, and they argued that, as they had just
demonstrated that the Sangamon was navigable (?),
they proposed to remove enough of the obstruc-
tion to let the boat through. Rowan Herndon,
describing it to me in 1865, said: "When we
struck the dam she hung. We then backed off and
threw the anchor over. We tore away part of the
dam and raising steam ran her over on the first
trial." The entire proceeding stirred up no little
feeling, in which mill owners, boat officers, and pas-
sengers took part. The effect the return trip of
the *Talisman* had on those who believed in the
successful navigation of the Sangamon is shrewdly
indicated by the pilot, who with laconic compla-
cency adds: "As soon as she was over, the company that chartered her was done with her." Lincoln and Herndon, in charge of the vessel, piloted
her through to Beardstown. There they were paid
forty dollars each, according to contract, and bidding adieu to the *Talisman's* officers and crew,
set out on foot for New Salem again. A few
months later the *Talisman* caught fire at the
wharf in St. Louis and went up in flames. The
experiment of establishing a steamboat line to

"And when we came to Salem dam,
   Up we went against it jam.
   We tried to cross with all our might,
   But found we couldn't and staid all night."

Springfield proved an unfortunate venture for its projector, Captain Bogue. Finding himself unable to meet his rapidly maturing obligations, incurred in aid of the enterprise, it is presumed that he left the country, for the *Journal* of that period is filled with notices of attachment proceedings brought by vigilant creditors who had levied on his goods.

CHAPTER V.

THE departure of the *Talisman* for deeper waters, the downfall of Denton Offut's varied enterprises and his disappearance from New Salem, followed in rapid succession, and before the spring of 1832 had merged into summer Lincoln found himself a piece of "floating driftwood" again. Where he might have lodged had not the Black Hawk war intervened can only be a matter of conjecture. A glance at this novel period in his life may not be out of keeping with the purpose of this book. The great Indian chief, Black Hawk, who on the 30th of June, 1831, had entered into an agreement, having all the solemnity of a treaty, with Governor Reynolds and General Gaines that none of his tribe should ever cross the Mississippi "to their usual place of residence, nor any part of their old hunting grounds east of the Mississippi, without permission of the President of the United States or the governor of the State of Illinois," had openly broken the compact. On the 6th of April, 1832, he recrossed the Mississippi and marched up Rock River Valley, accompanied by about five hundred warriors on horseback; while his women and children went up the river in canoes. The great chief was now sixty-seven years old, and believed that his plots

were all ripe and his allies fast and true. Although
warned by General Atkinson, then in command of
Fort Armstrong, against this aggression, and
ordered to return, he proudly refused, claiming that
he had "come to plant corn." On being informed
of the movement of Black Hawk Governor Reynolds
called for a thousand mounted volunteers to co-op-
erate with the United States forces under command
of General Atkinson, and drive the wily Indian
back across the Mississippi. The response to the
governor's call was prompt and energetic. In the
company from Sangamon county Lincoln enlisted,
and now for the first time entered on the vicissi-
tudinous and dangerous life of a soldier. That he
in fact regarded the campaign after the Indians as
a sort of holiday affair and chicken-stealing expedition is clearly shown in a speech he afterwards
made in Congress in exposure of the military pretensions of General Cass. However, in grim, sol-
dierly severity he marched with the Sangamon
county contingent to Rushville,* in Schuyler
county, where, much to his surprise, he was elected

---

* While at the rendezvous at Rushville and on the march to the
front Lincoln of course drilled his men, and gave them such meager
instruction in military tactics as he could impart. Some of the most
grotesque things he ever related were descriptions of these drills.
In marching one morning at the head of the company, who were
following in lines of twenty abreast, it became necessary to pass
through a gate much narrower than the lines. The captain could
not remember the proper command to turn the company *endwise*,
and the situation was becoming decidedly embarrassing, when one of
those thoughts born of the depths of despair came to his rescue.
Facing the lines, he shouted : " Halt ! This company will break ranks
for two minutes and form again on the other side of the gate." The
manœuvre was successfully executed.

captain of the company over William Kirkpatrick. A recital of the campaign that followed, in the effort to drive the treacherous Indians back, or a description of the few engagements—none of which reached the dignity of a battle—which took place, have in no wise been overlooked by the historians of Illinois and of the Black Hawk war. With the exception of those things which relate to Lincoln alone I presume it would be needless to attempt to add anything to what has so thoroughly and truthfully been told.

On being elected captain, Lincoln replied in a brief response of modest and thankful acceptance. It was the first official trust ever turned over to his keeping, and he prized it and the distinction it gave him more than any which in after years fell to his lot. His company savored strongly of the Clary's Grove order, and though daring enough in the presence of danger, were difficult to bring down to the inflexibilities of military discipline. Each one seemed perfectly able and willing to care for himself, and while the captain's authority was respectfully observed, yet, as some have said, they were none the less a crowd of "generous ruffians." I heard Mr. Lincoln say once on the subject of his career as captain in this company and the discipline he exercised over his men, that to the first order given one of them he received the response, "Go to the devil, sir!" Notwithstanding the interchange of many such unsoldierlike civilities between the officer and his men, a strong bond of affection united them together, and if a contest had arisen over the con-

8

flict of orders between the United States authorities and those emanating from Captain Lincoln or some other Illinois officer—as at one time was threatened —we need not be told to which side the Sangamon county company to a man would have gone. A general order forbidding the discharge of firearms within fifty yards of the camp was disobeyed by Captain Lincoln himself. For this violation of rule he was placed under arrest and deprived of his sword for a day. But this and other punishments in no way humiliated him in the esteem of his men ; if anything, they only clung the closer, and when Clary's Grove friendship asserted itself, it meant that firm and generous attachment found alone on the frontier—that bond, closer than the affinity of blood. which becomes stronger as danger approaches death.

A soldier of the Sangamon county company broke into the officers' quarters one night, and with the aid of a tomahawk and four buckets, obtained by stealth a good supply of wines and liquors, which he generously distributed to his appreciative comrades. The next morning at daybreak, when the army began to move, the Sangamon county company, much to their captain's astonishment, were unfit for the march. Their nocturnal expedition had been too much for them, and one by one they fell by the wayside, until but a mere handful remained to keep step with their gallant and astounded captain. Those who fell behind gradually overcame the effects of their carousal, but were hard pressed to overtake the command, and it was far into the night when the last one straggled into camp. The investigation which followed resulted only in the captain suffering the punishment for the more guilty men. For this infraction of military law he was put under arrest and made to carry a wooden sword for two days, "and this too," as one of his company has since assured me, "although he was entirely blameless in the matter."

Among the few incidents of Lincoln's career in the Black Hawk war that have found a place in history was his manly interference to protect an old Indian who strayed, hungry and helpless, into camp one day, and whom the soldiers were conspiring to kill on the ground that he was a spy. A letter from General Cass, recommending him for his past kind and faithful services to the whites, which the trembling old savage drew from beneath the folds of his blanket failed in any degree to appease the wrath of the men who confronted him. They had come out to fight the treacherous Indians, and here was one who had the temerity even to steal into their camp. "Make an example of him," they exclaimed. "The letter is a forgery and he is a spy." They might have put their threats into execution had not the tall form of their captain, his face "swarthy with resolution and rage," interposed itself between them and their defenseless victim. Lincoln's determined look and demand that "it must not be done" were enough. They sullenly desisted, and the Indian, unmolested, continued on his way.

Lincoln's famous wrestling match with the redoubtable Thompson, a soldier from Union county, who managed to throw him twice in succession, caused no diminution in the admiration and pride his men felt in their captain's muscle and prowess. They declared that unfair advantage had been taken of their champion, that Thompson had been guilty of foul tactics, and that, in the language of the sporting arena, it was a "dog-fall." Lincoln's magnanimous action, however, in according his opponent credit for fair dealing in the face of the wide-spread and adverse criticism that prevailed, only strengthened him in the esteem of all.*

At times the soldiers were hard pressed for food, but by a combination of ingenuity and labor in proportions known only to a volunteer soldier, they managed to avoid the unpleasant results of long-continued and unsatisfied hunger. "At an old Winnebago town called Turtle Village," narrates a member of the company, "after stretching our rations over nearly four days, one of our mess, an old acquaintance of Lincoln, G. B. Fanchier, shot a dove, and having a gill of flour left we made a gallon and a half of delicious soup in an old tin bucket that had been lost by Indians. This soup we divided among several messes that were hungrier

---

* William L. Wilson, a survivor of the war, in a letter under date of February 3, 1882, after detailing reminiscences of Stillman's defeat, says : "I have during that time had much fun with the afterwards President of the United States, Abraham Lincoln. I remember one time of wrestling with him, two best in three, and ditched him. He was not satisfied, and we tried it in a foot-race for a five-dollar bill. I won the money, and 'tis spent long ago. And many more reminiscences could I give, but am of the Quaker persuasion, and not much given to writing."

than we were and our own mess, by pouring in each
man's cup a portion of the esculent. Once more, at
another time, in the extreme northern part of Illinois,
we had been very hungry for two days, but suddenly
came upon a new cabin at the edge of the prairie
that the pioneer sovereign squatter family had vacated and 'skedaddled' from for fear of losing their
scalps. There were plenty of chickens about the
cabin, much hungrier than we ourselves were, if poverty is to test the matter, and the boys heard a voice
saying 'Slay and eat.' They at once went to running, clubbing, and shooting them as long as they
could be found. Whilst the killing was going on I
climbed to the ridge-pole of the smoke-house to see
distinctly what I saw obscurely from the ground,
and behold! the cleanest, sweetest jole I ever saw—
alone, half hid by boards and ridge-pole, stuck up
no doubt for future use. By this time many of the
chickens were on the fire, broiling, for want of grease
or gravy to fry them in. Some practical fellow
proposed to throw in with the fowls enough bacon
to convert broiling into frying; the proposition was
adopted, and they were soon fried. We began to
eat the tough, dry chickens with alternating mouthfuls of the jole, when Lincoln came to the repast
with the query, 'Eating chicken, boys?' 'Not
much, sir,' I responded, for we had operated principally on the jole, it being sweeter and more palatable
than the chickens. 'It is much like eating saddle-
bags,' he responded; 'but I think the stomach can
accomplish much to-day; but what have you got
there with the skeletons, George?' 'We did have

a sweet jole of a hog, sir,' I answered, ' but you are nearly too late for your share,' at the same time making room for him to approach the elm-bark dish. He ate the bacon a moment, then commenced dividing by mouthfuls to the boys from other messes, who came to ' see what Abe was at,' and saying many quaint and funny things suited to the time and the jole." The captain, it will be seen, by his " freedom without familiarity" and his " courtesy without condescension," was fast making inroads on the respect of his rude but appreciative men. He was doubtless looking a long way ahead, when both their friendship and respect would be of avail, for as the chronicler last quoted from continues: " He was acquainted with everybody, and he had determined, as he told me, to become a candidate for the next Legislature. The mess immediately pitched on him as our standard-bearer, and he accepted."

The term for which the volunteers had enlisted had now expired, and the majority, tiring of the service, the novelty of which had worn off, and longing for the comforts and good cheer of their homes, refused either to re-enlist or render further service. They turned their faces homeward, each with his appetite for military glory well satiated. But the war was not over, and the mighty Black Hawk was still east of the Mississippi. A few remained and re-enlisted. Among them was Lincoln. This time, eschewing the responsibility of a captaincy, and to avoid the possible embarrassment of dragging about camp a wooden sword, he entered the company of

Elijah Iles as a dignified private. It has pleased some of Mr. Lincoln's biographers to attribute this re-enlistment to pure patriotism on his part and a conscientious desire to serve his country. From the standpoint of sentiment that is a comfortable view to take of it; but I have strong reason to believe that Mr. Lincoln never entertained such serious notions of the campaign. In fact, I may say that my information comes from the best authority to be had in the matter—the soldier himself. Mr. Lincoln had no home; he had cut loose from his parents, from the Hankses and the Johnstons; he left behind him no anxious wife and children; and no chair before a warm fireside remained vacant for him. "I was out of work," he said to me once, "and there being no danger of more fighting, I could do nothing better than enlist again."

After his discharge from this last and brief period of service, along with the remainder of the Sangamon county soldiers, he departed from the scenes of recent hostilities for New Salem again. His soldier days had ended, and he returned now to enter upon a far different career. However much in later years he may have pretended to ridicule the disasters of the Black Hawk war, or the part he took in it, yet I believe he was rather proud of it after all. When Congress, along in the fifties, granted him a land warrant he was greatly pleased. He located it on some land in Iowa, and declared to me one day that he would die seized of that land, and although the tract never yielded him anything he never, so far as my knowledge extends parted with its ownership.*

The return of the Black Hawk warriors to New Salem occurred in the month of August, but a short time before the general election. A new Legislature was to be chosen, and as Lincoln had declared to his comrades in the army he would, and in obedience to the effusive declaration of principles which he had issued over his signature in March, before he went to the war, he presented himself to the people of his newly adopted county as a candidate for the Legislature. It is not necessary to enter into an account of the political conditions in Illinois at that time, or the effect had on the same by those

---

* "In regard to the Bounty Land Warrants issued to Abraham Lincoln for military services during the Black Hawk war as Captain of 4th Illinois Volunteers, the first warrant, No. 52,076, for forty acres (Act of 1850), was issued to Abraham Lincoln, Captain, etc. on the 16th of April, 1852, and was located in his name by his duly appointed attorney, John P. Davis, at Dubuque, Iowa, July 21, 1854, on the north-west quarter of the south-west quarter of section 20, in Township 84, north of Range 39, west, Iowa. A patent as recorded in volume 280, page 21, was issued for this tract to Abraham Lincoln on the 1st of June, 1855, and transmitted the 26th October, 1855, to the Register of delivery.

"Under the Act of 1855, another Land Warrant, No. 68,465, for 120 acres, was issued to Abraham Lincoln, Captain Illinois Militia, Black Hawk war, on the 22d April, 1856, and was located by himself at Springfield, Illinois, December 27, 1859, on the east half of the north-east quarter and the north-west quarter of the north-east quarter of section 18, in Township 84, north of Range 39, west; for which a patent, as recorded in volume 468, page 53, was issued September 10, 1860, and sent October 30, 1860, to the Register for delivery."—Letter Jos. S. Wilson Acting Commissioner Land Office, June 27, 1865.

who had in charge the governmental machinery. Lincoln's course is all that interests us. Though he may not have distinctly avowed himself a Whig, yet, as one of his friends asserted, "he stood openly on Whig principles." He favored a national bank, a liberal system of internal improvements, and a high protective tariff. The handbill or circular alluded to announcing his candidacy was a sort of literary fulmination, but on account of its length I deem it unnecessary to insert the whole of it here. I have been told that it was prepared by Lincoln, but purged of its most glaring grammatical errors by James McNamar, who afterwards became Lincoln's rival in an important love affair.*

The circular is dated March 9, 1832, and addressed to the "People of Sangamon County." In it he takes up all the leading questions of the day : railroads, river navigation, internal improvements, and usury. He dwells particularly on the matter of public education, alluding to it as the most important subject before the people. Realizing his own defects arising from a lack of school instruction he contends that every man and his children, however poor, should be permitted to obtain at least a moderate education, and thereby be enabled "to read the Scriptures and other works both of a moral and religious nature for themselves." The closing par-

---

* In a letter dated May 5, 1866, McNamar says :
"I corrected at his request some of the grammatical errors in his first address to the voters of Sangamon county, his principal hobby being the navigation of the Sangamon river."

agraph was so constructed as to appeal to the chivalrous sentiments of Clary's Grove. "I was born and have ever remained," he declares, "in the most humble walks of life. I have no wealthy or popular relatives or friends to recommend me. My case is thrown exclusively upon the independent voters of the county; and if elected they will have conferred a favor upon me for which I shall be unremitting in my labors to compensate. But if," he dryly concludes, "the good people in their wisdom shall see fit to keep me in the background, I have been too familiar with disappointments to be very much chagrined."

The election being near at hand only a few days remained for his canvass. One * who was with him at the time describing his appearance, says: "He wore a mixed jeans coat, clawhammer style, short in the sleeves and bobtail—in fact it was so short in the tail he could not sit on it; flax and tow-linen pantaloons, and a straw hat. I think he wore a vest, but do not remember how it looked. He wore pot-metal boots." His maiden effort on the stump was a speech on the occasion of a public sale at Pappsville, a village eleven miles west of Springfield. After the sale was over and speechmaking had begun, a fight—a "general fight," as one of the bystanders relates—ensued, and Lincoln, noticing one of his friends about to succumb to the energetic attack of an infuriated ruffian, interposed to prevent it. He did so most effectually.

---

* A. Y. Ellis, letter, June 5, 1866, MS.

Hastily descending from the rude platform he edged his way through the crowd, and seizing the bully by the neck and seat of his trowsers, threw him by means of his strength and long arms, as one witness stoutly insists, "twelve feet away." Returning to the stand and throwing aside his hat he inaugurated his campaign with the following brief but juicy declaration :

"Fellow Citizens, I presume you all know who I am. I am humble Abraham Lincoln. I have been solicited by many friends to become a candidate for the Legislature. My politics are short and sweet, like the old woman's dance. I am in favor of a national bank. I am in favor of the internal improvement system and a high protective tariff. These are my sentiments and political principles. If elected I shall be thankful ; if not it will be all the same."

I obtained this speech from A. Y. Ellis, who in 1865 wrote it out. Ellis was his friend and supporter, and took no little interest in his canvass. "I accompanied him," he relates, "on one of his electioneering trips to Island Grove, and he made a speech which pleased his party friends very well indeed, though some of the Jackson men tried to make sport of it. He told several anecdotes, and applied them, as I thought, very well. He also told the boys several stories which drew them after him. I remember them, but modesty and my veneration for his memory forbid me to relate them." His story-telling propensity, and the striking fitness of his yarns—many of them being of the bar-room order—in illustrating public questions, as we shall see further along in these chapters, was really one of the secrets of his popularity and strength. The election, as he had predicted, resulted in his defeat—the only defeat, as he himself afterward stated, that he ever suffered at the hands of the people. But there was little defeat in it after all. Out of the eight unsuccessful candidates he stood third from the head of the list, receiving 657 votes. Five others received less. The most gratifying feature of it all was the hearty support of his neighbors at New Salem. Of the entire 208 votes in the precinct he received every one save three.

It may not be amiss to explain the cause of this remarkable endorsement of Lincoln by the voters in New Salem. It arose chiefly from his advocacy of the improvement of the Sangamon river. He proposed the digging of a canal a few miles east of the point where the Sangamon enters the Illinois river, thereby giving the former two mouths. This, he explained to the farmers, would prevent the accumulation of back-water and consequent overflow of their rich alluvial bottom lands in the spring. It would also avert the sickness and evil results of stagnant pools, which formed in low places after the high waters receded. His scheme —that is the name by which it would be known to-day—commended itself to the judgment of his neighbors, and the flattering vote he received shows how they endorsed it.

The unsuccessful result of the election did not dampen his hopes nor sour his ambition. The extensive acquaintance, the practice in public speaking, the confidence gained with the people, together with what was augmented in himself, made a surplus of capital on which he was free to draw and of which he afterwards frequently availed himself. The election being over, however, he found himself without money, though with a goodly supply of experience, drifting again. His political experience had forever weaned him from the dull routine of common labor. Labor afforded him no time for study and no incentive to profitable reflection. What he seemed to want was some lighter work, employment in a store or tavern where he could meet the village celebrities, exchange views with strangers, discuss politics, horse-races, cock-fights, and narrate to listening loafers his striking and significant stories. In the communities where he had lived, the village store-keeper held undisturbed sway. He took the only newspapers, owned the only collection of books and half the property in the village; and in general was the social, and oftentimes the political head of the community. Naturally, therefore the prominence the store gave the merchant attracted Lincoln. But there seemed no favorable opening for him—clerks in New Salem were not in demand just then.

My cousins, Rowan and James Herndon, were at that time operating a store, and tiring of their investment and the confinement it necessitated, James sold his interest to an idle, shiftless fellow named William Berry. Soon after Rowan disposed of his to Lincoln. That the latter, who was with-

out means and in search of work, could succeed to
the ownership of even a half interest in a concern
where but a few days before he would in all probability gladly have exchanged his services for his
board, doubtless seems strange to the average
young business man of to-day. I once asked
Rowan Herndon what induced him to make such
liberal terms in dealing with Lincoln, whom he had
known for so short a time.

" I believed he was thoroughly honest," was the
reply, "and that impression was so strong in me I
accepted his note in payment of the whole. He
had no money, but I would have advanced him
still more had he asked for it."

Lincoln and Berry had been installed in business
but a short time until one Reuben Radford, the proprietor of another New Salem grocery, who, happen-
ing to incur the displeasure of the Clary's Grove
boys, decided suddenly one morning, in the commercial language of later days, to "retire from business." A visit by night of the Clary's Grove contingent always hastened any man's retirement from
business. The windows were driven in, and possession taken of the stock without either ceremony or
inventory. If, by break of day, the unfortunate
proprietor found any portion of his establishment
standing where he left it the night before, he might
count himself lucky. In Radford's case, fearing
" his bones might share the fate of his windows,"
he disposed of his stock and good-will to William
Greene for a consideration of four hundred dollars.
The latter employed Lincoln to make an inventory

of the goods, and when completed, the new merchant, seeing in it something of a speculation, offered Greene an advance of two hundred and fifty dollars on his investment. The offer was accepted, and the stock and fixtures passed into the ownership and control of the now enterprising firm of Lincoln & Berry. They subsequently absorbed the remnant of a store belonging to one Rutledge, which last transaction cleared the field of all competitors and left them in possession of the only mercantile concern in New Salem.

To effect these sales not a cent of money was required—the buyer giving the seller his note and the latter assigning it to someone else in another trade. Berry gave his note to James Herndon, Lincoln his to Rowan Herndon, while Lincoln & Berry as a firm, executed their obligation to Greene, Radford, and Rutledge in succession. Surely Wall Street at no time in its history has furnished a brace of speculators who in so brief a period accomplished so much and with so little money. A few weeks only were sufficient to render apparent Lincoln's ill adaptation to the requirements of a successful business career. Once installed behind the counter he gave himself up to reading and study, depending for the practical management of the business on his partner. A more unfortunate selection than Berry could not have been found ; for, while Lincoln at one end of the store was dispensing political information, Berry at the other was disposing of the firm's liquors, being the best customer for that article of merchandise himself. To put it more plainly, Lincoln's application to Shakespeare and Burns was only equalled by Berry's attention to spigot and barrel. That the latter in the end succeeded in squandering a good portion of their joint assets, besides wrecking his own health, is not to be wondered at. By the spring of 1833 they, like their predecessors, were ready to retire. Two brothers named Trent coming along, they sold to them on the liberal terms then prevalent the business and good-will; but before the latter's notes fell due, they in turn had failed and fled. The death of Berry following soon after, released him from the payment of any notes or debts, and thus Lincoln was left to meet the unhonored obligations of the ill-fated partnership, or avoid their payment by dividing the responsibility and pleading the failure of the business. That he assumed all the liability and set resolutely to work to pay everything, was strictly in keeping with his fine sense of honor and justice. He was a long time meeting these claims, even as late as 1848 sending to me from Washington portions of his salary as Congressman to be applied on the unpaid remnant of the Berry & Lincoln indebtedness—but in time he extinguished it all, even to the last penny.

Conscious of his many shortcomings as a merchant, and undaunted by the unfortunate complications from which he had just been released, Lincoln returned to his books. Rowan Herndon, with whom he had been living, having removed to the country, he became for the first time a sojourner at the tavern, as it was then called—a public-house kept by Rutledge, Onstatt, and Alley in succession. "It was a small log house," he explained to me in later years, "covered with clapboards, and contained four rooms." It was second only in importance to the store, for there he had the opportunity of meeting passing strangers—lawyers and others from the county seat, whom he frequently impressed with his knowledge as well as wit. He had, doubtless, long before determined to prepare himself for the law; in fact, had begun to read Blackstone while in the store, and now went at it with renewed zeal. He borrowed law-books of his former comrade in the Black Hawk war, John T. Stuart, who was practicing law in Springfield, frequently walking there to return one and borrow another. His determination to master any subject he undertook and his application to study were of the most intense order. On the road to and from Springfield he would read and recite from the book he carried open in his hand, and claimed to have mastered forty pages of Blackstone during the first day after his return from Stuart's office. At New Salem he frequently sat barefooted under the shade of a tree near the store, poring over a volume of Chitty or Blackstone, sometimes lying on his back, putting his feet up the tree, which provokes one of his biographers to denote the latter posture as one which might have been "unfavorable to mental application, in the case of a man with shorter extremities."

That Lincoln's attempt to make a lawyer of himself under such adverse and unpromising circumstances excited comment is not to be wondered at. Russell

9

Godby, an old man who still survives, told me in 1865, that he had often employed Lincoln to do farm work for him, and was surprised to find him one day sitting barefoot on the summit of a wood-pile and attentively reading a book. " This being an unusual thing for farm hands in that early day to do, I asked him," relates Godby, " what he was reading." ' I'm not reading,' he answered. ' I'm studying.' ' Studying what ?' I enquired. ' Law, sir,' was the emphatic response. It was really too much for me, as I looked at him sitting there proud as Cicero. ' Great God Almighty !' I exclaimed, and passed on."

But Lincoln kept on at his studies. Wherever he was and whenever he could do so the book was brought into use. He carried it with him in his rambles through the woods and his walks to the river. When night came he read it by the aid of any friendly light he could find. Frequently he went down to the cooper's shop and kindled a fire out of the waste material lying about, and by the light it afforded read until far into the night.

One of his companions at this time relates that, " while clerking in the store or serving as post-master he would apply himself as opportunity offered to his studies, if it was but five minutes time— would open his book which he always kept at hand, study it, reciting to himself ; then entertain the company present or wait on a customer without apparent annoyance from the interruption. Have frequently seen him reading while walking along the streets. Occasionally he would become absorbed with his book; would stop and stand for a few moments, then walk on, or pass from one house to another or from one crowd or squad of men to another. He was apparently seeking amusement, and with his thoughtful face and ill-fitting clothes was the last man one would have singled out for a student. If the company he was in was unappreciative, or their conversation at all irksome, he would open his book and commune with it for a time, until a happy thought suggested itself and then the book would again return to its wonted resting-place under his arm. He never appeared to be a hard student, as he seemed to master his studies with little effort, until he commenced the study of the law. In that he became wholly engrossed, and began for the first time to avoid the society of men, in order that he might have more time for study. He was not what is usually termed a quick-minded man, although he would usually arrive at his conclusions very readily. He seemed invariably to reflect and deliberate, and never acted from impulse so far as to force a wrong conclusion on a subject of any moment." *

It was not long until he was able to draw up deeds, contracts, mortgages, and other legal papers for his neighbors. He figured conspicuously as a pettifogger before the justice of the peace, but regarding it merely as a kind of preliminary practice, seldom made any charge for his services. Meanwhile he was reading not only law books but natural

---

* R. B. Rutledge, letter, Nov. 30. 1866, MS.

philosophy and other scientific subjects. He was a careful and patient reader of newspapers, the *Sangamon Journal*—published at Springfield—*Louisville Journal*, *St. Louis Republican*, and *Cincinnati Gazette* being usually within his reach. He paid a less degree of attention to historical works, although he read Rollin and Gibbon while in business with Berry. He had a more pronounced fondness for fictitious literature, and read with evident relish Mrs. Lee Hentz's novels, which were very popular books in that day, and which were kindly loaned him by his friend A. Y. Ellis. The latter was a prosperous and shrewd young merchant who had come up from Springfield and taken quite a fancy to Lincoln. The two slept together and Lincoln frequently assisted him in the store. He says that Lincoln was fond of short, spicy stories one and two columns long, and cites as specimens, "Cousin Sally Dillard," "Becky William's Courtship," "The Down-Easter and the Bull," and others, the very titles suggesting the character of the productions. He remembered everything he read, and could afterwards without apparent difficulty relate it. In fact, Mr. Lincoln's fame as a storyteller spread far and wide. Men quoted his sayings, repeated his jokes, and in remote places he was known as a story-teller before he was heard of either as lawyer or politician.

It has been denied as often as charged that Lincoln narrated vulgar stories; but the truth is he loved a story however extravagant or vulgar, if it had a good point. If it was merely a ribald recital and had no sting in the end, that is, if it exposed no weakness or pointed no moral, he had no use for it either in conversation or public speech; but if it had the necessary ingredients of mirth and moral no one could use it with more telling effect. As a mimic he was unequalled, and with his characteristic gestures, he built up a reputation for story-telling—although fully as many of his narratives were borrowed as original—which followed him through life. One who listened to his early stories in New Salem says: "His laugh was striking. Such awkward gestures belonged to no other man. They attracted universal attention, from the old sedate down to the schoolboy. Then in a few moments he was as calm and thoughtful as a judge on the bench, and as ready to give advice on the most important matters; fun and gravity grew on him alike."

Lincoln's lack of musical adaptation has deprived us of many a song. For a ballad or doggerel he sometimes had quite a liking. He could memorize or recite the lines but some one else had to do the singing. Listen to one in which he shows "*How St. Patrick Came to be Born on the 17th of March.*" Who composed it or where Lincoln obtained it I have never been able to learn. Ellis says he often inflicted it on the crowds who collected in his store of winter evenings. Here it is:

"The first factional fight in old Ireland, they say,
　　Was all on account of Saint Patrick's birthday,
　　It was somewhere about midnight without any doubt,
　　And certain it is, it made a great rout.

On the eighth day of March, as some people say,
St. Patrick at midnight he first saw the day;
While others assert 'twas the ninth he was born—
'Twas all a mistake—between midnight and morn.

Some blamed the baby, some blamed the clock;
Some blamed the doctor, some the crowing cock.
With all these close questions sure no one could know,
Whether the babe was too fast or the clock was too slow.

Some fought for the eighth, for the ninth some would die;
He who wouldn't see right would have a black eye.
At length these two factions so positive grew,
They each had a birthday, and Pat he had two.

Till Father Mulcahay who showed them their sins,
He said none could have two birthdays but as twins.
' Now Boys, don't be fighting for the eight or the nine
Don't quarrel so always, now why not combine.'

Combine eight with nine.   It is the mark;
Let that be the birthday.   Amen! said the clerk.
So all got blind drunk, which completed their bliss,
And they've kept up the practice from that day to this." *

As a salesman, Lincoln was lamentably deficient.
He was too prone to lead off into a discussion of
politics or morality, leaving someone else to finish
the trade which he had undertaken.   One of his
employers says: " He always disliked to wait on
the ladies, preferring, he said, to wait on the men
and boys.   I also remember he used to sleep on the
store counter when they had too much company at
the tavern.   He wore flax and tow linen pantaloons
—I thought about five inches too short in the legs
—and frequently had but one suspender, no vest or

---

* From MS., furnished by Ellis in August, 1866.

coat. He wore a calico shirt, such as he had in the Black Hawk war ; coarse brogans, tan color ; blue yarn socks and straw hat, old style, and without a band." His friend Ellis attributed his shyness in the presence of the ladies to the consciousness of his awkward appearance and the unpretentious condition of his wearing apparel. It was more than likely due to pure bashfulness. " On one occasion," continues Ellis, " while we boarded at the tavern, there came a family consisting of an old lady, her son, and three stylish daughters, from the State of Virginia, who stopped there for two or three weeks, and during their stay I do not remember of Mr. Lincoln's ever appearing at the same table with them."

As a society man, Lincoln was singularly deficient while he lived in New Salem, and even during the remainder of his life. He never indulged in gossip about the ladies, nor aided in the circulation of village scandal. For woman he had a high regard, and I can testify that during my long acquaintance with him his conversation was free from injurious comment in individual cases—freer from unpleasant allusions than that of most men. At one time Major Hill charged him with making defamatory remarks regarding his wife. Hill was insulting in his language to Lincoln who never lost his temper. When he saw a chance to edge a word in, Lincoln denied emphatically using the langauge or anything like that attributed to him. He entertained, he insisted, a high regard for Mrs. Hill, and the only thing he knew to her discredit was the fact that she was Major Hill's wife.

At this time in its brief history New Salem was what in the parlance of large cities would be called a fast place; and it was difficult for a young man of ordinary moral courage to resist the temptations that beset him on every hand. It remains a matter of surprise that Lincoln was able to retain his popularity with the hosts of young men of his own age, and still not join them in their drinking bouts and carousals. "I am certain," contends one of his companions, "that he never drank any intoxicating liquors—he did not even in those days smoke or chew tobacco." In sports requiring either muscle or skill he took no little interest. He indulged in all the games of the day, even to a horse-race or cock-fight. At one eventful chicken fight, where a fee of twenty-five cents for the entrance of each fowl was assessed, one Bap. McNabb brought a little red rooster, whose fighting qualities had been well advertised for days in advance by his owner. Much interest was naturally taken in the contest. As the outcome of these contests was generally a quarrel, in which each man, charging foul play, seized his victim, they chose Lincoln umpire, relying not only on his fairness but his ability to enforce his decisions. In relating what followed I cannot improve on the description furnished me in February, 1865, by one * who was present.

"They formed a ring, and the time having arrived,

---

* A. Y. Ellis, MS.

Lincoln, with one hand on each hip and in a squat-
ting position, cried, 'Ready.' Into the ring they
toss their fowls, Bap's red rooster along with the
rest. But no sooner had the little beauty discovered what was to be done than he dropped his tail
and ran. The crowd cheered, while Bap. in disappointment picked him up and started away, losing
his quarter and carrying home his dishonored fowl.
Once arrived at the latter place he threw his pet
down with a feeling of indignation and chagrin.
The little fellow, out of sight of all rivals, mounted
a wood pile and proudly flirting out his feathers,
crowed with all his might. Bap. looked on in disgust. 'Yes, you little cuss,' he exclaimed, irreverently, 'you're great on dress parade, but not worth a
d—n in a fight.'" It is said—how truthfully I do
not know—that at some period during the late war
Mr. Lincoln in conversation with a friend likened
McClellan to Bap. McNabb's rooster. So much
for New Salem sports.

While wooing that jealous-eyed mistress, the
law, Lincoln was earning no money. As another
has said, "he had a running board bill to pay, and
nothing to pay it with." By dint of sundry jobs
here and there, helping Ellis in his store to-day,
splitting rails for James Short to-morrow, he managed to keep his head above the waves. His
friends were firm—no young man ever had truer or
better ones—but he was of too independent a turn
to appeal to them or complain of his condition.
He never at any time abandoned the idea of becoming a lawyer. That was always a spirit which

beckoned him on in the darkest hour of his adversity. Someone, probably a Democrat who voted for him in the preceding fall, recommended him to John Calhoun, then surveyor of the county, as suitable material for an assistant. This office, in view of the prevailing speculation in lands and town lots, was the most important and possibly the most profitable in the county. Calhoun, the incumbent, was a Yankee and a typical gentleman. He was brave, intellectual, self-possessed, and cultivated. He had been educated for the law, but never practiced much after coming to Illinois—taught school in preference. As an instructor he was the popular one of his day and age. I attended the school he taught when I was a boy, in Springfield, and was in later years clerk of the city under his administration as Mayor. Lincoln, I know, respected and admired him. After Lincoln's removal to Springfield they frequently held joint debates on political questions. At one time I remember they discussed the tariff question in the court house, using up the better part of two evenings in the contest. Calhoun was polite, affable, and an honest debater, never dodging any question. This made him a formidable antagonist in argumentative controversy. I have heard Lincoln say that Calhoun gave him more trouble in his debates than Douglas ever did, because he was more captivating in his manner and a more learned man than Douglas.

But to resume. The recommendation of Lincoln's friends was sufficient to induce Calhoun to appoint him one of his deputies. At the time he received notice of his selection by Calhoun, Lincoln was out in the woods near New Salem splitting rails. A friend named Pollard Simmons, who still survives and has related the incident to me, walked out to the point where he was working with the cheering news. Lincoln, being a Whig and knowing Calhoun's pronounced Democratic tendencies, enquired if he had to sacrifice any principle in accepting the position. "If I can be perfectly free in my political action I will take the office," he remarked; "but if my sentiments or even expression of them is to be abridged in any way I would not have it or any other office." A young man hampered by poverty as Lincoln was at this time, who had the courage to deal with public office as he did, was certainly made of unalloyed material. No wonder in after years when he was defeated by Douglas he could inspire his friends by the admonition not to "give up after one nor one hundred defeats.'

After taking service with Calhoun, Lincoln found he had but little if any practical knowledge of surveying—all that had to be learned. Calhoun furnished him with books, directing him to study them till he felt competent to begin work. He again invoked the assistance of Mentor Graham, the schoolmaster, who aided him in his efforts at calculating the results of surveys and measurements. Lincoln was not a mathematician by nature, and hence, with him, learning meant labor. Graham's daughter is authority for the statement that her father and Lincoln frequently sat up till midnight engrossed in calculations, and only ceased when her mother drove them out after a fresh supply of wood for the fire. Meanwhile Lincoln was keeping up his law studies. " He studied to see the subject-matter clearly," says Graham, "and to express it truly and strongly. I have known him to study for hours the best way of three to express an idea." He was so studious and absorbed in his application at one time, that his friends, according to a statement made by one * of them, " noticed that he was so emaciated we feared he might bring on mental derangement." It was not long, however, until he had mastered surveying as a study, and then he was sent out to work by his superior—Calhoun. It has never been denied that his surveys were exact and just, and he was so manifestly fair that he was often chosen to settle disputed questions of corners and measurements. It is worthy of note here that, with all his knowledge of lands and their value and the opportunities that lay open to him for profitable and safe investments, he never made use of the information thus obtained from official sources, nor made a single speculation on his own account. The high value he placed on public office was more fully emphasized when as President, in answer to a delegation of gentlemen who called to press the claims of one of his warm personal friends for an important office, he declined on the ground that " he did not regard it as just to

---

* Henry McHenry, MS., Oct. 5, 1865.

the public to pay the debts of personal friendship with offices that belonged to the people."

As surveyor under Calhoun he was sent for at one time to decide or locate a disputed corner for some persons in the northern part of the county. Among others interested was his friend and admirer Henry McHenry. "After a good deal of disputing we agreed," says the latter, "to send for Lincoln and to abide by his decision. He came with compass, flag-staff, and chain. He stopped with me three or four days and surveyed the whole section. When in the neighborhood of the disputed corner by actual survey he called for his staff and driving it in the ground at a certain spot said, 'Gentlemen, here is the corner.' We dug down into the ground at the point indicated and, lo! there we found about six or eight inches of the original stake sharpened at the end, and beneath which was the usual piece of charcoal placed there by Rector the surveyor who laid the ground off for the government many years before." So fairly and well had the young surveyor done his duty that all parties went away completely satisfied. As late as 1865 the corner was preserved by a mark and pointed out to strangers as an evidence of the young surveyor's skill. Russell Godby, mentioned in the earlier pages of this chapter, presented to me a certificate of survey given to him by Lincoln. It was written January 14, 1834, and is signed " J. Calhoun, S. S. C., by A. Lincoln." " The survey was made by Lincoln," says Godby, " and I gave him as pay for his work two buckskins, which Hannah Armstrong 'foxed' on his pants so that the briers would not wear them out."

Honors were now crowding thick and fast upon him. On May 7, 1833, he was commissioned postmaster at New Salem, the first office he ever held under the Federal Government. The salary was proportionate to the amount of business done. Whether Lincoln solicited the appointment himself, or whether it was given him without the asking, I do not know ; but certain it is his " administration" gave general satisfaction. The mail arrived once a week, and we can imagine the extent of time and labor required to distribute it, when it is known that " he carried the office around in his hat." Mr. Lincoln used to tell me that when he had a call to go to the country to survey a piece of land, he placed inside his hat all the letters belonging to people in the neighborhood and distributed them along the way. He made head-quarters in Samuel Hill's store, and there the office may be said to have been located, as Hill himself had been postmaster before Lincoln. Between the revenue derived from the post-office and his income from land surveys Lincoln was, in the expressive language of the day, "getting along well enough." Suddenly, however, smooth sailing ceased and all his prospects of easy times ahead were again brought to naught. One Van Bergen brought suit against him and obtained judgment on one of the notes given in payment of the store debt—a relic of the unfortunate partnership with Berry. His personal effects were levied on and sold, his horse and surveying instruments going with the rest. But again a friend, one James Short, whose favor he had gained, interposed; bought in the property and restored it to the hopeless young surveyor. It will be seen now what kind of friends Lincoln was gaining. The bonds he was thus making were destined to stand the severest of tests. His case never became so desperate but a friend came out of the darkness to relieve him.

There was always something about Lincoln in his earlier days to encourage his friends. He was not only grateful for whatever aid was given him, but he always longed to help some one else. He had an unfailing disposition to succor the weak and the unfortunate, and was always, in his sympathy, struggling with the under dog in the fight. He was once overtaken when about fourteen miles from Springfield by one Chandler, whom he knew slightly, and who, having already driven twenty miles, was hastening to reach the land office before a certain other man who had gone by a different road. Chandler explained to Lincoln that he was poor and wanted to enter a small tract of land which adjoined his, that another man of considerable wealth had also determined to have it, and had mounted his horse and started for Springfield. "Meanwhile, my neighbors," continued Chandler, "collected and advanced me the necessary one hundred dollars, and now, if I can reach the land office first, I can secure the land." Lincoln noticed that Chandler's horse was too much fatigued to stand fourteen miles more of a forced march, and he therefore dismounted from his own and turned him over to Chandler, saying, " Here's my horse—he is fresh and full of grit ; there's no time to be lost ; mount him and put him through. When you reach Springfield put him up at Herndon's tavern and I'll call and get him." Thus encouraged Chandler moved on, leaving Lincoln to follow on the jaded animal. He reached Springfield over an hour in advance of his rival and thus secured the coveted tract of land. By nightfall Lincoln rode leisurely into town and was met by the now radiant Chandler, jubilant over his success. Between the two a friendship sprang up which all the political discords of twenty-five years never shattered nor strained.

About this time Lincoln began to extend somewhat his system—if he really ever had a system in anything—of reading. He now began to read the writings of Paine, Volney, and Voltaire. A good deal of religious skepticism existed at New Salem, and there were frequent discussions at the store and tavern, in which Lincoln took part. What views he entertained on religious questions will be more fully detailed in another place.

No little of Lincoln's influence with the men of New Salem can be attributed to his extraordinary feats of strength. By an arrangement of ropes and straps, harnessed about his hips, he was enabled one day at the mill to astonish a crowd of village celebrities by lifting a box of stones weighing near a thousand pounds. There is no fiction either, as suggested by some of his biographers, in the story that he lifted a barrel of whisky from the ground and drank from the bung; but in performing this latter almost incredible feat he did not stand erect and elevate the barrel, but squatted down and lifted it to his knees, rolling it over until his mouth came opposite the bung. His strength, kindness of manner, love of fairness and justice, his original and unique sayings, his power of mimicry, his perseverance—all made a combination rarely met with on the frontier. Nature had burnt him in her holy fire, and stamped him with the seal of her greatness.

In the summer of 1834 Lincoln determined to make another race for the legislature; but this time he ran distinctly as a Whig. He made, it is presumed, the usual number of speeches, but as the art of newspaper reporting had not reached the perfection it has since attained, we are not favored with even the substance of his efforts on the stump. I have Lincoln's word for it that it was more of a hand-shaking campaign than anything else. Rowan Herndon relates that he came to his house during harvest, when there were a large number of men at work in the field. He was introduced to them, but they did not hesitate to apprize him of their esteem for a man who could labor; and their admiration for a candidate for office was gauged somewhat by the amount of work he could do. Learning these facts, Lincoln took hold of a cradle, and handling it with ease and remarkable speed, soon distanced those who undertook to follow him. The men were satisfied, and it is presumed he lost no votes in that crowd. One Dr. Barrett, seeing Lincoln, enquired

10

of the latter's friends : "Can't the party raise any better material than that?" but after hearing his speech the doctor's opinion was considerably altered, for he declared that Lincoln filled him with amazement ; "that he knew more than all of the other candidates put together." The election took place in August. Lincoln's friend, John T. Stuart, was also a candidate on the legislative ticket. He encouraged Lincoln's canvas in every way, even at the risk of sacrificing his own chances. But both were elected. The four successful candidates were Dawson, who received 1390 votes,* Lincoln 1376, Carpenter 1170, and Stuart 1164.

At last Lincoln had been elected to the legislature, and by a very flattering majority. In order, as he himself said, "to make a decent appearance in the legislature," he had to borrow money to buy suitable clothing and to maintain his new dignity. Coleman Smoot, one of his friends, advanced him "two hundred dollars, which he returned, relates the generous Smoot, according to promise." Here we leave our rising young statesman, to take up a different but very interesting period of his history.

---

* In all former biographies of Lincoln, including the Nicolay and Hay history in the "Century Magazine," Dawson's vote is fixed at 1370, and Lincoln is thereby made to lead the ticket; but in the second issue of the *Sangamon Journal* after the election—August 16, 1834—the count is corrected, and Dawson's vote is increased to 1390. Dr. A. W. French, of Springfield, is the possessor of an official return of the votes cast at the New Salem precinct, made out in the handwriting of Lincoln, which also gives Dawson's vote at 1390.

CHAPTER VI.

Since the days when in Indiana Lincoln sat on the river's bank with little Kate Roby, dangling his bare feet in the water, there has been no hint in these pages of tender relations with any one of the opposite sex. Now we approach in timely order the "grand passion" of his life—a romance of much reality, the memory of which threw a melancholy shade over the remainder of his days. For the first time our hero falls in love. The courtship with Anne Rutledge and her untimely death form the saddest page in Mr. Lincoln's history. I am aware that most of his biographers have taken issue with me on this phase of Mr. Lincoln's life. Arnold says: "The picture has been somewhat too highly colored, and the story made rather too tragic." Dr. Holland and others omit the subject altogether, while the most recent biography—the admirable history by my friends Nicolay and Hay.—devotes but five lines to it. I knew Miss Rutledge myself, as well as her father and other members of the family, and have been personally acquainted with every one of the score or more of witnesses whom I at one time or another interviewed on this delicate subject. From my own knowledge and the information thus obtained, I therefore repeat, that the memory of Anne Rutledge was the saddest chapter in Mr. Lincoln's life.*

James Rutledge, the father of this interesting girl, was one of the founders of New Salem, having come there from Kentucky in 1829. He was born in South Carolina and belonged to the noted Rutledge family of that State. I knew him as early as 1833, and have often shared the hospitality of his home. My father was a politician and an extensive stock dealer in that early day, and he and Mr. Rutledge were great friends. The latter was a man of no little force of character; those who knew him best loved him the most. Like other Southern people he was warm,—almost to impulsiveness,—social, and generous. His hospitality, an inherited quality that flashed with him before he was born, developed by contact with the brave and broadminded people whom he met in Illinois. Besides his business interests in the store and mill at New Salem, he kept the tavern where Lincoln came to board in 1833. His family, besides himself and wife, consisted of nine children, three of whom were born in Kentucky, the remaining six in Illinois. Anne, the subject of this chapter, was the third child. She was a beautiful girl, and by her winning ways attached people to her so firmly that she soon became the most popular young lady in the village. She was quick of apprehension, industri-

---

* In a letter dated Dec. 4, 1866, one of Miss Rutledge's brothers writes: "When he first came to New Salem and up to the day of Anne's death Mr. Lincoln was all life and animation. He seemed to see the bright side of every picture."

ous, and an excellent housekeeper. She had a moderate education, but was not cultured except by contrast with those around her. One of her strong points was her womanly skill. She was dexterous in the use of the needle—an accomplishment of far more value in that day than all the acquirements of art in china painting and hammered brass are in this—and her needle-work was the wonder of the day. At every "quilting" Anne was a necessary adjunct, and her nimble fingers drove the needle more swiftly than anyone's else. Lincoln used to escort her to and from these quilting-bees, and on one occasion even went into the house— where men were considered out of place—and sat by her side as she worked on the quilt.

He whispered into her ear the old, old story. Her heart throbbed and her soul was thrilled with a joy as old as the world itself. Her fingers momentarily lost their skill. In her ecstasy she made such irregular and uneven stitches that the older and more sedate women noted it, and the owner of the quilt, until a few years ago still retaining it as a precious souvenir, pointed out the memorable stitches to such persons as visited her.

L. M. Greene, who remembered Anne well, says, "She was amiable and of exquisite beauty, and her intellect was quick, deep, and philosophic as well as brilliant. She had a heart as gentle and kind as an angel, and full of love and sympathy. Her sweet and angelic nature was noted by every one who met her. She was a woman worthy of Lincoln's love." This is a little overstated as to beauty—Greene writes as if he too had been in love with her—but is otherwise nearly correct.

"Miss Rutledge," says a lady * who knew her, "had auburn hair, blue eyes, fair complexion. She was pretty, slightly slender, but in everything a good hearted young woman. She was about five feet two inches high, and weighed in the neighborhood of a hundred and twenty pounds. She was beloved by all who knew her. She died as it were of grief. In speaking of her death and her grave Lincoln once said to me, ' My heart lies buried there.' "

Before narrating the details of Lincoln's courtship with Miss Rutledge, it is proper to mention briefly a few facts that occurred before their attachment began.

About the same time that Lincoln drifted into New Salem there came in from the Eastern States John McNeil, a young man of enterprise and great activity, seeking his fortune in the West. He went to work at once, and within a short time had accumulated by commendable effort a comfortable amount of property. Within three years he owned a farm, and a half interest with Samuel Hill in the leading store. He had good capacity for business, and was a valuable addition to that already pretentious village—New Salem. It was while living at James Cameron's house that this plucky and industrious young business man first saw Anne Rutledge. At that time she was attending the school

---

* Mrs. Hardin Bale.

of Mentor Graham, a pedagogue of local renown whose name is frequently met with in these pages, and who flourished in and around New Salem from 1829 to 1860. McNeil fell deeply in love with the school-girl—she was then only seventeen—and paid her the usual unremitting attentions young lovers of that age had done before him and are still doing to-day. His partner in the store, Samuel Hill, a young man of equal force of character, who afterwards amassed a comfortable fortune, and also wielded no little influence as a local politician, laid siege to the heart of this same attractive maiden, but he yielded up the contest early. Anne rejected him, and he dropped from the race. McNeil had clear sailing from this time forward. He was acquiring property and money day by day. As one of the pioneers puts it, " Men were honest then, and paid their debts at least once a year. The merchant surrounded by a rich country suffered little from competition. As he placed his goods on the shelf he added an advance of from seventy-five to one hundred and fifty per cent over cost price, and thus managed to get along." After " managing" thus for several years, McNeil, having disposed of his interest in the store to Hill, determined to return to New York, his native State, for a visit. He had accumulated up to this time, as near as we can learn, ten or possibly twelve thousand dollars. Before leaving he made to Anne a singular revelation. He told her the name McNeil was an assumed one ; that his real name was McNamar.

"I left behind me in New York," he said, "my parents and brothers and sisters. They are poor, and were in more or less need when I left them in 1829. I vowed that I would come West, make a fortune, and go back to help them. I am going to start now and intend, if I can, to bring them with me on my return to Illinois and place them on my farm." He expressed a sense of deep satisfaction in being able to clear up all mysteries which might have formed in the mind of her to whom he confided his love. He would keep nothing, he said, from her. They were engaged to be married, and she should know it all. The change of his name was occasioned by the fear that if the family in New York had known where he was they would have settled down on him, and before he could have accumulated any property would have sunk him beyond recovery. Now, however, he was in a condition to help them, and he felt overjoyed at the thought. As soon as the journey to New York could be made he would return. Once again in New Salem he and his fair one could consummate the great event to which they looked forward with undisguised joy and unbounded hope. Thus he explained to Anne the purpose of his journey—a story with some remarkable features, all of which she fully believed.

"She would have believed it all the same if it had been ten times as incredible. A wise man would have rejected it with scorn, but the girl's instinct was a better guide, and McNamar proved to be all that he said he was, although poor Anne never saw the proof which others got of it."*

At last McNamar, mounting an old horse that had participated in the Black Hawk war, began his journey. In passing through Ohio he became ill with a fever. For almost a month he was confined to his room, and a portion of the time was unconscious. As he approached a return to good health he grew nervous over the delay in his trip. He told no one around him his real name, destination, or business. He knew how his failure to write to New Salem would be construed, and the resulting irritation gave way to a feeling of desperation. In plainer language, he concluded it was "all up with him now." Meanwhile a different view of the matter was taken by Miss Rutledge. Her friends encouraged the idea of cruel desertion. The change of McNeil to McNamar had wrought in their minds a change of sentiment. Some contended that he had undoubtedly committed a crime in his earlier days, and for years had rested secure from apprehension under the shadow of an assumed name; while others with equal assurance whispered in the unfortunate girl's ear the old story of a rival in her affections. Anne's lady friends, strange to relate, did more to bring about a discordant feeling than all others. Women are peculiar creatures. They love to nettle and mortify one another; and when one of their own sex has fallen, how little sympathy they seem to have! But under all this

---

* Lamon, p. 161.

fire, in the face of all these insidious criticisms, Anne remained firm. She had faith, and bided her time.

McNamar, after much vexatious delay, finally reached his birthplace in New York, finding his father in the decline of years and health. He provided for his immediate needs, and by his assiduous attentions undertook to atone for the years of his neglect ; but all to no purpose. The old gentleman gradually faded from the world, and early one winter morning crossed the great river. McNamar was thus left to settle up the few unfinished details of his father's estate, and to provide for the pressing needs of the family. His detention necessitated a letter to Anne, explaining the nature and cause of the delay. Other letters followed ; but each succeeding one growing less ardent in tone, and more formal in phraseology than its predecessor, Anne began to lose faith. Had his love gradually died away like the morning wind ? was a question she often asked herself. She had stood firm under fire before, but now her heart grew sick with hope deferred. At last the correspondence ceased altogether.

At this point we are favored with the introduction of the ungainly Lincoln, as a suitor for the hand of Miss Rutledge. Lincoln had learned of McNamar's strange conduct, and conjecturing that all the silken ties that bound the two together had been sundered, ventured to step in himself. He had seen the young lady when a mere girl at Mentor Graham's school, and he, no doubt, then had formed a high opinion of her qualities.

But he was too bashful, as his friend Ellis declares, to tell her of it. No doubt, when he began to pay her attentions she was the most attractive young lady whom up to that time he had ever met. She was not only modest and winning in her ways, and full of good, womanly common-sense, but withal refined, in contrast with the uncultured people who surrounded both herself and Lincoln. "She had a secret, too, and a sorrow,—the unexplained and painful absence of McNamar,—which, no doubt, made her all the more interesting to him whose spirit was often even more melancholy than her own."

In after years, McNamar himself, describing her to me, said : " Miss Rutledge was a gentle, amiable maiden, without any of the airs of your city belles, but winsome and comely withal; a blonde in complexion, with golden hair, cherry-red lips, and a bonny blue eye. As to her literary attainments, she undoubtedly was as classic a scholar as Mr Lincoln. She had at the time she met him, I believe, attended a literary institution at Jacksonville, in company with her brother."

McNamar seems to have considered Lincoln's bashfulness as proof against the alluring charms of Miss Rutledge or anybody else, for he continues :

"Mr. Lincoln was not to my knowledge paying particular attention to any of the young ladies of my acquaintance when I left for my home in New York. There was no rivalry between us on that score ; on the contrary, I had every reason to believe him my warm, personal friend. But by-and-by I was left so far behind in the race I did not deem my chances worthy of notice. From this time forward he made rapid strides to that imperishable fame which justly fills a world."

Lincoln began to court Miss Rutledge in dead earnest. Like David Copperfield, he soon realized that he was in danger of becoming deeply in love, and as he approached the brink of the pit he trembled lest he should indeed fall in. As he pleaded and pressed his cause the Rutledges and all New Salem encouraged his suit. McNamar's unexplained absence and apparent neglect furnished outsiders with all the arguments needed to encourage Lincoln and convince Anne. Although the attachment was growing and daily becoming an intense and mutual passion, the young lady remained firm and almost inflexible. She was passing through another fire. A long struggle with her feelings followed ; but at length the inevitable moment came. She consented to have Lincoln, provided he gave her time to write to McNamar and obtain his release from her pledge. The slow-moving mails carried her tender letter to New York. Days and weeks—which to the ardent Lincoln must have seemed painfully long—passed, but the answer never came. In a half-hearted way she turned to Lincoln, and her looks told him that he had won. She accepted his proposal. Now that they were engaged he told her what she already knew, that he was poverty itself. She must grant him time to gather up funds to live on until he had completed his law studies. After this trifling delay " nothing on God's footstool," argued the emphatic lover, could keep them apart. To this the thoughtful Anne consented. To one of her brothers, she said : "As soon as his studies are completed we are to be married." But the ghost of another love would often rise unbidden before her. Within her bosom raged the conflict which finally undermined her health. Late in the summer she took to her bed. A fever was burning in her head. Day by day she sank, until all hope was banished. During the latter days of her sickness, her physician had forbidden visitors to enter her room, prescribing absolute quiet. But her brother relates that she kept enquiring for Lincoln so continuously, at times demanding to see him, that the family at last sent for him. On his arrival at her bedside the door was closed and he was left alone with her. What was said, what vows and revelations were made during this sad interview, were known only to him and the dying girl. A few days afterward she became unconscious and remained so until her death on the 25th day of August, 1835. She was buried in what is known as the Concord grave-yard, about seven miles north-west of the town of Petersburg.*

The most astonishing and sad sequel to this court-

---

* "I have heard mother say that Anne would frequently sing for Lincoln's benefit. She had a clear, ringing voice. Early in her illness he called, and she sang a hymn for which he always expressed a great preference. It begins :

'Vain man, thy fond pursuits forbear.'

You will find it in one of the standard hymn-books. It was likewise the last thing she ever sung."—Letter, John M. Rutledge, MS., Nov. 25, 1866.

ship was the disastrous effect of Miss Rutledge's death on Mr. Lincoln's mind. It operated strangely on one of his calm and stoical make-up. As he returned from the visit to the bedside of Miss Rutledge, he stopped at the house of a friend, who relates that his face showed signs of no little mental agony. "He was very much distressed," is the language of this friend, "and I was not surprised when it was rumored subsequently that his reason was in danger." One of Miss Rutledge's brothers* says: "The effect upon Mr. Lincoln's mind was terrible. He became plunged in despair, and many of his friends feared that reason would desert her throne. His extraordinary emotions were regarded as strong evidence of the existence of the tenderest relations between himself and the deceased." The truth is Mr. Lincoln was strangely wrought up over the sad ending of the affair. He had fits of great mental depression, and wandered up and down the river and into the woods woefully abstracted—at times in the deepest distress. If, when we read what the many credible persons who knew him at the time tell us, we do not conclude that he was deranged, we must admit that he walked on that sharp and narrow line which divides sanity from insanity. To one friend he complained that the thought " that the snows and rains fall upon her grave filled him with indescribable grief." † He was watched with especial vigilance

---

* R. B. Rutledge, MS., letter, Oct. 21, 1866.
† Letter, Wm. Greene, MS., May 29, 1865.

during damp, stormy days, under the belief that dark and gloomy weather might produce such a depression of spirits as to induce him to take his own life. His condition finally became so alarming, his friends consulted together and sent him to the house of a kind friend, Bowlin Greene, who lived in a secluded spot hidden by the hills, a mile south of town. Here he remained for some weeks under the care and ever watchful eye of this noble friend, who gradually brought him back to reason, or at least a realization of his true condition. In the years that followed Mr. Lincoln never forgot the kindness of Greene through those weeks of suffering and peril. In 1842, when the latter died, and Lincoln was selected by the Masonic lodge to deliver the funeral oration, he broke down in the midst of his address. "His voice was choked with deep emotion; he stood a few moments while his lips quivered in the effort to form the words of fervent praise he sought to utter, and the tears ran down his yellow and shrivelled cheeks. Every heart was hushed at the spectacle. After repeated efforts he found it impossible to speak, and strode away, bitterly sobbing, to the widow's carriage and was driven from the scene."

It was shortly after this that Dr. Jason Duncan placed in Lincoln's hands a poem called "Immortality." The piece starts out with the line, "Oh! why should the spirit of mortal be proud." Lincoln's love for this poem has certainly made it immortal. He committed these lines to memory, and any reference to or mention of Miss Rutledge would suggest them, as if "to celebrate a grief which lay with continual heaviness on his heart." There is no question that from this time forward Mr. Lincoln's spells of melancholy became more intense than ever. In fact a tinge of this desperate feeling of sadness followed him to Springfield. He himself was somewhat superstitious about it, and in 1840-41 wrote to Dr. Drake, a celebrated physician in Cincinnati, describing his mental condition in a long letter. Dr. Drake responded, saying substantially, "I cannot prescribe in your case without a personal interview." Joshua F. Speed, to whom Lincoln showed the letter addressed to Dr. Drake, writing to me from Louisville, November 30, 1866, says: "I think he (Lincoln) must have informed Dr. Drake of his early love for Miss Rutledge, as there was a part of the letter which he would not read." It is shown by the declaration of Mr. Lincoln himself made to a fellow member * of the Legislature within two years after Anne Rutledge's death that "although he seemed to others to enjoy life rapturously, yet when alone he was so overcome by mental depression he never dared to carry a pocket knife."

It may not be amiss to suggest before I pass from mention of McNamar that, true to his promise, he drove into New Salem in the fall of 1835 with his mother and brothers and sisters. They had come through from New York in a wagon, with all their portable goods. Anne Rutledge had

* Robert L. Wilson, MS., letter, Feb. 10, 1866

meanwhile died, and McNamar could only muse in silence over the fading visions of "what might have been." On his arrival he met Lincoln, who, with the memory of their mutual friend, now dead, constantly before him, "seemed desolate and sorely distressed." The little acre of ground in Concord cemetery contained the form of his first love, rudely torn from him, and the great world, throbbing with life but cold and heartless, lay spread before him.

CHAPTER VII.

BEFORE taking up an account of Lincoln's entry into the Legislature, which, following strictly the order of time, properly belongs here, I beg to digress long enough to narrate what I have gathered relating to another courtship—an affair of the heart which culminated in a sequel as amusing as the one with Anne Rutledge was sad. I experienced much difficulty in obtaining the particulars of this courtship. After no little effort I finally located and corresponded with the lady participant herself, who in 1866 furnished me with Lincoln's letters and her own account of the affair, requesting the suppression of her name and residence. Since then, however, she has died, and her children have not only consented to a publication of the history, but have furnished me recently with more facts and an excellent portrait of their mother made shortly after her refusal of Lincoln's hand.

Mary S. Owens—a native of Green county, Kentucky, born September 29, 1808—first became acquainted with Lincoln while on a visit to a sister, the wife of Bennet Able, an early settler in the country about New Salem. Lincoln was a frequent visitor at the house of Able, and a warm friend of the family. During the visit of Miss Owens in 1833, though only remaining a month, she lingered long enough to make an impression on Lincoln; but returned to Kentucky and did not reappear in New Salem till 1836. Meanwhile Anne Rutledge had died, and Lincoln's eyes began to wander after the dark-haired visitor from Kentucky. Miss Owens differed from Miss Rutledge in early education and the advantages of wealth. She had received an excellent education, her father being one of the wealthiest and most influential men of his time and locality. A portion of her schooling was obtained in a Catholic convent, though in religious faith she was a Baptist. According to a description furnished me by herself she "had fair skin, deep blue eyes, and dark curling hair; height five feet, five inches; weight about a hundred and fifty pounds." She was good-looking in girlhood; by many esteemed handsome, but became fleshier as she grew older. At the time of her second visit she reached New Salem on the day of the Presidential election, passing the polls where the men had congregated, on the way to her sister's house. One man in the crowd who saw her then was impressed with her beauty. Years afterwards, in relating the incident, * he wrote me:

"She was tall, portly, had large blue eyes and the finest trimmings I ever saw. She was jovial, social, loved wit and humor, had a liberal English education, and was considered wealthy. None of the poets or romance writers have ever given us a picture of a heroine so beautiful as a good description of Miss Owens in 1836 would be."

---

* L. M. Greene.

A lady friend* says she was "handsome, truly handsome, matronly-looking, over ordinary size in height and weight."

A gentleman † who saw her a few years before her death describes her as " a nervous, muscular woman, very intellectual, with a forehead massive and angular, square, prominent, and broad."

At the time of her advent into the society of New Salem she was polished in her manners, pleasing in her address, and attractive in many ways. She had a little dash of coquetry in her intercourse with that class of young men who arrogated to themselves claims of superiority, but she never yielded to this disposition to an extent that would willingly lend encouragement to an honest suitor sincerely desirous of securing her hand, when she felt she could not in the end yield to a proposal of marriage if he should make the offer. She was a good conversationalist and a splendid reader, very few persons being found to equal her in this accomplishment. She was light-hearted and cheery in her disposition, kind and considerate for those with whom she was thrown in contact.

One of Miss Owens' descendants is authority for the statement that Lincoln had boasted that " if Mary Owens ever returned to Illinois a second time he would marry her; " that a report of this came to her ears, whereupon she left her Kentucky home with a pre-determination to show him if she met

---

* Mrs. Hardin Bale.   † Johnson G. Greene.

him that she was not to be caught simply by the asking. On this second visit Lincoln paid her more marked attention than before, and his affections became more and more enlisted in her behalf. During the earlier part of their acquaintance, following the natural bent of her temperament she was pleasing and entertaining to him. Later on he discovered himself seriously interested in the blue-eyed Kentuckian, whom he had really under-estimated in his preconceived opinions of her. In the meantime she too had become interested, having discovered the sterling qualities of the young man who was paying her such devoted attention ; yet while she admired she did not love him. He was ungainly and angular in his physical make-up, and to her seemed deficient in the nicer and more delicate attentions which she felt to be due from the man whom she had pictured as an ideal husband. He had given her to understand that she had greatly charmed him ; but he was not himself certain that he could make her the husband with whom he thought she would be most happy. Later on by word and letter he told her so. His honesty of purpose showed itself in all his efforts to win her hand. He told her of his poverty, and while advising her that life with him meant to her who had been reared in comfort and plenty, great privation and sacrifice, yet he wished to secure her as a wife. She, however, felt that she did not entertain for him the same feeling that he professed for her and that she ought to entertain before accepting him, and so declined his offer. Judging from his letters alone it has been supposed by some that she, remembering the rumor she had heard of his determination to marry her, and not being fully certain of the sincerity of his purposes, may have purposely left him in the earlier stages of his courtship somewhat in uncertainty. Later on, however, when by his manner and repeated announcement to her that his hand and heart were at her disposal, he demonstrated the honesty and sincerity of his intentions, she declined his offer kindly but with no uncertain meaning.

The first letter I received from Mrs. Vineyard—for she was married to Jesse Vineyard, March 27, 1841—was written at Weston, Mo., May 1, 1866. Among other things she says: "After quite a struggle with my feelings I have at last decided to send you the letters in my possession written by Mr. Lincoln, believing as I do that you are a gentleman of honor and will faithfully abide by all you have said. My associations with your lamented friend were in Menard county whilst visiting a sister who then resided near Petersburg. I have learned that my maiden name is now in your possession; and you have ere this, no doubt, been informed that I am a native Kentuckian."

The letters written by Lincoln not revealing enough details of the courtship, I prepared a list of questions for the lady to answer in order that the entire history of their relations might be clearly shown. I perhaps pressed her too closely in such a delicate matter, for she responded in a few days as follows:

MARY S. OWENS.

From a daguerreotype loaned by her son.

"WESTON, MO., May 22, 1866.

"MR. W. H. HERNDON,

"MY DEAR SIR: Really, you catechise me in true lawyer style; but I feel you will have the goodness to excuse me if I decline answering all your questions in detail, being well assured that few women would have ceded as much as I have under all the circumstances.

"You say you have heard why our acquaintance terminated as it did. I too have heard the same bit of gossip; but I never used the remark which Madame Rumor says I did to Mr. Lincoln. I think I did on one occasion say to my sister, who was very anxious for us to be married, that I thought Mr. Lincoln was deficient in those little links which make up the chain of woman's happiness—at least it was so in my case. Not that I believed it proceeded from a lack of goodness of heart; but his training had been different from mine; hence there was not that congeniality which would otherwise have existed.

"From his own showing you perceive that his heart and hand were at my disposal; and I suppose that my feelings were not sufficiently enlisted to have the matter consummated. About the beginning of the year 1838 I left Illinois, at which time our acquaintance and correspondence ceased, without ever again being renewed.

"My father, who resided in Green county, Kentucky, was a gentleman of considerable means; and I am persuaded that few persons placed a higher estimate on education than he did.

"Respectfully yours,

"MARY S. VINEYARD."

The reference to Lincoln's deficiency "in those little links which make up the chain of woman's happiness" is of no little significance. It proved that his training had indeed been different from hers. In a short time I again wrote Mrs. Vineyard to enquire as to the truth of a story current in New Salem, that one day as she and Mrs. Bowlin Greene were climbing up the hill to Able's house they were joined by Lincoln; that Mrs. Greene was obliged to carry her child, a fat baby boy, to the summit; that Lincoln strolled carelessly along, offering no assistance to the woman who bent under the load. Thereupon Miss Owens, censuring him for his neglect, reminded him that in her estimation he would not make a good husband. In due time came her answer:

"WESTON, MO., July 22, 1866.

"Mr. W. H. HERNDON:

"DEAR SIR: I do not think you are pertinacious in asking the question relative to old Mrs. Bowlin Greene, because I wish to set you right on that question. Your information, no doubt, came through my cousin, Mr. Gaines Greene, who visited us last winter. Whilst here, he was laughing at me about Mr. Lincoln, and among other things spoke about the circumstance in connection with Mrs. Greene and child. My impression is now that I tacitly admitted it, for it was a season of trouble with me, and I gave but little heed to the matter. We never had any hard feelings towards each other that I know of. On no occasion did I say to Mr. Lincoln that I did not believe he would make a kind husband, because he did not tender his services to Mrs. Greene in helping of her carry her babe. As I said to you in a former letter, I thought him lacking in smaller attentions. One circumstance presents itself just now to my mind's eye. There was a company of us going to Uncle

Billy Greene's. Mr. Lincoln was riding with me, and we had a very bad branch to cross. The other gentlemen were very officious in seeing that their partners got safely over. We were behind, he riding in, never looking back to see how I got along. When I rode up beside him, I remarked, 'You are a nice fellow! I suppose you did not care whether my neck was broken or not.' He laughingly replied (I suppose by way of compliment), that he knew I was plenty smart to take care of myself.

"In many things he was sensitive almost to a fault. He told me of an incident: that he was crossing a prairie one day and saw before him, 'a hog mired down,' to use his own language. He was rather 'fixed up,' and he resolved that he would pass on without looking at the shoat. After he had gone by, he said the feeling was irresistible; and he had to look back, and the poor thing seemed to say wistfully, 'There now, my last hope is gone;' that he deliberately got down and relieved it from its difficulty.

"In many things we were congenial spirits. In politics we saw eye to eye, though since then we differed as widely as the South is from the North. But methinks I hear you say, 'Save me from a political woman!' So say I.

"The last message I ever received from him was about a year after we parted in Illinois. Mrs. Able visited Kentucky, and he said to her in Springfield, 'Tell your sister that I think she was a great fool because she did not stay here and marry me.' Characteristic of the man!

"Respectfully yours,

"MARY S. VINEYARD."

We have thus been favored with the lady's side of this case, and it is but fair that we should hear the testimony of her honest but ungainly suitor. Fortunately for us and for history we have his view of the case in a series of letters which have been preserved with zealous care by the lady's family.* The first letter was written from Vandalia, December 13, 1836, where the Legislature to which he belonged was in session. After reciting the progress of legislation and the flattering prospect that then existed for the removal of the seat of government to Springfield, he gets down to personal matters by apprising her of his illness for a few days, coupled with the announcement that he is mortified by daily trips to the post-office in quest of her letter, which it seemed never would arrive. "You see," he complains, "I am mad about that old letter yet. I don't like to risk you again. I'll try you once more, anyhow." Further along in the course of the missive, he says: "You recollect, I mentioned at the outset of this letter, that I had been unwell. That is the fact, though I believe I am about well now; but that, with other things I cannot account for, have conspired, and have gotten my spirits so low that I feel that I would rather be in any place in the world than here. I really cannot endure the thought of staying here ten weeks. Write back as soon as you get this, and if possible, say something that will please me; for really, I have not been pleased since I left you.

---

* The copies of these letters were carefully made by Mr. Weil from the originals, now in the possession of B. R. Vineyard, St. Joseph, Mo.

This letter is so dry and stupid," he mournfully concludes, " that I am ashamed to send it, but with my present feelings I cannot do any better."

After the adjournment of the Legislature he returned to Springfield, from which point it was a matter of easy driving to reach New Salem, where his lady-love was sojourning, and where he could pay his addresses in person. It should be borne in mind that he had by this time removed to Springfield, the county seat, and entered on the practice of the law. In the gloom resulting from lack of funds and the dim prospect for business, he found time to communicate with the friend whose case was constantly uppermost in his mind. Here is one characteristic letter:

"SPRINGFIELD, May 7, 1837.

FRIEND MARY:

" I have commenced two letters to send you before this, both of which displeased me before I got half done, and so I tore them up. The first I thought wasn't serious enough, and the second was on the other extreme. I shall send this, turn out as it may.

" This thing of living in Springfield is rather a dull business after all—at least it is so to me. I am quite as lonesome here as [I] ever was anywhere in my life. I have been spoken to by but one woman since I've been here, and should not have been by her if she could have avoided it. I've never been to church yet, and probably shall not be soon. I stay away because I am conscious I should not know how to behave myself. I am often thinking of what we said of your coming to live· at Springfield. I am afraid you would not be satisfied. There is a great deal of flourishing about in carriages here, which it would be your doom to see without sharing in it. You would have to be poor without the means of hiding your poverty. Do you believe you could bear that patiently? Whatever woman may cast her lot with mine, should anyone ever do so, it is my intention to do all in my power to make her happy and contented, and there is nothing I can imagine that would make me more unhappy than to fail in the effort. I know I should be much happier with you than the way I am, provided I saw no signs of discontent in you.

"What you have said to me may have been in jest or I may have misunderstood it. If so, then let it be forgotton; if otherwise I much wish you would think seriously before you decide. For my part I have already decided. What I have said I will most positively abide by, provided you wish it. My opinion is you had better not do it. You have not been accustomed to hardship, and it may be more severe than you imagine. I know you are capable of thinking correctly on any subject; and if you deliberate maturely upon this before you decide, then I am willing to abide your decision.

"You must write me a good long letter after you get this. You have nothing else to do, and though it might not seem interesting to you after you have written it, it would be a good deal of company in this busy wilderness. Tell your sister I don't want to hear any more about selling out and moving. That gives me the hypo whenever I think of it.

"Yours, etc.
"LINCOLN."

Very few if any men can be found who in fond pursuit of their love would present their case voluntarily in such an unfavorable light. In one breath he avows his affection for the lady whose image is constantly before him, and in the next furnishes her reasons why she ought not to marry him! During the warm, dry summer months he kept up the siege without apparent diminution of zeal. He was as assiduous as ever, and in August was anxious to force a decision. On the 16th he had a meeting with her which terminated much like a drawn battle—at least it seems to have afforded him but little encouragement, for on his return to Springfield he immediately indulged in an epistolary effusion stranger than any that preceded it.

" Friend Mary :
"You will no doubt think it rather strange that I should write you a letter on the same day on which we parted; and I can only account for it by supposing that seeing you lately makes me think of you more than usual, while at our late meeting we had but few expressions of thoughts. You must know that I cannot see you or think of you with entire indifference; and yet it may be that you are mistaken in regard to what my real feelings towards you are. If I knew you were not, I should not trouble you with this letter. Perhaps any other man would know enough without further information, but I consider it my peculiar right to plead ignorance and your bounden duty to allow the plea.
" I want in all cases to do right; and most particularly so in all cases with women. I want, at this particular time, more than anything else, to do right with you, and if I knew it would be doing right, as I rather suspect it would, to let you alone, I would do it. And for the purpose of making the matter as plain as possible, I now say, that you can now drop the subject, dismiss your thoughts (if you

ever had any) from me forever, and leave this letter unanswered, without calling forth one accusing murmur from me. And I will even go farther, and say, that if it will add anything to your comfort or peace of mind to do so, it is my sincere wish that you should. Do not understand by this that I wish to cut your acquaintance. I mean no such thing. What I do wish is that our further acquaintance shall depend upon yourself. If such further acquaintance would contribute nothing to your happiness, I am sure it would not to mine. If you feel yourself in any degree bound to me, I am now willing to release you, provided you wish it ; while, on the other hand, I am willing and even anxious to bind you faster if I can be convinced that it will in any considerable degree add to your happiness. This, indeed, is the whole question with me. Nothing would make me more miserable, nothing more happy, than to know you were so.

"In what I have now said, I think I cannot be misunderstood ; and to make myself understood is the sole object of this letter.

"If it suits you best to not answer this—farewell —a long life and a merry one attend you. But if you conclude to write back, speak as plainly as I do. There can be neither harm nor danger in saying to me anything you think, just in the manner you think it.

"My respects to your sister.

"Your friend,

"LINCOLN."

For an account of the final outcome of this *affaire du cœur* the reader is now referred to the most ludicrous letter Mr. Lincoln ever wrote. It has been said, but with how much truth I do not know, that during his term as President the lady to

whom it was written—Mrs. O. H. Browning, wife of
a fellow-member of the Legislature—before giving
a copy of it to a biographer, wrote to Lincoln asking
his consent to the publication, but that he answered
warning her against it because it was too full of
truth. The only biographer who ever did insert it
apologized for its appearance in his book, regarding
it for many reasons as an extremely painful duty.
"If it could be withheld," he laments, "and the
act decently reconciled to the conscience of a biographer * professing to be honest and candid, it
should never see the light in these pages. Its grotesque humor, its coarse exaggerations in describing
the person of a lady whom the writer was willing to
marry ; its imputation of toothless and weather-
beaten old age to a woman really young and handsome ; its utter lack of that delicacy of tone and
sentiment which one naturally expects a gentleman
to adopt when he thinks proper to discuss the
merits of his late mistress—all these, and its defective orthography, it would certainly be more agreeable to suppress than to publish. But if we begin
by omitting or mutilating a document which sheds
so broad a light upon one part of his life and one
phase of his character, why may we not do the like
as fast and as often as the temptation arises? and
where shall the process cease?"

I prefer not to take such a serious view of the
letter or its publication. My idea is, that Mr.
Lincoln got into one of his irresistible moods of
humor and fun—a state of feeling into which he

---

* Lamon, p. 181.

frequently worked himself to avert the overwhelming effects of his constitutional melancholy—and in
the inspiration of the moment penned this letter,
which many regard as an unfortunate composition.
The class who take such a gloomy view of the
matter should bear in mind that the letter was
written by Mr. Lincoln in the fervor of early manhood, just as he was emerging from a most embarrassing situation, and addressed to a friend who, he
supposed, would keep it sacredly sealed from the
public eye. As a matter of fact Mr. Lincoln was
not gifted with a ready perception of the propriety
of things in all cases. Nothing with him was
intuitive. To have profound judgment and just
discrimination he required time to think ; and if
facts or events were forced before him in too rapid
succession the machinery of his judgment failed to
work. A knowledge of this fact will account for
the letter, and also serve to rob the offence—if any
was committed—of half its severity.

The letter was written in the same month Miss
Owens made her final departure from Illinois.

"SPRINGFIELD, April 1, 1838.

"DEAR MADAM :—

"Without apologizing for being egotistical, I
shall make the history of so much of my life as
has elapsed since I saw you the subject of this
letter. And, by the way, I now discover that, in
order to give a full and intelligible account of the
things I have done and suffered since I saw you, I
shall necessarily have to relate some that happened
before.

"It was, then, in the autumn of 1836 that a married lady of my acquaintance and who was a great friend of mine, being about to pay a visit to her father and other relatives residing in Kentucky, proposed to me that on her return she would bring a sister of hers with her on condition that I would engage to become her brother-in-law with all convenient despatch. I, of course, accepted the proposal, for you know I could not have done otherwise, had I really been averse to it; but privately, between you and me I was most confoundedly well pleased with the project. I had seen the said sister some three years before, thought her intelligent and agreeable, and saw no good objection to plodding life through hand in hand with her. Time passed on, the lady took her journey, and in due time returned, sister in company sure enough. This astonished me a little; for it appeared to me that her coming so readily showed that she was a trifle too willing; but, on reflection, it occurred to me that she might have been prevailed on by her married sister to come, without anything concerning me ever having been mentioned to her; and so I concluded that, if no other objection presented itself, I would consent to waive this. All this occurred to me on hearing of her arrival in the neighborhood; for, be it remembered, I had not yet seen her, except about three years previous, as above mentioned. In a few days we had an interview; and, although I had seen her before, she did not look as my imagination had pictured her. I knew she was over-size, but she now appeared a fair match for Falstaff. I knew she was called an 'old maid,' and I felt no doubt of the truth of at least half of the appellation; but now, when I beheld her, I could not for my life avoid thinking of my mother; and this, not from withered features, for her skin was too full of fat to permit of its contracting into wrinkles, but from her want of teeth,

12

weather-beaten appearance in general, and from a kind of notion that ran in my head that nothing could have commenced at the size of infancy and reached her present bulk in less than thirty-five or forty years ; and, in short, I was not at all pleased with her. But what could I do ? I had told her sister I would take her for better or for worse ; and I made a point of honor and conscience in all things to stick to my word, especially if others had been induced to act on it, which in this case I had no doubt they had ; for I was now fairly convinced that no other man on earth would have her, and hence the conclusion that they were bent on holding me to my bargain. ' Well,' thought I, ' I have said it, and, be the consequences what they may, it shall not be my fault if I fail to do it.' At once I determined to consider her my wife ; and, this done, all my powers of discovery were put to work in search of perfections in her which might be fairly set off against her defects. I tried to imagine her handsome, which, but for her unfortunate corpulency, was actually true. Exclusive of this, no woman that I have ever seen has a finer face. I also tried to convince myself that the mind was much more to be valued than the person ; and in this she was not inferior, as I could discover, to any with whom I had been acquainted.

"Shortly after this, without coming to any positive understanding with her, I set out for Vandalia, when and where you first saw me. During my stay there I had letters from her which did not change my opinion of either her intellect or intention, but on the contrary confirmed it in both.

" All this while, although I was fixed, ' firm as the surge-repelling rock,' in my resolution, I found I was continually repenting the rashness which had led me to make it. Through life, I have been in no bondage, either real or imaginary, from the thral-

dom of which I so much desired to be free. After
my return home, I saw nothing to change my opinions of her in any particular. She was the same,
and so was I. I now spent my time in planning how
I might get along through life after my contemplated change of circumstances should have taken
place, and how I might procrastinate the evil day
for a time, which I really dreaded as much, perhaps
more, than an Irishman does the halter.

"After all my suffering upon this deeply interesting subject, here I am, wholly, unexpectedly, completely, out of the ' scrape'; and now I want to
know if you can guess how I got out of it—out,
clear, in every sense of the term ; no violation of
word, honor, or conscience. I don't believe you can
guess, and so I might as well tell you at once. As
the lawyer says, it was done in the manner following, to-wit : After I had delayed the matter as long
as I thought I could in honor do (which, by the
way, had brought me round into the last fall), I
concluded I might as well bring it to a consumma-
tion without further delay ; and so I mustered my
resolution, and made the proposal to her direct ;
but, shocking to relate, she answered, No. At first
I supposed she did it through an affectation of
modesty, which I thought but ill became her under
the peculiar circumstances of her case ; but on my
renewal of the charge, I found she repelled it with
greater firmness than before. I tried it again and
again, but with the same success, or rather with the
same want of success.

"I finally was forced to give it up ; at which I
very unexpectedly found myself mortified almost
beyond endurance. I was mortified, it seemed to
me, in a hundred different ways. My vanity was
deeply wounded by the reflection that I had been
too stupid to discover her intentions, and at the
same time never doubting that I understood them

perfectly ; and also that she, whom I had taught myself to believe nobody else would have, had actually rejected me with all my fancied greatness. And, to cap the whole, I then for the first time began to suspect that I was really a little in love with her. But let it all go. I'll try and outlive it. Others have been made fools of by the girls ; but this can never with truth be said of me. I most emphatically, in this instance, made a fool of myself. I have now come to the conclusion never again to think of marrying, and for this reason: I can never be satisfied with any one who would be blockhead enough to have me.

" When you receive this, write me a long yarn about something to amuse me. Give my respects to Mr. Browning.

" Your sincere friend,
" A. LINCOLN."

MRS. O. H. BROWNING.

As before mentioned Miss Owens was afterwards married and became the mother of five children. Two of her sons served in the Confederate army. She died July 4, 1877. Speaking of Mr. Lincoln a a short time before her death she referred to him as " a man with a heart full of kindness and a head full of sense."

CHAPTER VIII.

In December, 1834, Lincoln prepared himself for the Legislature to which he had been elected by such a complimentary majority. Through the generosity of his friend Smoot he purchased a new suit of clothes, and entering the stage at New Salem, rode through to Vandalia, the seat of government. He appreciated the dignity of his new position, and instead of walking to the capitol, as some of his biographers have contended, availed himself of the usual mode of travel. At this session of the Legislature he was anything but conspicuous. In reality he was very modest, but shrewd enough to impress the force of his character on those persons whose influence might some day be of advantage to him. He made but little stir, if we are to believe the record, during the whole of this first session. Made a member of the committee on Public Accounts and Expenditures, his name appears so seldom in the reports of the proceedings that we are prone to conclude that he must have contented himself with listening to the flashes of border oratory and absorbing his due proportion of parliamentary law. He was reserved in manner, but very observant; said little, but learned much; made the acquaintance of all the members and many influential per-

sons on the outside. The lobby at that day contained the representative men of the state—men of
acknowledged prominence and respectability, many
of them able lawyers, drawn thither in advocacy
of some pet bill. Schemes of vast internal improvements attracted a retinue of log-rollers, who
in later days seem to have been an indispensable
necessity in the movement of complicated legislative machinery. Men of capital and brains were
there. He early realized the importance of knowing all these, trusting to the inspiration of some
future hour to impress them with his skill as an
organizer or his power as an orator. Among the
members of the outside or "third body" was
Stephen A. Douglas, whom Lincoln then saw for
the first time. Douglas had come from Vermont
only the year before, but was already undertaking
to supplant John J. Hardin in the office of States
Attorney for the district in which both lived.
What impression he made on Lincoln, what opinions each formed of the other, or what the extent
of their acquaintance then was, we do not know. It
is said that Lincoln afterwards in mentioning their
first meeting observed of the newly-arrived Ver-
monter that he was the "least man he had ever
seen." The Legislature proper contained the youth
and blood and fire of the frontier. Some of the
men who participated in these early parliamentary battles were destined to carry the banners
of great political parties, some to lead in war and
some in the great council chamber of the nation.
Some were to fill the Governor's office, others to

wear the judicial ermine, and one was destined to be Chief Magistrate and die a martyr to the cause of human liberty.

The society of Vandalia and the people attracted thither by the Legislature made it, for that early day, a gay place indeed. Compared to Lincoln's former environments, it had no lack of refinement and polish. That he absorbed a good deal of this by contact with the men and women who surrounded him there can be no doubt. The "drift of sentiment and the sweep of civilization" at this time can best be measured by the character of the legislation. There were acts to incorporate banks, turnpikes, bridges, insurance companies, towns, railroads, and female academies. The vigor and enterprise of New England fusing with the illusory prestige of Kentucky and Virginia was fast forming a new civilization to spread over the prairies! At this session Lincoln remained quietly in the background, and contented himself with the introduction of a resolution in favor of securing to the State a part of the proceeds of sales of public lands within its limits. With this brief and modest record he returned to his constituents at New Salem. With zealous perseverance, he renewed his application to the law and to surveying, continuing his studies in both departments until he became, as he thought, reliable and proficient. By reason of a change in the office of Surveyor for the county he became a deputy under Thomas M. Neale, who had been elected to succeed John Calhoun. The speculation in lands made a brisk business for the

new surveyor, who even added Calhoun, his predecessor, to the list of deputies. Lincoln had now
become somewhat established in the good-will and
respect of his constituents. His bashfulness and
timidity was gradually giving way to a feeling of
self-confidence, and he began to exult over his ability to stand alone. The brief taste of public office
which he had just enjoyed, and the distinction it
gave him only whetted his appetite for further honors. Accordingly, in 1836 we find him a candidate
for the Legislature again. I well remember this
campaign and the election which followed, for my
father, Archer G. Herndon, was also a candidate,
aspiring to a seat in the State Senate. The Legislature at the session previous had in its apportion-
ment bill increased the delegation from Sangamon
county to seven Representatives and two Senators. Party conventions had not yet been invented,
and there being no nominating machinery to interfere, the field was open for any and all to run.
Lincoln again resorted, in opening his canvass, to
the medium of the political handbill. Although it
had not operated with the most satisfactory results
in his first campaign, yet he felt willing to risk it
again. Candidates of that day evinced far more
willingness to announce their position than political
aspirants do now. Without waiting for a convention to construct a platform, or some great political leader to " sound the key-note of the campaign,"
they stepped to the forefront and blew the bugle
themselves. This custom will account for the bold-
ness of Lincoln's utterances and the unequivocal

tone of his declarations. His card—a sort of politi-cal fulmination—was as follows:

"NEW SALEM, June 13, 1836.

" *To the Editor of The Journal :*

"In your paper of last Saturday I see a com-munication over the signature of "Many Voters" in which the candidates who are announced in the *Journal* are called upon to ' show their hands.' Agreed. Here's mine :

"I go for all sharing the privileges of the govern-ment who assist in bearing its burdens. Conse-quently, I go for admitting all whites to the right of suffrage who pay taxes or bear arms (by no means excluding females).

"If elected I shall consider the whole people of Sangamon my constituents, as well those that oppose as those that support me.

"While acting as their Representative, I shall be governed by their will on all subjects upon which I have the means of knowing what their will is ; and upon all others I shall do what my own judg-ment teaches me will best advance their interests. Whether elected or not, I go for distributing the proceeds of the sales of public lands to the several States to enable our State, in common with others, to dig canals and construct railroads without bor-rowing money and paying the interest on it.

"If alive on the first Monday in November, I shall vote for Hugh L. White, for President.

"Very respectfully,

"A. LINCOLN."

It is generally admitted that the bold and decided stand Lincoln took—though too audacious and emphatic for statesmen of a later day—suited the temper of the times. Leaving out of sight his expressed preference for White of Tennessee,—on whom all the anti-Jackson forces were disposed to concentrate, and which was but a mere question of men,—there is much food for thought in the second paragraph. His broad plan for universal suffrage certainly commends itself to the ladies, and we need no further evidence to satisfy our minds of his position on the subject of "Woman's Rights," had he lived. In fact, I cannot refrain from noting here what views he in after years held with reference to the great questions of moral and social reforms, under which he classed universal suffrage, temperance, and slavery. "All such questions," he observed one day, as we were discussing temperance in the office, "must first find lodgment with the most enlightened souls who stamp them with their approval. In God's own time they will be organized into law and thus woven into the fabric of our institutions."

The canvass which followed this public avowal of creed, was more exciting than any which had preceded it. There were joint discussions, and, at times, much feeling was exhibited. Each candidate had his friends freely distributed through the crowd, and it needed but a few angry interruptions or insinuating rejoinders from one speaker to another to bring on a conflict between their friends. Frequently the speakers led in the battle themselves, as in the case of Ninian W. Edwards—afterwards a brother-in-law of Lincoln—who, in debate, drew a pistol on his opponent Achilles Morris, a prominent Democrat. An interesting relic of this canvass recently came to light, in a letter which Mr. Lincoln wrote a week after he had announced his candidacy. It is addressed to Colonel Robert Allen, a Democratic politician of local prominence, who had been circulating some charges intended to affect Lincoln's chances of election. The affair brought to the surface what little satire there was in Lincoln's nature, and he administers—by way of innuendo—such a flaying as the gallant colonel doubtless never wanted to have repeated. The strangest part of it all is that the letter was recently found and given to the public by Allen's own son.* It is as follows:

"NEW SALEM, June 21, 1836.
" DEAR COLONEL:
"I am told that during my absence last week you passed through the place and stated publicly that you were in possession of a fact or facts, which if known to the public would entirely destroy the prospects of N. W. Edwards and myself at the ensuing election, but that through favor to us you would forbear to divulge them. No one has needed favors more than I, and generally few have been less unwilling to accept them, but in this case favor to me would be injustice to the public, and therefore I must beg your pardon for declining it. That I once had the confidence of the people of Sangamon county is sufficiently evident; and if I have done anything, either by design or misadventure, which if known would subject me to a forfeiture of that confidence, he that knows of that thing, and conceals it, is a traitor to his country's interest.

---

* The MS. is now in possession of the Lincoln Monument Association of Springfield.

"I find myself wholly unable to form any conjecture of what fact or facts, real or supposed, you spoke; but my opinion of your veracity will not permit me for a moment to doubt that you at least believed what you said. I am flattered with the personal regard you manifested for me; but I do hope that on mature reflection you will view the public interest as a paramount consideration and therefore let the worst come.

"I assure you that the candid statement of facts on your part, however low it may sink me, shall never break the ties of personal friendship between us.

"I wish an answer to this, and you are at liberty to publish both if you choose.

"Very respectfully,
"A. LINCOLN."

COL. ROBERT ALLEN.

Lincoln was sure the letter never would be published or answered, because Allen had no facts whatever upon which to base any such charges. He also knew that Allen, who was a hide-bound Democrat, was in politics the most unreliable man in Sangamon county. A vein of irony runs all through the letter, especially where in such a delicate way he pays tribute to the veracity of Allen, who, although a generous fellow in the ordinary sense of the term, was unlimited in exaggeration and a veritable bag of wind. The effort to smoke him out seems to have been of little effect, but enough appears in Lincoln's letter to show that he was thoroughly warmed up.

A joint debate in which all the candidates participated, took place on the Saturday preceding the election. "The speaking began in the forenoon," says one of the participants, "the candidates speaking alternately until everyone who could speak had had his turn, generally consuming the whole afternoon." Dr. Early, a Democratic candidate, in his speech took issue with Ninian W. Edwards, stigmatizing some of the latter's statements as untrue. This brought Edwards to his feet with a similar retort. His angry tone and menacing manner, as he mounted a table and with clenched fist hurled defiance at his challenger, foreboded a tumultuous scene. "The excitement that followed," relates another one of the candidates,* "was intense—so much so that fighting men thought a duel must settle the difficulty. Mr. Lincoln by the programme followed Early. Taking up the subject in dispute, he handled it so fairly and with such ability, all were astonished and pleased." The turbulent spirits were quieted and the difficulty was easily overcome.

Lincoln's friend Joshua F. Speed relates that during this campaign he made a speech in Springfield a few days before the election. "The crowd was large," says Speed, "and great numbers of his friends and admirers had come in from the country. I remember that his speech was a very able one, using with great power and originality all the arguments used to sustain the principles of the Whig party as against its great rival, the Democratic party of that day. The speech produced a profound impression—the crowd was with him.

* R. L. Wilson, letter, Feb. 10, 1866, MS.

George Forquer, an old citizen, a man of recognized prominence and ability as a lawyer, was present. Forquer had been a Whig—one of the champions of the party—but had then recently joined the Democratic party, and almost simultaneous with the change had been appointed Register of the Land Office, which office he then held. Just about that time Mr. Forquer had completed a neat frame house—the best house then in Springfield—and over it had erected a lightning rod, the only one in the place and the first one Mr. Lincoln had ever seen. He afterwards told me that seeing Forquer's lightning rod had led him to the study of the properties of electricity and the utility of the rod as a conductor. At the conclusion of Lincoln's speech the crowd was about dispersing, when Forquer rose and asked to be heard. He commenced by saying that the young man would have to be taken down, and was sorry the task devolved on him. He then proceeded to answer Lincoln's speech in a style which, while it was able and fair, in his whole manner asserted and claimed superiority." Lincoln stood a few steps away with arms folded, carefully watching the speaker and taking in everything he said. He was laboring under a good deal of suppressed excitement. Forquer's sting had roused the lion within him. At length Forquer concluded, and he mounted the stand to reply.

"I have heard him often since," continued Speed, "in the courts and before the people, but never saw him appear and acquit himself so well as upon that occasion. His reply to Forquer was characterized by great dignity and force. I shall never forget the conclusion of that speech: 'Mr. Forquer commenced his speech by announcing that the young man would have to be taken down. It is for you, fellow citizens, not for me to say whether I am up or down. The gentleman has seen fit to allude to my being a young man; but he forgets that I am older in years than I am in the tricks and trades of politicians. I desire to live, and I desire place and distinction ; but I would rather die now than, like the gentleman, live to see the day that I would change my politics for an office worth three thousand dollars a year, and then feel compelled to erect a lightning rod to protect a guilty conscience from an offended God.' " The effect of this rejoinder was wonderful, and gave Forquer and his lightning rod a notoriety the extent of which no one envied him.

In the election which followed, Sangamon county in a political sense was entirely turned over. Hitherto the Democrats had always carried it, but now the Whigs gained control by an average majority of four hundred. This time Lincoln led his ticket. The nine elected were, Abraham Lincoln, Ninian W. Edwards, John Dawson, Andrew McCormick, Dan Stone, Wm. F. Elkin, Robert L. Wilson, Job Fletcher, and Archer G. Herndon. The last two were senators. On assembling at Vandalia they were at once, on account of their stature, dubbed the "Long Nine." In height they averaged over six feet, and in weight over two hundred pounds. "We were not only noted," says one * of them, "for our number and length, but for our combined influence. All the bad or objectional laws passed at that session of the Legislature and for many years afterwards were chargeable to the management and influence of the 'Long Nine.'" It is not my purpose to enter into a detailed account of legislation at this period or to rehearse the history of the political conditions. Many and ingenious were the manœuvres, but it would fill page after page to narrate them. One thing which deserves mention in passing was "that Yankee contrivance," the convention system, which for the first time was brought into use. The Democrats, in obedience to the behests of Jackson, had adopted it, and, singularly enough, among the very first named for office under the operation of the new system was Stephen A. Douglas, who was elected to the Legislature from Morgan county. Its introduction was attributed to Ebenezer Peck, of Chicago, a Democrat who had once, it was said, served in the Canadian Parliament. This latter supposed connection with a monarchical institution was sufficient to bring down on his head the united hostility of the Whigs, a feeling in which even Lincoln joined. But after witnessing for a time the wonderful effects of its discipline in Democratic ranks, the Whigs too fell in, and resorted to the use of the improved machinery.

The Legislature of which Mr. Lincoln thus be-

---

* R. L. Wilson, MS.

came a member was one that will never be forgotten in Illinois. Its legislation in aid of the
so-called internal improvement system was significantly reckless and unwise. The gigantic and
stupendous operations of the scheme dazzled the
eyes of nearly everybody, but in the end it rolled
up a debt so enormous as to impede the otherwise
marvelous progress of Illinois. The burdens imposed by this Legislature under the guise of
improvements became so monumental in size it is
little wonder that at intervals for years afterward the
monster of repudiation often showed its hideous
face above the waves of popular indignation.
These attempts at a settlement of the debt brought
about a condition of things which it is said led the
Little Giant, in one of his efforts on the stump, to
suggest that "Illinois ought to be honest if she
never paid a cent." However much we may regret
that Lincoln took part and aided in this reckless legislation, we must not forget that his party and all his
constituents gave him their united endorsement.
They gave evidence of their approval of his course
by two subsequent elections to the same office. It
has never surprised me in the least that Lincoln fell
so harmoniously in with the great system of improvement. He never had what some people call
"money sense." By reason of his peculiar nature
and construction he was endowed with none of the
elements of a political economist. He was enthusiastic and theoretical to a certain degree;
could take hold of, and wrap himself up in, a great
moral question; but in dealing with the financial

13

and commercial interests of a community or government he was equally as inadequate as he was ineffectual in managing the economy of his own household. In this respect alone I always regarded Mr. Lincoln as a weak man.

One of his biographers, describing his legislative career at this time, says of him: "He was big with prospects: his real public service was just now about to begin. In the previous Legislature he had been silent, observant, studious. He had improved the opportunity so well that of all men in this new body, of equal age in the service, he was the smartest parliamentarian and cunningest 'log roller.' He was fully determined to identify himself conspicuously with the liberal legislation in contemplation, and dreamed of a fame very different from that which he actually obtained as an anti-slavery leader. It was about this time he told his friend Speed that he aimed at the great distinction of being called the 'DeWitt Clinton of Illinois.'"

The representatives in the Legislature from Sangamon county had been instructed by a mass convention of their constituents to vote "for a general system of internal improvements." Another convention of delegates from all the counties in the State met at Vandalia and made a similar recommendation to the members of the Legislature, specifying that it should be "commensurate with the wants of the people." Provision was made for a gridiron of railroads. The extreme points of the State, east and west, north and south, were to be brought together by thirteen hundred miles of iron

rails. Every river and stream of the least importance was to be widened, deepened, and made
navigable. A canal to connect the Illinois River
and Lake Michigan was to be dug, and thus the
great system was to be made "commensurate with
the wants of the people." To effect all these great
ends, a loan of twelve million dollars was authorized
before the session closed. Work on all these gigantic enterprises was to begin at the earliest prac-
ticable moment ; cities were to spring up everywhere ; capital from abroad was to come pouring in ;
attracted by the glowing reports of marvelous
progress and great internal wealth, people were to
come swarming in by colonies, until in the end
Illinois was to outstrip all the others, and herself
become the Empire State of the Union.

Lincoln served on the Committee on Finance,
and zealously labored for the success of the great
measures proposed, believing they would ultimately
enrich the State, and redound to the glory of all
who aided in their passage. In advocating these
extensive and far-reaching plans he was not alone.
Stephen A. Douglas, John A. McClernand, James
Shields, and others prominent in the subsequent
history of the State, were equally as earnest in espousing the cause of improvement, and sharing
with him the glory that attended it. Next in
importance came the bill to remove the seat of
government from Vandalia. Springfield, of course,
wanted it. So also did Alton, Decatur, Peoria,
Jacksonville, and Illiopolis. But the Long Nine,
by their adroitness and influence, were too much

for their contestants.   They made a bold fight for
Springfield, intrusting the management of the bill
to Lincoln.   The friends of other cities fought
Springfield bitterly, but under Lincoln's leadership
the Long Nine contested with them every inch of
the way.   The struggle was warm and protracted.
" Its enemies," relates one of Lincoln's colleagues,*
" laid it on the table twice.   In those darkest hours
when our bill to all appearances was beyond resusci-
tation, and all our opponents were jubilant over our
defeat, and when friends could see no hope, Mr.
Lincoln never for one moment despaired ; but
collecting his colleagues to his room for consulta-
tion, his practical common-sense, his thorough
knowledge of human nature, then made him an
overmatch for his compeers and for any man that I
have ever known."   The friends of the bill at last
surmounted all obstacles, and only a day or two
before the close of the session secured its passage
by a joint vote of both houses.

Meanwhile the great agitation against human
slavery, which like a rare plant had flourished amid
the hills of New England in luxuriant growth,
began to make its appearance in the West.   Mis-
sionaries in the great cause of human liberty were
settling everywhere.   Taunts, jeers, ridicule, persecution, assassination even, were destined to prove
ineffectual in the effort to suppress or exterminate
these pioneers of Abolitionism.   These brave but
derided apostles carried with them the seed of a

---

* R. S. Wilson, MS.

great reform. Perhaps, as was then said of them, they were somewhat in advance of their season, and perhaps too, some of the seed might be sown in sterile ground and never come to life, but they comforted themselves with the assurance that it would not all die. A little here and there was destined to grow to life and beauty.

It is not surprising, I think, that Lincoln should have viewed this New England importation with mingled suspicion and alarm. Abstractly, and from the standpoint of conscience, he abhorred slavery. But born in Kentucky, and surrounded as he was by slave-holding influences, absorbing their prejudices and following in their line of thought, it is not strange, I repeat, that he should fail to estimate properly the righteous indignation and unrestrained zeal of a Yankee Abolitionist. On the last day but one of the session, he solicited his colleagues to sign with him a mild and carefully worded protest against certain resolutions on the subject of domestic slavery, which had been passed by both houses of the Legislature. They all declined, however, save one, Dan Stone,* who with

---

*Following are the resolutions against the passage of which Lincoln and Stone made their protest :

Resolved by the General Assembly of the State of Illinois : That we highly disapprove of the formation of Abolition societies and of the doctrines promulgated by them,

That the right of property in slaves is sacred to the slave-holding States by the Federal Constitution, and that they cannot be deprived of that right without their consent,

That the General Government cannot abolish slavery in the

his associate will probably be known long after mention of all other members of the Long Nine has dropped from history. The language and sentiment are clearly Lincolnian, and over twenty years afterward, when it was charged that Lincoln was an Abolitionist, and this protest was cited as proof, it was only necessary to call for a careful reading of the paper for an unqualified and over-whelming refutation of the charge. The records of the Legislature for March 3, 1837, contain this entry:

"Resolutions upon the subject of domestic slavery having passed both branches of the General Assembly at its present session, the undersigned hereby protest against the passage of the same.

"They believe that the institution of slavery is founded on both injustice and bad policy, but that the promulgation of abolition doctrines tends rather to increase than abate its evils.

"They believe that the Congress of the United States has no power under the Constitution to interfere with the institution of slavery in the different States.

"They believe that the Congress of the United States has the power under the Constitution to abolish slavery in the District of Columbia, but that the power ought not to be exercised unless at the request of the people of the District.

District of Columbia against the consent of the citizens of said District, without a manifest breach of good faith,

That the Governor be requested to transmit to the States of Virginia, Alabama, Mississippi, New York, and Connecticut, a copy of the foregeing report and resolutions.

"The difference between these opinions and those contained in the above resolutions is their reason for entering this protest.

"DAN STONE,
"A. LINCOLN,

"Representatives from the county of Sangamon."

This document so adroitly drawn and worded, this protest pruned of any offensive allusions, and cautiously framed so as to suit the temper of the times, stripped of its verbal foliage reveals in naked grandeur the solemn truth that "the institution of slavery is founded on both injustice and bad policy." A quarter of a century later finds one of these protesters righting the injustice and correcting the bad policy of the inhuman and diabolical institution.

The return of the "Long Nine" to Springfield was the occasion of much enthusiasm and joy. The manifestations of public delight had never been equalled before, save when the steamer *Talisman* made its famous trip down the Sangamon in 1831. The returning legislators were welcomed with public dinners and the effervescent buncombe of local orators. Amid the congratulations of warm friends and the approval of their enthusiastic constituents, in which Lincoln received the lion's share of praise, they separated, each departing to his own home.

After his return from the Legislature, Lincoln determined to remove to Springfield, the county seat, and begin the practice of the law. Having been so instrumental in securing the removal of the

State Capital from Vandalia, and having received such encouraging assurances from Major John T. Stuart and other leading citizens, he felt confident of a good start.* He had little, if any, money, but hoped to find in Springfield, as he had in New Salem, good and influential friends, who, recognizing alike his honesty and his nobility of character, would aid him whenever a crisis came and their help was needed. In this hope he was by no means in error, for his subsequent history shows that he indeed united his friends to himself with hooks of steel. I had up to this time frequently seen Mr. Lincoln—had often, while visiting my cousins, James and Rowan Herndon, at New Salem, met him at their house—but became warmly attached to him soon after his removal to Springfield. There was something in his tall and angular frame, his ill-fitting garments, honest face, and lively humor that imprinted his individuality on my affection and regard. What impression I made on him I had no means of knowing till many years afterward. He was my senior by nine years, and I looked up to him, naturally enough, as my superior in everything— a thing I continued to do till the end of his days.

---

* Lincoln used to come to our office—Stuart's and mine—in Springfield from New Salem and borrow law-books. Sometimes he walked but generally rode. He was the most uncouth looking young man I ever saw. He seemed to have but little to say ; seemed to feel timid, with a tinge of sadness visible in the countenance, but when he did talk all this disappeared for the time and he demonstrated that he was both strong and acute. He surprised us more and more at every visit."—Henry E. Dummer, Statement, Sept. 16th, 1865.

SPRINGFIELD COURT-HOUSE.

STUART AND LINCOLN'S OFFICE (IN 1839), SECOND FLOOR, OVER FURNITURE-STORE.

Photographed in 1888.

Now that the State capital was to be located at Springfield, that place began, by way of asserting its social superiority, to put on a good many airs. Wealth made its gaudy display, and thus sought to attain a pre-eminence from which learning and refinement are frequently cut off. Already, people had settled there who could trace their descent down a long line of distinguished ancestry. The established families were mainly from Kentucky. They re-echoed the sentiments and reflected the arrogance and elegance of a slave-holding aristocracy. "The Todds, Stuarts, and Edwardses were there, with priests, dogs, and servants;" there also were the Mathers, Lambs, Opdykes, Forquers, and Fords. Amid all "the flourishing about in carriages" and the pretentious elegance of that early day was Lincoln. Of origin, doubtful if not unknown; "poor, without the means of hiding his poverty," he represented yet another importation from Kentucky which is significantly comprehended by the term, "the poor whites." Springfield, containing between one and two thousand people, was near the northern line of settlement in Illinois. Still it was the center of a limited area of wealth and refinement. Its citizens were imbued with the spirit of push and enterprise. Lincoln therefore could not have been thrown into a better or more appreciative community.

In March, 1837, he was licensed to practice law. His name appears for the first time as attorney for the plaintiff in the case of Hawthorne *vs.* Woolridge. He entered the office and became the partner of his comrade in the Black Hawk war, John T. Stuart, who had gained rather an extensive practice, and who, by the loan of sundry textbooks several years before, had encouraged Lincoln to continue in the study of law. Stuart had emigrated from Kentucky in 1828, and on account of his nativity, if for no other reason, had great influence with the leading people in Springfield. He used to relate that on the next morning after his arrival in Springfield he was standing in front of the village store, leaning against a post in the sidewalk and wondering how to introduce himself to the community, when he was approached by a well-dressed old gentleman, who, interesting himself in the newcomer's welfare, enquired after his history and business. "I'm from Kentucky," answered Stuart, "and my profession is that of a lawyer, sir. What is the prospect here?" Throwing his head back and closing his left eye the old gentleman reflected a moment. "Young man, d——d slim chance for that kind of a combination here," was the response.

At the time of Lincoln's entry into the office, Stuart was just recovering from the effects of a congressional race in which he had been the loser. He was still deeply absorbed in politics, and was preparing for the next canvass, in which he was finally successful—defeating the wily and ambitious Stephen A. Douglas. In consequence of the political allurements, Stuart did not give to the law his undivided time or the full force of his energy and intellect. Thus more or less responsibility in the management of business and the conduct of cases soon devolved on Lincoln. The entries in the account books of the firm are all in the handwriting of Lincoln. Most of the declarations and pleas were written by him also. This sort of exercise was never congenial to him, and it was the only time, save a brief period under Judge Logan, that he served as junior partner and performed the labor required of one who serves in that rather subordinate capacity. He had not yet learned to love work. The office of the firm was in the upper story of a building opposite the north-west corner of the present Court-house Square. In the room underneath, the county court was held. The furniture was in keeping with the pretensions of the firm—a small lounge or bed, a chair containing a buffalo robe, in which the junior member was wont to sit and study, a hard wooden bench, a feeble attempt at a book-case, and a table which answered for a desk. Lincoln's first attempt at settlement in Springfield, which preceded a few days his partnership with Stuart, has been graphically described by his friend, Joshua F. Speed, who generously offered to share his quarters with the young legal aspirant. Speed, who was a prosperous young merchant, reports that Lincoln's personal effects consisted of a pair of saddle-bags containing two or three law books and a few pieces of clothing. " He had ridden into town on a borrowed horse," relates Speed, " and engaged from the only cabinet-maker in the village a single bedstead. He came into my store, set his saddle-bags on the counter, and enquired what the furniture for a single bedstead would cost. I took slate and pencil, made a calculation, and found the sum for furniture complete would amount to seventeen dollars in all. Said he: 'It is probably cheap enough; but I want to say that, cheap as it is, I have not the money to pay. But if you will credit me until Christmas, and my experiment here as a lawyer is a success, I will pay you then. If I fail in that I will probably never pay you at all.' The tone of his voice was so melancholy that I felt for him. I looked up at him and I thought then, as I think now, that I never saw so gloomy and melancholy a face in my life. I said to him, ' So small a debt seems to affect you so deeply, I think I can suggest a plan by which you will be able to attain your end without incurring any debt. I have a very large room and a very large double bed in it, which you are perfectly welcome to share with me if you choose.' 'Where is your room?' he asked. 'Upstairs,' said I, pointing to the stairs leading from the store to my room. Without saying a word he took his saddle-bags on his arm, went upstairs, set them down on the floor, came down again, and with a face beaming with pleasure and smiles, exclaimed, 'Well, Speed, I'm moved.'"

William Butler, who was prominent in the removal of the capital from Vandalia to Springfield, took no little interest in Lincoln, while a member of the Legislature. After his removal to Springfield, Lincoln boarded at Butler's house for several years. He became warmly attached to the family, and it is probable the matter of pay never entered Butler's mind. He was not only able but willing to befriend the young lawyer in this and many other ways.

Stephen T. Logan was judge of the Circuit court, and Stephen A. Douglas was prosecuting attorney. Among the attorneys we find many promising spirits. Edward D. Baker, John T. Stuart, Cyrus Walker, Samuel H. Treat, Jesse B. Thomas, George Forquer, Dan Stone, Ninian W. Edwards, John J. Hardin, Schuyler Strong, A. T. Bledsoe, and Josiah Lamborn—a galaxy of names, each destined to shed more or less lustre on the history of the State. While I am inclined to believe that Lincoln did not, after entering Stuart's office, do as much deep and assiduous studying as people generally credit him with, yet I am confident he absorbed not a little learning by contact with the great minds who thronged about the courts and State Capitol. The books of Stuart and Lincoln, during 1837, show a practice more extensive than lucrative, for while they received a number of fees, only two or there of them reached fifty dollars; and one of these has a credit of: "Coat to Stuart, $15.00," showing that they were compelled, now and then, even to "trade out" their earnings. The litigation was as limited in importance as in extent. There were no great corporations, as in this progressive day, retaining for counsel the brains of the bar in every county seat, but the greatest as well as the least had to join the general scramble for practice. The courts consumed as much time deciding who had committed an assault or a trespass on a neighbor's ground, as it spent in the solution of questions arising on contracts, or unravelling similar legal complications. Lawyers depended for success, not on their knowledge of the law or their familiarity with its underlying principles, but placed their reliance rather on their frontier oratory and the influence of their personal bearing before the jury.

Lincoln made Speed's store headquarters. There politics, religion, and all other subjects were discussed. There also public sentiment was made. The store had a large fire-place in the rear, and around it the lights of the town collected every evening. As the sparks flew from the crackling logs, another and more brilliant fire flashed when these great minds came into collision. Here were wont to gather Lincoln, Douglas, Baker, Calhoun, Browning, Lamborn, Jesse B. Thomas and others. Only those who were present and listened to these embryonic statesmen and budding orators will ever be able to recall their brilliant thoughts and appreciate their youthful enthusiasm. In the fall and winter of 1837, while I was attending college at Jacksonville, the persecution and death of Elijah P. Lovejoy at Alton took place. This cruel and uncalled-for murder had aroused the anti-slavery sentiment everywhere. It penetrated the college, and both faculty and students were loud and unrestrained in their denunciation of the crime. My father, who was thoroughly pro-slavery in his ideas, believing that, the college was too strongly permeated with the virus of Abolitionism, forced me to withdraw from the institution and return home. But it was too late. My soul had absorbed too much of what my father believed was rank poison. The murder of Lovejoy filled me with more desperation than the slave scene in New Orleans did Lincoln ; for while he believed in non-interference with slavery, so long as the Constitution permitted and authorized its existence, I, although acting nominally with the Whig party up to 1853, struck out for Abolitionism pure and simple.

On my return to Springfield from college, I hired to Joshua F. Speed as clerk in his store. My salary, seven hundred dollars per annum, was considered good pay then. Speed, Lincoln, Charles R. Hurst, and I slept in the room upstairs over the store. I had worked for Speed before going to college, and after hiring to him this time again, continued in his employ for several years. The young men who congregated about the store formed a society for the encouragement of debate and literary efforts. Sometimes we would meet in a lawyer's office and often in Speed's room. Besides the debates, poems and other original productions were read. Unfortunately we ruled out the ladies. I am free to admit I would not encourage a similar thing nowadays ; but in that early day the young men had not the comforts of books and newspapers which are within the reach of every boy now. Some allowance therefore should be made for us. I have forgotten the name of the society—if it had any—and can only recall a few of its leading spirits. Lincoln, James Matheney,

Noah Rickard, Evan Butler, Milton Hay, and Newton Francis were members. I joined also. Matheney was secretary.* We were favored with all sorts of literary productions. Lincoln one night entertained us with a few lines of rhyme intended to illustrate some weakness in woman—her frailty, perhaps. Unfortunately, the manuscript has not been preserved. Matheney was able, several years ago, to repeat a single stanza, but claimed that after the lapse of so many years it was all he could recall. Perhaps in the end it is best his memory was no more retentive. Reproduced here exactly as in the original, it might suggest more than one construction or offend against the canons of approved taste; in either event I shall omit it.

Besides this organization we had a society in Springfield, which contained and commanded all

---

* Near Hoffman's Row, where the courts were held in 1839-40, lived a shoemaker who frequently would get drunk and invariably whipped his wife. Lincoln, hearing of this, told the man if he ever repeated it he would thrash him soundly himself. Meanwhile he told Evan Butler, Noah Rickard, and myself of it, and we decided if the offense occurred again to join with Lincoln in suppressing it. In due course of time we heard of it. We dragged the offender up to the court-house, stripped him of his shirt, and tied him to a post or pump which stood over the well in the yard back of the building. Then we sent for his wife and arming her with a good limb bade her " light in." We sat on our haunches and watched the performance. The wife did her work lustily and well. When we thought the culprit had had enough Lincoln released him; we helped him on with his shirt and he crept sorrowfully homeward. Of course he threatened vengeance, but still we heard no further reports of wife-whipping from him.—James H. Matheney.

the culture and talent of the place. Unlike the other one its meetings were public, and reflected great credit on the community. We called it the "Young Men's Lyceum." Late in 1837, Lincoln delivered before the society a carefully prepared address on the "Perpetuation of Our Free Institutions." * The inspiration and burthen of it was law and order. It has been printed in full so often, and is always to be found in the list of Lincoln's public speeches, that I presume I need not reproduce it here. It was highly sophomoric in character and abounded in striking and lofty metaphor. In point of rhetorical effort it excels anything he ever afterward attempted. Probably it was the thing people expect from a young man of twenty-eight. The address was published in the *Sangamon Journal* and created for the young orator a reputation which soon extended beyond the limits of the locality in which he lived. As illustrative of his style of oratory, I beg to introduce the concluding paragraph of the address. Having characterized the surviving soldiers of the Revolution as "living histories," he closes with this thrilling flourish: "But these histories are gone. They can be read no more forever. They were a fortress of strength; but what invading foeman never could do, the silent artillery of time has—the levelling of its

---

* Mr. Lincoln's speech was brought out by the burning of a negro in St. Louis a few weeks before by a mob. Lincoln took this incident as a sort of text for his remarks. James Matheney was appointed by the Lyceum to request of Lincoln a copy of his speech and see to its publication.

14

walls. They are gone. They were a forest of
giant oaks; but the all-resistless hurricane has swept
over them, and left only here and there a lonely
trunk, despoiled of its verdure, shorn of its foliage,
unshading and unshaded. to murmur in a few more
gentle breezes, and to combat with its mutilated
limbs a few more rude storms, then to sink and be
no more. They were pillars of the temple of liberty, and now that they have crumbled away, that
temple must fall, unless we, their descendants,
supply their places with other pillars hewn from the
same solid quarry of sober reason. Passion has
helped us, but can do so no more. It will in future
be our enemy. Reason—cold, calculating, unim-
passioned reason—must furnish all the materials
for our future support and defense. Let these
materials be moulded into general intelligence,
sound morality, and in particular, a reverence for
the Constitution and the laws. * * * Upon these
let the proud fabric of freedom rest as the rock of
its basis, and as truly as has been said of the only
greater institution, 'The gates of hell shall not
prevail against it.' "

In time Lincoln's style changed: he became more
eloquent but with less gaudy ornamentation. He
grew in oratorical power, dropping gradually the
alliteration and rosy metaphor of youth, until he
was able at last to deliver that grandest of all
orations—the Gettysburg address.

One evening, while the usual throng of loungers
surrounded the inviting fireplace in Speed's store,
the conversation turned on political matters. The

First Presbyterian Church, Springfield.

disputants waxed warm and acrimonious as the discussion proceeded. Business being over for the day, I strolled back and seating myself on a keg listened with eager interest to the battle going on among these would-be statesmen. Douglas, I recollect, was leading on the Democratic side. He had already learned the art of dodging in debate, but still he was subtle, fiery, and impetuous. He charged the Whigs with every blunder and political crime he could imagine. No vulnerable spot seemed to have escaped him. At last, with great vehemence, he sprang up and abruptly made a challenge to those who differed with him to discuss the whole matter publicly, remarking that, "This store is no place to talk politics." In answer to Douglas's challenge the contest was entered into. It took place in the Presbyterian Church. Douglas, Calhoun, Lamborn, and Thomas represented the Democrats ; and Logan, Baker, Browning, and Lincoln, in the order named, presented the Whig side of the question. One evening was given to each man, and it therefore required over a week to complete the tournament. Lincoln occupied the last evening, and although the people by that time had necessarily grown a little tired of the monotony and well-worn repetition, yet Lincoln's manner of presenting his thoughts and answering his Democratic opponents excited renewed interest. So deep was the impression he created that he was asked to furnish his speech to the *Sangamon Journal* for publication, and it afterwards appeared in the columns of that organ.

Meanwhile Mr. Lincoln had attended one special session of the Legislature in July, 1837. The session was called to take some action with regard to the financial condition of the State. The Bank of the United States and the New York and Philadelphia Banks had suspended specie payments. This action had precipitated general ruin among business men and interests over the entire country. The called session of the Legislature was intended to save the Illinois banks from impending dissolution. Lincoln retained his position on the Committee on Finance, and had lost none of his enthusiasm over the glorious prospects of internal improvements. The Legislature, instead of abridging, only extended the already colossal proportions of the great system. In this they paid no heed to the governor, whose head seems to have been significantly clear on the folly of the enterprise.

In 1838 Mr. Lincoln was again elected to the Legislature. At this session, as the nominee of the Whig party, he received thirty-eight votes for Speaker. Wm. L. D. Ewing, his successful competitor, the Democratic candidate, received forty-three votes, and was elected. Besides retaining his place on the Finance Committee, Lincoln was assigned to the Committee on Counties. The enthusiasm and zeal of the friends of internal improvements began to flag now in view of the fact that the bonds issued were beginning to find their true level in point of value. Lincoln, together with others of kindred views, tried to bolster the "system" up; but soon the discouraging fact became apparent that no more money could be obtained, and the Legislature began to descant on what part of the debt was lawful and what unlawful. Repudiation seemed not far off. Mr. Lincoln despaired now of ever becoming the "DeWitt Clinton of Illinois." We find him admitting "his share of the responsibility in the present crisis," and finally concluding that he was "no financier" after all. No sooner had the Legislature adjourned than he decided—if he had not already so determined—to run for the same place again. He probably wanted it for a vindication. He was pursued now more fiercely than ever, and he was better able to endure the vilification of a political campaign than when he first offered himself to the voters in New Salem.

Among the Democratic orators who stumped the county at this time was one Taylor—commonly known as Col. Dick Taylor. He was a showy, bombastic man, with a weakness for fine clothes and other personal adornments. Frequently he was pitted against Lincoln, and indulged in many bitter flings at the lordly ways and aristocratic pretensions of the Whigs. He had a way of appealing to "his horny-handed neighbors," and resorted to many other artful tricks of a demagogue. When he was one day expatiating in his accustomed style, Lincoln, in a spirit of mischief and, as he expressed it, "to take the wind out of his sails," slipped up to the speaker's side, and catching his vest by the lower edge gave it a sharp pull. The latter instantly opened and revealed to his astonished hearers a ruffled shirt-front glittering with watch-chain, seals, and other golden jewels. The effect was startling. The speaker stood confused and dumbfounded, while the audience roared with laughter. When it came Lincoln's turn to answer he covered the gallant colonel over in this style: "While Colonel Taylor was making these charges against the Whigs over the country, riding in fine carriages, wearing ruffled shirts, kid gloves, massive gold watch-chains with large gold seals, and flourishing a heavy gold-headed cane, I was a poor boy, hired on a flat-boat at eight dollars a month, and had only one pair of breeches to my back, and they were buckskin. Now if you know the nature of buckskin when wet and dried by the sun, it will shrink; and my breeches kept shrinking until they left several inches of my legs bare between the tops of my socks and the lower part of my breeches; and whilst I was growing taller they were becoming shorter, and so much tighter that they left a blue streak around my legs that can be seen to this day. If you call this aristocracy I plead guilty to the charge." *

It was during this same canvass that Lincoln by his manly interference protected his friend E. D. Baker from the anger of an infuriated crowd. Baker was a brilliant and effective speaker, and quite as full too of courage as invective. He was addressing a crowd in the court room, which was immediately underneath Stuart and Lincoln's office. Just above the platform on which the speaker stood

---

* From MS. of Ninian W. Edwards.

was a trap door in the floor, which opened into Lincoln's office. Lincoln at the time, as was often his habit, was lying on the floor looking down through the door at the speaker. I was in the body of the crowd. Baker was hot-headed and impulsive, but brave as a lion. Growing warm in his arraignment of the Democratic party, he charged that "wherever there was a land office there was a Democratic newspaper to defend its corruptions." This angered the brother of the editor of our town paper, who was present, and who cried out, "Pull him down," at the same time advancing from the crowd as if to perform the task himself. Baker, his face pale with excitement, squared himself for resistance. A shuffling of feet, a forward movement of the crowd, and great confusion followed. Just then a long pair of legs were seen dangling from the aperture above, and instantly the figure of Lincoln dropped on the platform. Motioning with his hands for silence and not succeeding, he seized a stone water-pitcher standing near by, threatening to break it over the head of the first man who laid hands on Baker. "Hold on, gentlemen," he shouted, "this is the land of free speech. Mr. Baker has a right to speak and ought to be heard. I am here to protect him, and no man shall take him from this stand if I can prevent it." His interference had the desired effect. Quiet was soon restored, and the valiant Baker was allowed to proceed. I was in the back part of the crowd that night, and an enthusiastic Baker man myself. I knew he was a brave man, and even if Lincoln had not interposed, I felt sure he wouldn't have been pulled from the platform without a bitter struggle.

This canvass—1840—was Mr. Lincoln's last campaign for the Legislature. Feeling that he had had enough honor out of the office he probably aspired for a place of more distinction. Jesse B. Thomas, one of the men who had represented the Democratic side in the great debate in the Presbyterian Church, in a speech at the court-house during this campaign, indulged in some fun at the expense of the "Long Nine," reflecting somewhat more on Lincoln than the rest. The latter was not present, but being apprised by his friends of what had been said, hastened to the meeting, and soon after Thomas closed, stepped upon the platform and responded. The substance of his speech on this occasion was not so memorable as the manner of its delivery. He felt the sting of Thomas's allusions, and for the first time, on the stump or in public, resorted to mimicry for effect. In this, as will be seen later along, he was without a rival. He imitated Thomas in gesture and voice, at times caricaturing his walk and the very motion of his body. Thomas, like everybody else, had some peculiarities of expression and gesture, and these Lincoln succeeded in rendering more prominent than ever. The crowd yelled and cheered as he continued. Encouraged by these demonstrations, the ludicrous features of the speaker's performance gave way to intense and scathing ridicule. Thomas, who was obliged to sit near by and endure the pain of this unique ordeal, was ordinarily sensitive ; but the exhibition goaded him to desperation. He was so thoroughly wrought up with suppressed emotion that he actually gave way to tears. I was not a witness of this scene, but the next day it was the talk of the town, and for years afterwards it was called the "skinning" of Thomas. Speed was there, so were A. Y. Ellis, Ninian W. Edwards, and David Davis, who was just then coming into prominence. The whole thing was so unlike Lincoln, it was not soon forgotten either by his friends or enemies. I heard him afterwards say that the recollection of his conduct that evening filled him with the deepest chagrin. He felt that he had gone too far, and to rid his good-nature of a load, hunted up Thomas and made ample apology. The incident and its sequel proved that Lincoln could not only be vindictive but manly as well.

He was selected as an Elector on the Harrison ticket for President in 1840, and as such stumped over a good portion of the State. In debate he frequently met Douglas, who had already become the standard-bearer and exponent of Democratic principles. These joint meetings were spirited affairs sometimes; but at no time did he find the Little Giant averse to a conflict. "He was very sensitive," relates one of his colleagues on the stump, "where he thought he had failed to meet the expectations of his friends. I remember a case. He was pitted by the Whigs in 1840 to debate with Mr. Douglas, the Democratic champion. Lincoln did not come up to the requirements of the occasion. He was conscious of his failure, and I never saw any man so much distressed. He begged to be permitted to try it again, and was reluctantly indulged; and in the next effort he transcended our highest expectations.* I never heard and never expect to hear such a triumphant vindication as he then gave of Whig measures or policy. He never after, to my knowledge, fell below himself."

The campaign ended in his election to the Legislature. He was again the caucus nominee of the Whigs for Speaker, receiving thirty-six votes; but his former antagonist, William L. D. Ewing, was elected by a majority of ten votes over him. The proceedings of, and laws enacted by, this Legislature are so much a matter of history and so generally known that it seems a needless task on my part to enter into details. It is proper to note, however, in passing, that Mr. Lincoln was neither prompt nor constant in his attendance during the session. He had been to a certain extent " upset " by another love affair, the particulars of which must be assigned to a future chapter.

---

* Joseph Gillespie, MS. letter, June 5, '66.

CHAPTER IX.

THE year 1840 finds Mr. Lincoln entering his thirty-second year and still unmarried. "I have come to the conclusion," he suggests in a facetious letter, two years before, "never again to think of marrying." But meanwhile he had seen more of the world. The State Capital had been removed to Springfield, and he soon observed the power and influence one can exert with high family and social surroundings to draw upon. The sober truth is that Lincoln was inordinately ambitious. He had already succeeded in obtaining no inconsiderable political recognition, and numbered among his party friends men of wealth and reputation ; but he himself was poor, besides lacking the graces and ease of bearing obtained through mingling in polite society—in fact, to use the expressive language of Mary Owens, he was "deficient in those little links which make up the chain of woman's happiness." Conscious, therefore, of his humble rank in the social scale, how natural that he should seek by marriage in an influential family to establish strong connections and at the same time foster his political fortunes ! This may seem an audacious thing to insinuate, but on no other basis can we reconcile the strange course of his courtship and the tempestuous chapters in his married life. It is a curious history, and the facts, long chained down, are gradually coming to the surface. When all is at last known, the world I believe will divide its censure between Lincoln and his wife.

Mary Todd, who afterwards became the wife of Mr. Lincoln, was born in Lexington, Kentucky, December 13, 1818. "My mother," related Mrs. Lincoln to me in 1865, "died when I was still young. I was educated by Madame Mantelli, a lady who lived opposite Mr. Clay's, and who was an accomplished French scholar. Our conversation at school was carried on entirely in French—in fact we were allowed to speak nothing else. I finished my education at Mrs. Ward's Academy, an institution to which many people from the North sent their daughters. In 1837 I visited Springfield, Illinois, remaining three months. I returned to Kentucky, remaining till 1839, when I again set out for Illinois, which State finally became my home."

The paternal grandfather of Mary Todd, General Levi Todd, was born in 1756, was educated in Virginia, and studied law in the office of General Lewis of that State. He emigrated to Kentucky, was a lieutenant in the campaigns conducted by General George Rogers Clark against the Indians, and commanded a battalion in the battle of Blue Licks, August 18, 1782, where his brother, John Todd, was killed. He succeeded Daniel Boone in command of the militia, ranking as major-general, and was one of the first settlers in Lexington, Ky. February 25, 1779, he married Miss Jane Briggs. The seventh child of this union, born February 25, 1791, was Robert S. Todd, the father of Mrs. Lincoln. On her maternal side Mrs. Lincoln was highly connected. Her great-grandfather, General Andrew Porter, was in the war of the Revolution. He succeeded Peter Muhlenberg as major-general of the Pennsylvania militia. Her great uncles, George B. Porter, who was governor of Michigan, James Madison Porter, secretary of the navy under President Tyler, and David R. Porter, governor of Pennsylvania, were men of ability and distinction. Her mother, Anne Eliza Parker, was a cousin of her father, Robert S. Todd. The latter had served in both houses of the Kentucky Legislature, and for over twenty years was president of the Bank of Kentucky at Lexington. He died July 16, 1849.

To a young lady in whose veins coursed the blood that had come down from this long and distinguished ancestral line, who could even go back in the genealogical chart to the sixth century, Lincoln, the child of Nancy Hanks, whose descent was dimmed by the shadow of tradition, was finally united in marriage.

When Mary Todd came to her sister's house in Springfield in 1839, she was in her twenty-first year. She was a young woman of strong, passionate nature and quick temper, and had " left her home in Kentucky to avoid living under the same roof with a stepmother." * She came to live with her oldest sister, Elizabeth, who was the wife of Lin-

---

* Mrs. Edwards, statement, Aug. 3, 1887.

coln's colleague in the Legislature, Ninian W. Edwards. She had two other sisters, Frances, married to Dr. William Wallace, and Anne, who afterwards became the wife of C. M. Smith, a prominent and wealthy merchant. They all resided in Springfield. She was of the average height, weighing when I first saw her about a hundred and thirty pounds. She was rather compactly built, had a well rounded face, rich dark-brown hair, and bluish-gray eyes. In her bearing she was proud, but handsome and vivacious. Her education had been in no wise defective; she was a good conversationalist, using with equal fluency the French and English languages. When she used a pen, its point was sure to be sharp, and she wrote with wit and ability. She not only had a quick intellect but an intuitive judgment of men and their motives. Ordinarily she was affable and even charming in her manners; but when offended or antagonized, her agreeable qualities instantly disappeared beneath a wave of stinging satire or sarcastic bitterness, and her entire better nature was submerged. In her figure and physical proportions, in education, bearing, temperament, history—in everything she was the exact reverse of Lincoln.

On her return to Springfield she immediately entered society, and soon became one of the belles, leading the young men of the town a merry dance. She was a very shrewd observer, and discreetly and without apparent effort kept back all the unattractive elements in her unfortunate organization. Her trenchant wit, affability, and candor pleased the

JOSHUA FRY SPEED AND WIFE.

From an oil-painting in possession of the family.

young men not less than her culture and varied
accomplishments impressed the older ones with
whom she came in contact. The first time I met
her was at a dance at the residence of Col. Robert
Allen, a gentleman mentioned in the preceding
chapter. I engaged her for a waltz, and as we
glided through it I fancied I never before had
danced with a young lady who moved with such
grace and ease. A few moments later, as we were
promenading through the hall, I thought to compliment her graceful dancing by telling her that
while I was conscious of my own awkward movements, she seemed to glide through the waltz with
the ease of a serpent. The strange comparison was
as unfortunate as it was hideous. I saw it in an
instant, but too late to recall it. She halted
for a moment, drew back, and her eyes flashed
as she retorted: " Mr. Herndon, comparison to a
serpent is rather severe irony, especially to a newcomer."

Through the influence of Joshua F. Speed, who
was a warm friend of the Edwardses, Lincoln was
led to call on Miss Todd. He was charmed with her
wit and beauty, no less than by her excellent social
qualities and profound knowledge of the strong and
weak points in individual character. One visit succeeded another. It was the old story. Lincoln
had again fallen in love. "I have often happened
in the room where they were sitting," relates Mrs.
Edwards, describing this courtship, "and Mary
invariably led the conversation. Mr. Lincoln would
sit at her side and listen. He scarcely said a word,

but gazed on her as if irresistibly drawn towards her by some superior and unseen power. He could not maintain himself in a continued conversation with a lady reared as Mary was. He was not educated and equipped mentally to make himself either interesting or attractive to the ladies. He was a good, honest, and sincere young man whose rugged, manly qualities I admired ; but to me he somehow seemed ill-constituted by nature and education to please such a woman as my sister. Mary was quick, gay, and in the social world somewhat brilliant. She loved show and power, and was the most ambitious woman I ever knew. She used to contend when a girl, to her friends in Kentucky, that she was destined to marry a President. I have heard her say that myself, and after mingling in society in Springfield she repeated the seemingly absurd and idle boast. Although Mr. Lincoln seemed to be attached to Mary, and fascinated by her wit and sagacity, yet I soon began to doubt whether they could always be so congenial. In a short time I told Mary my impression that they were not suited, or, as some persons who believe matches are made in heaven would say, not intended for each other."

But Mrs. Edwards' advice was seed sown on rocky soil. The courtship ran on smoothly to the point of engagement, when a new and disturbing element loomed up ahead in their paths. It was no less than the dashing and handsome Stephen A. Douglas, who now appeared on the scene in the guise of a rival. As a society man Douglas was infinitely more accomplished, more attractive and influential than Lincoln, and that he should supplant the latter in the affections of the proud and aristocratic Miss Todd is not to be marveled at. He was unremitting in his attentions to the lady, promenaded the streets arm-in-arm with her— frequently passing Lincoln—and in every way made plain his intention to become the latter's rival. There are those who believe this warm reciprocation of young Douglas' affection was a mere flirtation on Mary Todd's part, intended to spur Lincoln up, to make him more demonstrative, and manifest his love more positively and with greater fervor. But a lady relative who lived with Lincoln and his wife for two years after their marriage is authority for the statement coming from Mrs. Lincoln herself that "she loved Douglas, and but for her promise to marry Lincoln would have accepted him." The unfortunate attitude she felt bound to maintain between these two young men ended in a spell of sickness. Douglas, still hopeful, was warm in the race, but the lady's physician,—her brother-in-law,— Dr. William Wallace, to whom she confided the real cause of her illness, saw Douglas and induced him to end his pursuit,* which he did with great reluctance.

If Miss Todd intended by her flirtation with Douglas to test Lincoln's devotion, she committed a grievous error. If she believed, because he was ordinarily so undemonstrative, that he was without

---

* Mrs. Harriett Chapman, statement, Nov. 8, 1887.
15

will-power and incapable of being aroused, she certainly did not comprehend the man. Lincoln began now to feel the sting. Miss Todd's spur had certainly operated and with awakening effect. One evening Lincoln came into our store and called for his warm friend Speed. Together they walked back to the fireplace, where Lincoln, drawing from his pocket a letter, asked Speed to read it. "The letter," relates Speed, "was addressed to Mary Todd, and in it he made a plain statement of his feelings, telling her that he had thought the matter over calmly and with great deliberation, and now felt that he did not love her sufficiently to warrant her in marrying him. This letter he desired me to deliver. Upon my declining to do so he threatened to intrust it to some other person's hand. I reminded him that the moment he placed the letter in Miss Todd's hand, she would have the advantage over him. 'Words are forgotten,' I said, 'misunderstood, unnoticed in a private conver-sation, but once put your words in writing and they stand a living and eternal monument against you.' Thereupon I threw the unfortunate letter in the fire. 'Now,' I continued, 'if you have the courage of manhood, go see Mary yourself; tell her, if you do not love her, the facts, and that you will not marry her. Be careful not to say too much, and then leave at your earliest opportunity.' Thus admonished, he buttoned his coat, and with a rather determined look started out to perform the serious duty for which I had just given him explicit direc-tions."

That night Speed did not go upstairs to bed with us, but under pretense of wanting to read, remained in the store below. He was waiting for Lincoln's return. Ten o'clock passed, and still the interview with Miss Todd had not ended. At length, shortly after eleven, he came stalking in. Speed was satisfied, from the length of Lincoln's stay, that his directions had not been followed.

"Well, old fellow, did you do as I told you and as you promised?" were Speed's first words.

"Yes, I did," responded Lincoln, thoughtfully, "and when I told Mary I did not love her, she burst into tears and almost springing from her chair and wringing her hands as if in agony, said something about the deceiver being himself deceived." Then he stopped.

"What else did you say?" inquired Speed, drawing the facts from him.

"To tell you the truth, Speed, it was too much for me. I found the tears trickling down my own cheeks. I caught her in my arms and kissed her."

"And that's how you broke the engagement," sneered Speed. "You not only acted the fool, but your conduct was tantamount to a renewal of the engagement, and in decency you cannot back down now."

"Well," drawled Lincoln, "if I am in again, so be it. It's done, and I shall abide by it." *

Convinced now that Miss Todd regarded the engagement ratified,—instead of broken, as her tall

---

* Statement, Joshua F. Speed, Sep. 17, 1866, MS.

suitor had at first intended,—Lincoln continued his visits, and things moved on smoothly as before. Douglas had dropped out of the race, and everything pointed to an early marriage. It was probably at this time that Mr. and Mrs. Edwards began to doubt the wisdom of the marriage, and now and then to intimate the same to the lady; but they went no farther in their opposition and placed no obstacle in their paths.

The time fixed for the marriage was the first day in January, 1841. Careful preparations for the happy occasion were made at the Edwards mansion. The house underwent the customary renovation; the furniture was properly arranged, the rooms neatly decorated, the supper prepared, and the guests invited. The latter assembled on the evening in question, and awaited in expectant pleasure the interesting ceremony of marriage. The bride, bedecked in veil and silken gown, and nervously toying with the flowers in her hair, sat in the adjoining room. Nothing was lacking but the groom. For some strange reason he had been delayed. An hour passed, and the guests as well as the bride were becoming restless. But they were all doomed to disappointment. Another hour passed; messengers were sent out over town, and each returning with the same report, it became apparent that Lincoln, the principal in this little drama, had purposely failed to appear! The bride, in grief, disappeared to her room; the wedding supper was left untouched; the guests quietly and wonderingly withdrew; the lights in the Edwards mansion were blown out, and dark-

ness settled over all for the night. What the feelings of a lady as sensitive, passionate, and proud as
Miss Todd were we can only imagine—no one can
ever describe them. By daybreak, after persistent
search, Lincoln's friends found him. Restless,
gloomy, miserable, desperate, he seemed an object
of pity. His friends, Speed among the number,
fearing a tragic termination, watched him closely in
their rooms day and night. " Knives and razors,
and every instrument that could be used for self-
destruction were removed from his reach." * Mrs.
Edwards did not hesitate to regard him as insane,
and of course her sister Mary shared in that view.
But the case was hardly so desperate. His condition
began to improve after a few weeks, and a letter
written to his partner Stuart, on the 23d of January,
1841, three weeks after the scene at Edwards' house,
reveals more perfectly how he felt. He says: " I
am now the most miserable man living. If what I
feel were equally distributed to the whole human
family, there would not be one cheerful face on
earth. Whether I shall ever be better, I cannot tell ;
I awfully forebode I shall not. To remain as I am is
impossible. I must die or be better, as it appears
to me. . . I fear I shall be unable to attend to any
business here, and a change of scene might help me.
If I could be myself I would rather remain at home
with Judge Logan. I can write no more."

During all this time the Legislature to which Lincoln belonged was in special session, but for a time

---

* J. F. Speed, MS. letter, January 6, 1866.

he was unable to attend.* Towards the close
of the session, however, he resumed his seat. He
took little if any part in the proceedings, made no
speeches, and contented himself with answers to
the monotonous roll-call, and votes on a few of the
principal measures. After the adjournment of the
Legislature, his warm friend Speed, who had disposed of his interests in Springfield, induced Lincoln to accompany him to Kentucky. Speed's
parents lived in a magnificent place a few miles
from Louisville. Their farm was well stocked, and
they, in the current phrase, " lived well." Thither
he was taken, and there amid the quiet surroundings
he found the " change of scene " which he told
Stuart might help him. He was living under the
cloud of melancholia, and sent to the *Sangamon
Journal* a few lines under the gloomy title of " Suicide." They were published in the paper, and a
few years since I hunted over the files, and coming
across the number containing them, was astonished
to find that some one had cut them out. I have
always supposed it was done by Lincoln or by some
one at his instigation.

Speed's mother was much impressed with the
tall and swarthy stranger her son had brought
with him. She was a God-fearing mother, and besides aiding to lighten his spirits, gave him a Bible,

---

* His illness and consequent incapacity for duty in the Legislature,
continued for almost three weeks. On the 19th of January, 1841,
John J. Hardin announced his illness in the House. Four days
afterward he wrote the letter to Stuart from which I have quoted
a few lines.

advising him to read it and by adopting its precepts obtain a release from his troubles which no other agency, in her judgment, could bring him. " He was much depressed. At first he almost contemplated suicide. In the deepest of his depression he said one day he had done nothing to make any human being remember that he had lived ; and that to connect his name with the events transpiring in his day and generation, and so impress himself upon them as to link his name with something that would redound to the interest of his fellow-men, was what he desired to live for." * The congenial associations at the Speed farm,† the freedom from unpleasant reminders, the company of his staunch friend, and above all the motherly care and delicate attentions of Mrs. Speed exerted a marked influence over Lincoln. He improved gradually, day by day gaining strength and confidence in himself, until at last the great cloud lifted and passed away. In the fall he and Speed returned to Springfield. At this point, as affording us the most reliable account of Mr. Lincoln's condition and views, it is proper to insert a portion of his correspondence with Mr. Speed. For some time Mr. Speed was reluctant to give these

---

* Letter, J. F. Speed, February 9, 1866, MS.

† At the time of Lincoln's visit at the Speed mansion, James Speed, a brother of Joshua, and afterward Attorney-General in Lincoln's Cabinet, was practicing law in Louisville. Lincoln came into his office daily. " He read my books," related Mr. Speed in after years ; " talked with me about his life, his reading, his studies, his aspirations." Mr. Speed discredits the thought that Lincoln was insane at the time, although he understood he was saddened and melancholy over an unfortunate love affair.

letters to the world. After some argument, however, he at last shared my view that they were properly a matter of history, and sent them to me, accompanied by a letter, in which he says :

" I enclose you copies of all the letters of any interest from Mr. Lincoln to me. Some explanation may be needed that you may rightly understand their import. In the winter of 1840 and 1841, he was unhappy about his engagement to his wife—not being entirely satisfied that his heart was going with his hand. How much he suffered then on that account none knew so well as myself ; he disclosed his whole heart to me.*

" In the summer of 1841 I became engaged to my wife. He was here on a visit when I courted her ; and, strange to say, something of the same feeling which I regarded as so foolish in him took possession of me and kept me very unhappy from the time of my engagement until I was married. This will explain the deep interest he manifested in his letters on my account.

" One thing is plainly discernible ; if I had not been married and happy—far more happy than I ever expected to be—he would not have married."

The first of these letters is one which he gave

---

* Lincoln wrote a letter—a long one which he read to me—to Dr. Drake of Cincinnati, descriptive of his case. Its date would be in December, 1840, or early in January, 1841. I think that he must have informed Dr. Drake of his early love for Miss Rutledge, as there was a part of the letter which he would not read. . . I remember Dr. Drake's reply, which was, that he would not undertake to prescribe for him without a personal interview."—Joshua F. Speed, MS. letter, November 30, 1866.

Speed when the latter started on his journey from Illinois to Kentucky. It bears no date, but was handed him January 1, 1842, as Speed has testified, in another letter to me, that he left Springfield on that day. It is full of consolation and advice how best to conduct himself when the periods of gloom which he feels sure will follow come upon his friend. " I know," he says, " what the painful point with you is at all times when you are unhappy ; it is an apprehension that you do not love her as you should. What nonsense ! How came you to court her ? . . . Did you court her for her wealth ? Why, you say she had none. But you say you reasoned yourself into it. What do you mean by that ? Was it not that you found yourself unable to reason yourself out of it ? Did you not think, and partly form the purpose, of courting her the first time you ever saw her or heard of her ? What had reason to do with it at that early stage ? There was nothing at that time for reason to work upon. Whether she was moral, amiable, sensible, or even of good character, you did not nor could then know, except perhaps you might infer the last from the company you found her in. . . . Say candidly, were not those heavenly black eyes the whole basis of all your reasoning on the subject ? After you and I had once been at the residence, did you not go and take me all the way to Lexington and back for no other purpose but to get to see her again on our return on that evening to take a trip for that express object ? "

The next paragraph is significant as affording us

an idea of how the writer perhaps viewed Miss Todd's flirtation with Douglas : "What earthly consideration," he asks, " would you take to find her scouting and despising you and giving herself up to another ? But of this you need have no apprehension, and therefore you cannot bring it home to your feelings."

February 3, he writes again, acknowledging receipt of a letter dated January 25. The object of Speed's affection had been ill, and her condition had greatly intensified his gloomy spirits. Lincoln proffers his sympathy. "I hope and believe," he continues, "that your present anxiety about her health and her life must and will forever banish those horrid doubts which I know you sometimes felt as to the truth of your affection for her. If they can once and forever be removed (and I almost feel a presentiment that the Almighty has sent your present affliction expressly for that object), surely nothing can come in their stead to fill their immeasurable measure of misery . . .

"It really appears to me that you yourself ought to rejoice and not sorrow at this indubitable evidence of your undying affection for her. Why, Speed, if you did not love her, although you might not wish her death, you would most certainly be resigned to it. Perhaps this point is no longer a question with you, and my pertinacious dwelling upon it is a rude intrusion upon your feelings. If so you must pardon me. You know the hell I have suffered on that point, and how tender I am upon it. You know I do not mean wrong. I have been quite clear of hypo since you left, even better than I was along in the fall."

The next letter, February 13, was written on the eve of Speed's marriage. After assurances of his desire to befriend him in everything, he suggests : " But you will always hereafter be on ground that I have never occupied, and consequently, if advice were needed, I might advise wrong. I do fondly hope, however, that you will never again need any comfort from abroad . . . I incline to think it probable that your nerves will occasionally fail you for awhile ; but once you get them firmly graded now, that trouble is over forever. If you went through the ceremony calmly or even with suffi- cient composure not to excite alarm in any present, you are safe beyond question, and in two or three months, to say the most, will be the happiest of men."

Meanwhile Lincoln had been duly informed of Speed's marriage, and on the 25th he responds: " Yours of the 16th, announcing that Miss Fanny and you are 'no more twain, but one flesh,' reached me this morning. I have no way of telling how much happiness I wish you both, though I believe you both can conceive it. I feel somewhat jealous of both of you now. You will be so exclusively concerned for one another that I shall be forgotten entirely . . . I shall be very lonesome without you. How miserably things seem to be arranged in this world! If we have no friends we have no pleasure ; and if we have them we are sure to lose them, and be doubly pained by the loss."

In another letter, written the same day, he says, " I have no doubt it is the peculiar misfortune of both you and me to dream dreams of Elysium far exceeding all that anything earthly can realize. Far short of your dreams as you may be, no woman could do more to realize them than that same black-eyed Fanny. If you could but contemplate her through my imagination, it would appear ridiculous to you that any one should for a moment think of being unhappy with her. My old father used to have a saying, that, ' If you make a bad bargain hug it all the tighter,' and it occurs to me that if the bargain just closed can possibly be called a bad one it is certainly the most pleasant one for applying that maxim to which my fancy can by any effort picture."

Speed having now safely married, Lincoln's mind began to turn on things nearer home. His relations with Mary Todd were still strained, but reminders of his period of gloom the year before began now to bring her again into view. In a letter to Speed, March 27, he says :

" It cannot be told how it thrills me with joy to hear you say you are ' far happier than you ever expected to be.' That much, I know, is enough. I know you too well to suppose your expectations were not at least sometimes extravagant, and if the reality exceeds them all, I say, ' Enough, dear Lord.' I am not going beyond the truth when I tell you that the short space it took me to read your last letter gave me more pleasure than the total sum of all I have enjoyed since that fatal first of January, 1841. Since then it seems to me I should have been entirely happy but for the never-absent idea that there is one still unhappy whom I have contributed to make so. That kills my soul. I cannot but reproach myself for even wishing to be happy while she is otherwise. She accompanied a large party on the railroad cars to Jacksonville last Monday, and on her return spoke, so that I heard of it, of having enjoyed the trip exceedingly. God be praised for that!"

The last paragraph of this letter contains a bit of sentiment by Lincoln in acknowledgment of a violet. In the margin of the letter which he gave me, Speed made this note in pencil: "The violet was sent by my wife, who dropped it in the letter as I was in the act of sealing it. How beautiful the acknowledgment!" This is the paragraph: "The sweet violet you enclosed came safely to hand, but it was so dry, and mashed so flat, that it crumbled to dust at the first attempt to handle it. The juice that mashed out of it stained a place in the letter, which I mean to preserve and cherish for the sake of her who procured it to be sent. My renewed good wishes to her."

Meanwhile the coldness that existed between Lincoln and his "Mary" was gradually passing away, and with it went all of Lincoln's resolution never to renew the engagement. In a letter, July 4, he says: "I must gain confidence in my own ability to keep my resolves when they are made. In that ability I once prided myself as the only chief gem of my character; that gem I lost, how and where you know too well. I have not regained it; and until I do I cannot trust myself in any matter of much importance. I believe now that had you understood my case at the time as well as I understood yours afterwards, by the aid you would have given me I should have sailed through clear; but that does not now afford me sufficient confidence to begin that or the like of that again. . . . I always was superstitious; I believe God made me one of the instruments of bringing Fanny and you together, which union I have no doubt he had foreordained. Whatever he designs he will do for me yet. 'Stand still and see the salvation of the Lord,' is my text just now. If, as you say, you have told Fanny all, I should have no objection to her seeing this letter, but for its reference to our friend here; let her seeing it depend upon whether she has ever known anything of my affairs; and if she has not, do not let her. I do not think I can come to Kentucky this season. I am so poor and make so little headway in the world that I drop back in a month of idleness as much as I gain in a year's sowing."

The last letter, and the one which closes this series, was written October 5, 1842. In it he simply announces his "duel with Shields," and then goes on to "narrate the particulars of the duelling business, which still rages in this city." This referred to a challenge from the belligerent Shields to William Butler, and another from General Whitesides to Dr. Merryman. In the latter, Lincoln acted as the "friend of Merryman," but in neither case was there any encounter, and both ended in smoke. The concluding paragraph of this letter is the most singular in the entire correspondence. I give it entire without further comment :

"But I began this letter not for what I have been writing, but to say something on that subject which you know to be of such infinite solicitude to me. The immense sufferings you endured from the first days of September till the middle of February you never tried to conceal from me, and I well understood. You have now been the husband of a lovely woman nearly eight months. That you are happier now than the day you married her, I well know, for without, you could not be living. But I have your word for it, too, and the returning elasticity of spirits which is manifested in your letters. But I want to ask a close question : 'Are you in *feeling* as well as *judgment* glad you are married as you are?' From anybody but me this would be an impudent question, not to be tolerated, but I know you will pardon it in me. Please answer it quickly, as I am impatient to know."

Lincoln again applied himself to the law. He re-entered the practice, after the long hiatus of rest, with renewed vigor. He permitted the memory of his engagement with Mary Todd to trouble him no longer. Their paths had diverged, the pain of the separation was over, and the whole thing was a history of the past. And so it might ever have remained but for the intervention of a very shrewd and sagacious lady—one who was capable of achieving success anywhere in the ranks of diplomacy. This lady was the wife of Simeon Francis, the editor of the *Sangamon Journal.* She was a warm friend of Mary Todd and a leader in society. Her husband was warmly attached to Lincoln. He ran the Whig organ, and entertained great admiration for Lincoln's brains and noble qualities. The esteem was mutual, and it is no stretch of the truth to say that for years Lincoln exercised undisputed control of the columns of the *Journal* himself. Whatever he wrote or had written, went into the editorial page without question. Mrs. Francis, sharing her husband's views of Lincoln's glorious possibilities, and desiring to do Mary Todd a kindly act, determined to bring about a reconciliation. She knew that Miss Todd had by letter a few days after " that fatal first of January, 1841," as Lincoln styled it, released him from the engagement, and that since then their relations had been strained, if not entirely broken off. As she viewed it, a marriage between a man as promising in the political world as Lincoln, and a woman as accomplished and brilliant in society as Mary Todd, would certainly add to the attractions of Springfield and reflect great credit on those who brought the union about. She was a great social entertainer, and one day arranged a gathering at her house for the express purpose of bringing these two people together. Both were invited and both attended ; but neither suspected the other's presence. Having arranged things so ingeniously and with so much discretion, it was no difficult task for the hostess to bring the couple together by a warm introduction and the encouraging admonition, "Be friends again." Much to the surprise of both they found the web woven around them. They entered into the spirit of the reconciliation, and found Mrs. Francis' roof an inviting place for many succeeding meetings. A wall reared itself between them and the past, and they started again under the auspicious omens of another engagement. The tact of a woman and the diplomacy of society had accomplished what love had long since despaired of ever doing or seeing done.

The meetings in the parlor of Mrs. Francis' house were conducted with no little privacy. At first even Mrs. Edwards knew nothing of it, but presently it came to her ears. "I asked Mary," said this lady, "why she was so secretive about it. She said evasively that after all that had occurred, it was best to keep the courtship from all eyes and ears. Men and women and the whole world were uncertain and slippery, and if misfortune befell the engagement all knowledge of it would be hidden from the world." *

It is unnecessary to prolong the account of this strange and checkered courtship. The intervention of the affair with Shields, which will be detailed in a subsequent chapter, in no way impeded, if it did not hasten the marriage. One morning in November, Lincoln, hastening to the room of his friend James H. Matheney before the latter had arisen from bed, informed him that he was to be married

---

* Statement, January 10, 1866, MS.

16

that night, and requested him to attend as best man.* That same morning Miss Todd called on her friend Julia M. Jayne, who afterward married Lyman Trumbull, and made a similar request. The Edwardses were notified, and made such meager preparations as were possible on so short notice. License was obtained during the day, the minister, Charles N. Dresser,† was sent for, and in the evening of November 4, 1842, "as pale and trembling as if

---

* "Marriages in Springfield up to that time had been rather commonplace affairs. Lincoln's was perhaps the first one ever performed with all the requirements of the Episcopal ceremony. A goodly number of friends had gathered, and while witnessing the ceremony one of the most amusing incidents imaginable occurred. No description on paper can do it justice. Among those present was Thomas C. Brown, one of the judges of the Supreme Court. He was in truth an "old-timer," and had the virtue of saying just what he thought, without regard to place or surroundings. He had been on the bench for many years and was not less rough than quaint and curious. There was, of course, a perfect hush in the room as the ceremony progressed. Brown was standing just behind Lincoln. Old Parson Dresser, in canonical robes, with much and impressive solemnity recited the Episcopal service. He handed Lincoln the ring, who, placing it on the bride's finger, repeated the Church formula, 'With this ring I thee endow with all my goods and chattels, lands and tenements.' Brown, who had never witnessed such a proceeding, was struck with its utter absurdity. 'God Almighty! Lincoln,' he ejaculated, loud enough to be heard by all, 'the statute fixes all that!' This unlooked-for interruption almost upset the old parson; he had a keen sense of the ridiculous, and for the moment it seemed as if he would break down; but presently recovering his gravity, he hastily pronounced them husband and wife."—Letter, James H. Matheney, MS., Aug. 21, 1888.

† "My father, Rev. Charles Dresser, was a graduate of Brown University, Providence, R. I., of the class of 1823."—Thomas W. Dresser, MS. letter, Sept. 17, 1888.

The Edwards Residence, Springfield,

In which Lincoln and Mary Todd were married, and in which the latter died

being driven to slaughter," Abraham Lincoln was at last married to Mary Todd.*

One great trial of his life was now over, and another still greater one was yet to come. To me it has always seemed plain that Mr. Lincoln married Mary Todd to save his honor, and in doing that he sacrificed his domestic peace. He had searched himself subjectively, introspectively, thoroughly : he knew he did not love her, but he had promised to marry her ! The hideous thought came up like a nightmare. As the " fatal first of January, 1841," neared, the clouds around him blackened the heavens and his life almost went out with the storm. But soon the skies cleared. Friends interposed their aid to avert a calamity, and at last he stood face to face with the great conflict between honor and domestic peace. He chose the former, and with it years of self-torture, sacrificial pangs, and the loss forever of a happy home.

With Miss Todd a different motive, but one equally as unfortunate, prompted her adherence to the union. To marry Lincoln meant not a life of luxury and ease, for Lincoln was not a man to accumulate wealth ; but in him she saw position in society, prominence in the world, and the grandest social distinction. By that means her ambition would be satisfied. Until that fatal New Year's day in 1841 she may have loved him, but his action on

---

* While dressing for the wedding in his room at Butler's house, the latter's little boy, Speed, seeing Lincoln so handsomely attired, in boyish innocence asked him where he was going ? " To hell, I suppose," was Lincoln's reply.

that occasion forfeited her affection. He had crushed her proud, womanly spirit. She felt degraded in the eyes of the world. Love fled at the approach of revenge. Some writer—it is Junius, I believe—has said that, "Injuries may be forgiven and forgotten, but insults admit of no compensation: they degrade the mind in its own self-esteem and force it to recover its level by revenge." Whether Mrs. Lincoln really was moved by the spirit of revenge or not she acted along the lines of human conduct. She led her husband a wild and merry dance. If, in time, she became soured at the world it was not without provocation, and if in later years she unchained the bitterness of a disappointed and outraged nature, it followed as logically as an effect does the cause.

I have told this sad story as I know and have learned it. In rehearsing the varied scenes of the drama,* I have unearthed a few facts that seem half-

---

* For many years I had reason to believe that Sarah Rickard, who was a sister of Mrs. William Butler, had been the recipient of some attentions at the hand of Mr. Lincoln. The lady, long since married, is now living in a Western State. I applied to her for information recently, and after some entreaty received this answer in her own handwriting: "As an old friend I will answer the question propounded to me, though I can scarcely see what good it can do history. Mr. Lincoln did make a proposal of marriage to me in the summer, or perhaps later, in the year of 1840. He brought to my attention the accounts in the Bible of the patriarch Abraham's marriage to Sarah, and used that historical union as an argument in his own behalf. My reason for declining his proposal was the wide difference in our ages. I was then only sixteen, and had given the subject of matrimony but very little, if any, thought. I entertained the highest regard for Mr. Lincoln. He seemed almost like an older brother, being, as it were, one of my sister's family."

buried, perhaps, but they were not destined to lay buried deep or long. The world will have the truth as long as the name of Lincoln is remembered by mankind.

There were two things Mr. Lincoln always seemed willing to forget. One was his unparliamentary escape with Joseph Gillespie from the Legislature by jumping through the church window, in 1839, and the other was the difficulty with James Shields, or, as he expressed it in a letter to Speed, the "duel with Shields." Other incidents in his career he frequently called up in conversation with friends, but in after years he seldom if ever referred to the affair with Shields. People in Illinois did gradually forget or, at least, cease mention of it, but in more remote quarters where Mr. Lincoln was less extensively known, the thing, much to his regret, kept rising to the surface. During a visit which I made to the Eastern States in 1858, I was often asked for an account of the so-called duel; so often, in fact, that on my return home I told Mr. Lincoln of it. "If all the good things I have ever done," he said regretfully, "are remembered as long and well as my scrape with Shields, it is plain I shall not soon be forgotten."

James Shields, a "gallant, hot-headed bachelor from Tyrone county, Ireland," and a man of inordinate vanity, had been elected Auditor of State. Encouraged somewhat by the prominence the office gave him, he at once assumed a conspicuous position in the society of Springfield. He was extremely sensitive by nature, but exposed himself to merciless ridicule by attempting to establish his supremacy as a beau among the ladies. Blind to his own defects, and very pronounced in support of every act of the Democratic party, he made himself the target for all the bitterness and ridicule of the day. It happened that the financial resources of the State, owing to the collapse of the great internal improvement system, were exceedingly limited, and people were growing restless under what they deemed excessive taxation. The State officers were all Democrats, and during the summer they issued an order declining to receive any more State Bank-notes or bills in payment of taxes. This made the tax-payer's burdens greater than ever, as much of this paper remained outstanding in the hands of the people. The order met with opposition from every quarter—the Whigs of course losing no opportunity to make it as odious as possible. It was perfectly natural, therefore, that such an ardent Whig as Lincoln should join in the popular denunciation. Through the columns of the *Springfield Journal*, of which he had the undisputed use, he determined to encourage the opposition by the use of his pen. No object seemed to merit more ridicule and caricature than the conspicuous figure of the Auditor of State. At this time Lincoln was enjoying stolen conferences under the hospitable roof of Mrs. Francis with Mary Todd and her friend Julia M. Jayne. These two young ladies, to whom he confided his purpose, encouraged it and offered to lend their aid. Here he caught the idea of puncturing

Shields. The thing took shape in an article pub-lished in the *Journal*, purporting to have come from a poor widow, who with her pockets full of State Bank paper was still unable to obtain the coveted receipt for her taxes. It was written by Lincoln and was headed:

A Letter from the Lost Townships.

LOST TOWNSHIPS, August 27, 1842.
DEAR MR. PRINTER,

I see you printed that long letter I sent you a spell ago. I'm quite encouraged by it, and can't keep from writing again. I think the printing of my letters will be a good thing all round—it will give me the benefit of being known by the world, and give the world the advantage of knowing what's going on in the Lost Townships, and give your paper respectability besides. So here comes another. Yesterday afternoon I hurried through cleaning up the dinner dishes and stepped over to neighbor S—— to see if his wife Peggy was as well as mout be expected, and hear what they called the baby. Well, when I got there and just turned round the corner of his log cabin, there he was, set-ting on the doorstep reading a newspaper. "How are you, Jeff?" says I. He sorter started when he heard me, for he hadn't seen me before. "Why," says he, "I'm mad as the devil, Aunt 'Becca!" "What about?" says I; "ain't its hair the right color? None of that nonsense, Jeff; there ain't an honester women in the Lost Townships than"—— "Than who?" says he; "what the mischief are you about?" I began to see I was running the wrong trail, and so says I, "Oh! nothing: I guess I was mistaken a little, that's all. But what is it you're mad about?"

"Why," says he, "I've been tugging ever since

harvest, getting out wheat and hauling it to the river to raise State Bank paper enough to pay my tax this year and a little school debt I owe ; and now, just as I've got it, here I open this infernal *Extra Register*, expecting to find it full of ' Glorious Democratic Victories' and ' High Comb'd Cocks,' when, lo and behold! I find a set of fellows, calling themselves officers of the State, have forbidden the tax collectors and school commissioners to receive State paper at all; and so here it is dead on my hands. I don't now believe all the plunder I've got will fetch ready cash enough to pay my taxes and that school debt."

I was a good deal thunderstruck myself ; for that was the first I had heard of the proclamation, and my old man was pretty much in the same fix with Jeff. We both stood a moment staring at one another without knowing what to say. At last says I, " Mr. S——, let me look at that paper." He handed it to me, when I read the proclamation over.

" There now," says he, " did you ever see such a piece of impudence and imposition as that?" I saw Jeff was in a good tune for saying some ill-natured things, and so I tho't I would just argue a little on the contrary side, and make him rant a spell if I could. " Why," says I, looking as dignified and thoughtful as I could, " it seems pretty tough, to be sure, to have to raise silver where there's none to be raised ; but then, you see, ' there will be danger of loss' if it ain't done."

" Loss! damnation!" says he. " I defy Daniel Webster, I defy King Solomon, I defy the world— I defy—I defy—yes, I defy even you, Aunt 'Becca, to show how the people can lose anything by paying their taxes in State paper."

" Well," says I, " you see what the officers of State say about it, and they are a desarnin' set of men,

But," says I, "I guess you're mistaken about what the proclamation says. It don't say the people will lose anything by the paper money being taken for taxes. It only says 'there will be danger of loss'; and though it is tolerable plain that the people can't lose by paying their taxes in something they can get easier than silver, instead of having to pay silver; and though it's just as plain that the State can't lose by taking State Bank paper, however low it may be, while she owes the bank more than the whole revenue, and can pay that paper over on her debt, dollar for dollar;—still there is danger of loss to the 'officers of State'; and you know, Jeff, we can't get along without officers of State."

"Damn officers of State!" says he; "that's what Whigs are always hurrahing for."

"Now, don't swear so, Jeff," says I; "you know I belong to the meetin', and swearin' hurts my feelings."

"Beg pardon, Aunt 'Becca," says he; "but I do say it's enough to make Dr. Goddard swear, to have tax to pay in silver, for nothing only that Ford may get his two thousand a year, and Shields his twenty-four hundred a year, and Carpenter his sixteen hundred a year, and all without 'danger of loss' by taking it in State paper. Yes, yes : it's plain enough now what these officers of State mean by 'danger of loss.' Wash, I s'pose, actually lost fifteen hundred dollars out of the three thousand that two of these 'officers of State' let him steal from the treasury, by being compelled to take it in State paper. Wonder if we don't have a proclamation before long, commanding us to make up this loss to Wash in silver."

And so he went on till his breath run out, and he had to stop. I couldn't think of anything to say just then, and so I begun to look over the paper again. "Ay! here's another proclamation, or something like it."

"Another?" says Jeff; "and whose egg is it, pray?"

I looked to the bottom of it, and read aloud, "Your obedient servant, James Shields, Auditor."

"Aha!" says Jeff, "one of them same three fellows again. Well, read it, and let's hear what of it."

I read on till I came to where it says, "The object of this measure is to suspend the collection of the revenue for the current year."

"Now stop, now stop!" says he; "that's a lie a'ready, and I don't want to hear of it."

"Oh! may be not," says I.

"I say it—is—a—lie. Suspend the collection, indeed! Will the collectors, that have taken their oaths to make the collection, dare to suspend it? Is there anything in law requiring them to perjure themselves at the bidding of James Shields?

"Will the greedy gullet of the penitentiary be satisfied with swallowing him instead of all of them, if they should venture to obey him? And would he not discover some 'danger of loss,' and be off about the time it came to taking their places?

"And suppose the people attempt to suspend, by refusing to pay; what then? The collectors would just jerk up their horses and cows, and the like, and sell them to the highest bidder for silver in hand, without valuation or redemption. Why, Shields didn't believe that story himself: it was never meant for the truth. If it was true, why was it not writ till five days after the proclamation? Why didn't Carlin and Carpenter sign it as well as Shields? Answer me that, Aunt 'Becca. I say it's a lie, and not a well told one at that. It grins out like a copper dollar. Shields is a fool as well as a liar. With him truth is out of the question; and as for getting a good, bright, passable lie out of him, you might as well try to strike fire from a cake of tallow. I stick to it, it's all an infernal Whig lie!"

"A Whig lie! Highty tighty!"

"Yes, a Whig lie; and it's just like everything the cursed British Whigs do. First they'll do some divilment, and then they'll tell a lie to hide it. And they don't care how plain a lie it is: they think they can cram any sort of a one down the throats of the ignorant Locofocos, as they call the Democrats."

"Why, Jeff, you're crazy: you don't mean to say Shields is a Whig!"

"Yes, I do."

"Why, look here! the proclamation is in your own Democratic paper, as you call it."

"I know it; and what of that? They only printed it to let us Democrats see the deviltry the Whigs are at."

"Well, but Shields is the auditor of this Loco— I mean this Democratic State."

"So he is, and Tyler appointed him to office."

"Tyler appointed him?"

"Yes (if you must chaw it over), Tyler appointed him; or, if it wasn't him, it was old Granny Harrison, and that's all one. I tell you, Aunt 'Becca, there's no mistake about his being a Whig. Why, his very looks shows it; everything about him shows it: if I was deaf and blind, I could tell him by the smell. I seed him when I was down in Springfield last winter. They had a sort of a gatherin' there one night among the grandees, they called a fair. All the gals about town was there, and all the handsome widows and married women, finickin' about trying to look like gals, tied as tight in the middle, and puffed out at both ends, like bundles of fodder that hadn't been stacked yet, but wanted stackin' pretty bad.   And then they had tables all around the house kivered over with [   ] caps and pincushions and ten thousand such little knic-knacks, tryin' to sell 'em to the fellows that were bowin' and scrapin' and kungeerin' about 'em.   They wouldn't let no Democrats in, for fear they'd disgust the ladies, or scare the little gals, or dirty the floor.   I looked in at the window, and there was this same fellow Shields floatin' about on the air, without heft or earthly substances, just like a lock of cat fur where cats had been fighting.

"He was paying his money to this one, and that one, and t'other one, and sufferin' great loss because it wasn't silver instead of State paper; and the sweet distress he seemed to be in,—his very features, in the ecstatic agony of his soul, spoke audibly and distinctly, 'Dear girls, it is distressing, but I cannot marry you all.   Too well I know how much you suffer ; but do, do remember, it is not my fault that I am so handsome and so interesting.'

"As this last was expressed by a most exquisite contortion of his face, he seized hold of one of their hands, and squeezed, and held on to it about a quarter of an hour.   'Oh, my good fellow !' says I to myself, 'if that was one of our Democratic gals in the Lost Townships, the way you'd get a brass pin let into you would be about up to the head.'   He a Democrat ! Fiddlesticks ! I tell you, Aunt 'Becca, he's a Whig, and no mistake : nobody but a Whig could make such a conceity dunce of himself."

"Well," says I, "maybe he is ; but, if he is, I'm mistaken the worst sort.   Maybe so, maybe so; but, if I am, I'll suffer by it ; I'll be a Democrat if it turns out that Shields is a Whig, considerin' you shall be a Whig if he turns out a Democrat."

"A bargain, by jingoes !" says he ; "but how will we find out ?"

" Why," says I, " we'll just write and ax the printer."

"Agreed again!" says he; "and by thunder! if
it does turn out that Shields is a Democrat, I never
will " —

" Jefferson! Jefferson!"

" What do you want, Peggy?"

"Do get through your everlasting clatter some
time, and bring me a gourd of water; the child's
been crying for a drink this livelong hour."

"Let it die, then; it may as well die for water as
to be taxed to death to fatten officers of State."

Jeff run off to get the water, though, just like he
hadn't been saying anything spiteful for he's a
raal good-hearted fellow, after all, once you get at
the foundation of him.

I walked into the house, and," Why, Peggy," says
I, " I declare we like to forgot you altogether."

" Oh, yes," says she, " when a body can't help
themselves, everybody soon forgets 'em; but, thank
God! by day after to-morrow I shall be well
enough to milk the cows, and pen the calves, and
wring the contrary ones' tails for 'em, and no
thanks to nobody."

" Good evening, Peggy," says I, and so I sloped,
for I seed she was mad at me for making Jeff neglect her so long.

And now, Mr. Printer, will you be sure to let us
know in your next paper whether this Shields is a
Whig or a Democrat? I don't care about it for my
self, for I know well enough how it is already; but
I want to convince Jeff. It may do some good to let
him, and others like him, know who and what these
officers of State are. It may help to send the present hypocritical set to where they belong, and to fill
the places they now disgrace, with men who will do
more work for less pay, and take a fewer airs while
they are doing it. It ain't sensible to think that the

same men who get us into trouble will change their course; and yet it's pretty plain if some change for the better is not made, it's not long that either Peggy or I or any of us will have a cow left to milk, or a calf's tail to wring.

Yours truly,
REBECCA ———.

Within a week another epistle from Aunt Rebecca appeared, in which, among other things, she offered the gallant Shields her hand. This one was written by Miss Todd and Miss Jayne. I insert it without further comment:

LOST TOWNSHIPS, September 8, 1842.
DEAR MR. PRINTER:

I was a-standin' at the spring yesterday a-washin' out butter when I seed Jim Snooks a-ridin' up towards the house for very life, when, jist as I was a-wonderin' what on airth was the matter with him, he stops suddenly, and ses he, "Aunt 'Becca, here's somethin' for you;" and with that he hands out your letter. Well, you see, I steps out towards him, not thinkin' that I had both hands full of butter; and seein' I couldn't take the letter, you know, without greasin' it, I ses, "Jim, jist you open it, and read it for me." Well, Jim opens it and reads it; and would you believe it, Mr. Editor, I was so completely dumfounded and turned into stone that there I stood in the sun a-workin' the butter, and it a-running on the ground, while he read the letter, that I never thunk what I was about till the hull on't run melted on the ground and was lost. Now, sir, it's not for the butter, nor the price of the butter, but, the Lord have massy on us, I wouldn't have sich another fright for a whole firkin of it. Why, when I found out that it was the man what Jeff seed down to the fair that had demanded the author of my letters, threatnin' to take personal satisfaction of the writer, I was so skart that I tho't I should quill-wheel right where I was.

You say that Mr. S—— is offended at being compared to cats' fur, and is as mad as a March hare (that ain't fur), because I told about the squeezin'. Now I want you to tell Mr. S—— that, rather than fight, I'll make any apology; and, if he wants personal satisfaction, let him only come here, and he may squeeze my hand as hard as I squeezed the butter, and, if that ain't personal satisfaction, I can only say that he is the fust man that was not satisfied with squeezin' my hand. If this should not answer, there is one thing more that I would rather do than get a lickin'. I have long expected to die a widow; but, as Mr. S—— is rather good-looking than otherwise, I must say I don't care if we compromise the matter by—really, Mr. Printer, I can't help blushin'—but I—it must come out—I—but widowed modesty—well, if I must, I must—wouldn't he—may be sorter let the old grudge drap if I was to consent to be—be— h-i-s w-i-f-e? I know he's a fightin' man, and would rather fight than eat; but isn't marryin' better than fightin', though it does sometimes run in to it? And I don't think, upon the whole, that I'd be sich a bad match neither: I'm not over sixty, and am jist four feet three in my bare feet, and not much more around the girth; and for color, I wouldn't turn my back to nary a gal in the Lost Townships. But, after all, maybe I'm countin' my chickins before they are hatched, and dreamin' of matrimonial bliss when the only alternative reserved for me may be a lickin'. Jeff tells me the way these fire-eaters do is to give the challenged party choice of weapons, etc., which bein' the case, I'll tell you in confidence that I never fights with anything but broomsticks or hot water or a shovelful of coals or some such thing;

the former of which, being somewhat like a shilla-
lah, may not be very objectional to him. I will give
him choice, however, in one thing, and that is,
whether, when we fight, I shall wear breeches or
he petticoats, for, I presume that change is sufficient to place us on an equality.

Yours, etc.,

REBECCA ——.

P. S.—Jist say to your friend, if he concludes to
marry rather than fight, I shall only inforce one
condition, that is, if he should ever happen to
gallant any young gals home of nights from our
house, he must not squeeze their hands.

Not content with their epistolary efforts, the
ladies invoked the muse. "Rebecca" deftly trans-
formed herself into "Cathleen," and in jingling
rhyme sang the praises of Shields, and congratulated
him over the prospect of an early marriage to the
widow. Following are the verses, rhyme, metre,
and all:

Ye Jew's-harps awake! The Auditor's won.
Rebecca the widow has gained Erin's son;
The pride of the north from Emerald Isle
Has been wooed and won by a woman's smile.
The combat's relinquished, old loves all forgot:
To the widow he's bound. Oh, bright be his lot!
In the smiles of the conquest so lately achieved.
Joyful be his bride, "widowed modesty" relieved,
The footsteps of time tread lightly on flowers,
May the cares of this world ne'er darken his hours!
But the pleasures of life are fickle and coy
As the smiles of a maiden sent off to destroy.
Happy groom! in sadness far distant from thee
The fair girls dream only of past times of glee

Enjoyed in thy presence ; whilst the soft blarnied store
Will be fondly remembered as relics of yore,
And hands that in rapture you oft would have pressed,
In prayer will be clasped that your lot may be blest.
                                        CATHLEEN.

The satire running through these various compositions, and the publicity their appearance in the
Journal gave them, had a most wonderful effect on
the vain and irascible Auditor of State. He could no
longer endure the merriment and ridicule that met
him from every side. A man of cooler head might
have managed it differently, but in the case of a
high-tempered man like Shields he felt that his
integrity had been assailed and that nothing but
an "affair of honor" would satisfy him. Through
General John D. Whiteside he demanded of editor Francis the name of the author. The latter
hunted up Lincoln, who directed him to give his
name and say nothing about the ladies. The further proceedings in this grotesque drama were so
graphically detailed by the friends of both parties
in the columns of the *Journal* at that time, that I
copy their letters as a better and more faithful
narrative than can be obtained from any other
source. The letter of Shields' second, General
Whiteside, appearing first in the *Journal,* finds the
same place in this chapter :

                         "SPRINGFIELD, Oct. 3, 1842.
" *To the Editor of the Sangamon Journal :*
"SIR : To prevent misrepresentation of the
recent affair between Messrs. Shields and Lincoln,
I think it proper to give a brief narrative of the
17

facts of the case, as they came within my knowledge; for the truth of which I hold myself responsible, and request you to give the same publication. An offensive article in relation to Mr.
Shields appeared in the *Sangamon Journal* of the
2d of September last; and, on demanding the
author, Mr. Lincoln was given up by the editor.
Mr. Shields, previous to this demand, made
arrangements to go to Quincy on public business;
and before his return Mr. Lincoln had left for
Tremont to attend the court, with the intention,
as we learned, of remaining on the circuit several
weeks. Mr. Shields, on his return, requested me to
accompany him to Tremont; and, on arriving
there, we found that Dr. Merryman and Mr. Butler
had passed us in the night, and got there before us.
We arrived in Tremont on the 17th ult., and Mr.
Shields addressed a note to Mr. Lincoln immediately, informing him that he was given up as the
author of some articles that appeared in the *Sangamon Journal* (one more over the signature having
made its appearance at this time), and requesting
him to retract the offensive allusions contained in
said articles in relation to his private character.
Mr. Shields handed this note to me to deliver to
Mr. Lincoln, and directed me, at the same time,
not to enter into any verbal communication, or be
the bearer of any verbal explanation, as such were
always liable to misapprehension. This note was
delivered by me to Mr. Lincoln, stating, at the
same time, that I would call at his convenience for
an answer. Mr. Lincoln, in the evening of the
same day, handed me a letter addressed to Mr.
Shields. In this he gave or offered no explanation,
but stated therein that he could not submit to
answer further, on the ground that Mr. Shields's
note contained an assumption of facts and also a
menace. Mr. Shields then addressed him another

note, in which he disavowed all intention to men-ace, and requested to know whether he (Mr. Lin-coln) was the author of either of the articles which appeared in the *Journal*, headed 'Lost Townships,' and signed 'Rebecca'; and, if so, he repeated his request of a retraction of the offensive matter in relation to his private character; if not, his denial would be held sufficient. This letter was returned to Mr. Shields unanswered, with a verbal statement 'that there could be no further negotiation be-tween them until the first note was withdrawn.' Mr. Shields thereupon sent a note designating me as a friend, to which Mr. Lincoln replied by desig-nating Dr. Merryman. These three last notes passed on Monday morning, the 19th. Dr. Merry-man handed me Mr. Lincoln's last note when by ourselves. I remarked to Dr. Merryman that the matter was now submitted to us, and that I would propose that he and myself should pledge our words of honor to each other to try to agree upon terms of amicable arrangement, and compel our principals to accept of them. To this he readily assented, and we shook hands upon the pledge. It was then mutually agreed that we should adjourn to Springfield, and there procrastinate the matter, for the purpose of effecting the secret arrangement between him and myself. All this I kept concealed from Mr. Shields. Our horse had got a little lame in going to Tremont, and Dr. Merryman invited me to take a seat in his buggy. I accepted the invita-tion the more readily, as I thought that leaving Mr. Shields in Tremont until his horse would be in better condition to travel would facilitate the pri-vate agreement between Dr. Merryman and myself. I travelled to Springfield part of the way with him, and part with Mr. Lincoln; but nothing passed between us on the journey in relation to the matter in hand. We arrived in Springfield on Monday

night. About noon on Tuesday, to my astonishment, a proposition was made to meet in Missouri,
within three miles of Alton, on the next Thursday!
The weapons, cavalry broadswords of the largest
size ; the parties to stand on each side of a barrier,
and to be confined to a limited space. As I had
not been consulted at all on the subject, and considering the private understanding between Dr.
Merryman and myself, and it being known that Mr.
Shields was left at Tremont, such a proposition
took me by surprise. However, being determined
not to violate the laws of the State, I declined
agreeing upon the terms until we should meet in
Missouri. Immediately after, I called upon Dr.
Merryman and withdrew the pledge of honor between him and myself in relation to a secret arrangement. I started after this to meet Mr. Shields, and
met him about twenty miles from Springfield. It
was late on Tuesday night when we both reached the
city and learned that Dr. Merryman had left for
Missouri, Mr. Lincoln having left before the proposition was made, as Dr. Merryman had himself
informed me. The time and place made it necessary to start at once. We left Springfield at eleven
o'clock on Tuesday night, travelled all night, and
arrived in Hillsborough on Wednesday morning,
where we took in General Ewing. From there we
went to Alton, where we arrived on Thursday ; and,
as the proposition required three friends on each
side, I was joined by General Ewing and Dr. Hope,
as the friends of Mr. Shields. We then crossed to
Missouri, where a proposition was made by General
Hardin and Dr. English (who had arrived there in
the mean time as mutual friends) to refer the
matter to, I think, four friends for a settlement.
This I believed Mr. Shields would refuse, and declined seeing him ; but Dr. Hope, who conferred
with him upon the subject, returned and stated that

Mr. Shields declined settling the matter through any other than the friends he had selected to stand by him on that occasion. The friends of both the parties finally agreed to withdraw the papers (temporarily) to give the friends of Mr. Lincoln an opportunity to explain. Whereupon the friends of Mr. Lincoln, to wit, Messrs. Merryman, Bledsoe, and Butler, made a full and satisfactory explanation in relation to the article which appeared in the *Sangamon Journal* of the 2d, the only one written by him. This was all done without the knowledge or consent of Mr. Shields, and he refused to accede to it, until Dr. Hope, General Ewing, and myself declared the apology sufficient, and that we could not sustain him in going further. I think it necessary to state further, that no explanation or apology had been previously offered on the part of Mr. Lincoln to Mr. Shields, and that none was ever communicated by me to him, nor was any even offered to me, unless a paper read to me by Dr. Merryman after he had handed me the broadsword proposition on Tuesday. I heard so little of the reading of the paper, that I do not know fully what it purported to be; and I was the less inclined to inquire, as Mr. Lincoln was then gone to Missouri, and Mr. Shields not yet arrived from Tremont. In fact, I could not entertain any offer of the kind, unless upon my own responsibility; and that I was not disposed to do after what had already transpired.

"I make this statement, as I am about to be absent for some time, and I think it due to all concerned to give a true version of the matter before I leave.

"Your obedient servant,
"JOHN D. WHITESIDE."

SPRINGFIELD, October 8, 1842.

Editors of the Journal:

GENTS:—By your paper of Friday, I discover that General Whiteside has published his version of the late affair between Messrs. Shields and Lincoln, I now bespeak a hearing of my version of the same affair, which shall be true and full as to all material facts.

On Friday evening, the 16th of September, I learned that Mr. Shields and General Whiteside had started in pursuit of Mr. Lincoln, who was at Tremont, attending court. I knew that Mr. Lincoln was wholly unpractised both as to the diplomacy and weapons commonly employed in similar affairs; and I felt it my duty, as a friend, to be with him, and, so far as in my power, to prevent any advantage being taken of him as to either his honor or his life. Accordingly, Mr. Butler and myself started, passed Shields and Whiteside in the night, and arrived at Tremont ahead of them on Saturday morning. I told Mr. Lincoln what was brewing, and asked him what course he proposed to himself. He stated that he was wholly opposed to duelling, and would do anything to avoid it that might not degrade him in the estimation of himself and friends; but, if such degradation or a fight were the only alternatives, he would fight.

In the afternoon Shields and Whiteside arrived, and very soon the former sent to Mr. Lincoln, by the latter, the following note or letter:—

TREMONT, September 17, 1842.

A. LINCOLN, Esq.:—I regret that my absence on public business compelled me to postpone a matter of private consideration a little longer than I could have desired. It will only be necessary, however, to account for it by informing you that I have been to Quincy on business that would not admit of delay. I will now state briefly the reasons of my troubling you with this communication, the disagreeable nature of which I regret, as I had hoped to avoid any difficulty with any one in Springfield while residing there, by endeavoring to conduct myself in such a way amongst both my political friends and opponents, as to escape the necessity of any. Whilst thus abstaining from giving provocation, I have become the object of slander, vituperation, and personal abuse which, were I capable of submitting to, I would prove myself worthy of the whole of it.

In two or three of the last numbers of the *Sangamon Journal*, articles of the most personal nature, and calculated to degrade me, have made their appearance. On inquiring, I was informed by the editor of that paper, through the medium of my friend, General Whiteside, that you are the author of those articles. This information satisfies me that I have become, by some means or other, the object of secret hostility. I will not take the trouble of inquiring into the reason of all this, but I will take the liberty of requiring a full, positive, and absolute retraction of all offensive allusions used by you in these communications, in relation to my private character and standing as a man, as an apology for the insults conveyed in them.

This may prevent consequences which no one will regret more than myself.

Your ob't serv't,

JAS. SHIELDS.

About sunset, General Whiteside called again, and secured from Mr. Lincoln the following answer to Mr. Shields's note :—

TREMONT, September 17, 1842.

JAS. SHIELDS, Esq. :—Your note of to-day was handed me by General Whiteside. In that note you say you have been informed, through the medium of the editor of the *Journal*, that I am the author of certain articles in that paper which you deem personally abusive of you ; and, without stopping to inquire whether I really am the author, or to point out what is offensive in them, you demand an unqualified retraction of all that is offensive, and then proceed to hint at consequences.

Now, sir, there is in this so much assumption of facts, and so much of menace as to consequences, that I cannot submit to answer that note any further than I have, and to add, that the consequences to which I suppose you allude would be matter of as great regret to me as it possibly could to you.

Respectfully,

A. LINCOLN.

In about an hour, General Whiteside called again with another note from Mr. Shields ; but after conferring with Mr. Butler for a long time, say two or three hours, returned without presenting the note to Mr. Lincoln. This was in consequence of an assurance from Mr. Butler that Mr. Lincoln could not receive any communication from Mr. Shields, unless it were a withdrawal of his first note, or a challenge. Mr. Butler further stated to General Whiteside, that, on the withdrawal of the first note, and a proper and gentlemanly request for an explanation, he had no doubt one would be given. General Whiteside admitted that that was the course Mr. Shields ought to pursue, but deplored that his furious and intractable temper prevented his having any influence with him to that end. General Whiteside then requested us to wait with him until Monday morning, that he might endeavor to bring Mr. Shields to reason.

On Monday morning he called and presented Mr. Lincoln the same note as Mr. Butler says he had brought on Saturday evening. It was as follows :—

TREMONT, September 17, 1842.

A. LINCOLN, Esq. :—In your reply to my note of this date, you intimate that I assume facts and menace consequences, and that you cannot submit to answer it further. As now, sir, you desire it, I will be a little more

GEN. JAMES SHIELDS.

Photographed in 1871.

particular. The editor of the *Sangamon Journal* gave me to understand that you are the author of an article which appeared, I think, in that paper of the 2d September inst., headed "The Lost Townships" and signed Rebecca or 'Becca. I would therefore take the liberty of asking whether you are the author of said article, or any other of the same signature which has appeared in any of the late numbers of that paper. If so, I repeat my request of an absolute retraction of all offensive allusions contained therein in relation to my private character and standing.

If you are not the author of any of the articles, your denial will be sufficient. I will say further, it is not my intention to menace, but to do myself justice.

Your ob't serv't,

JAS. SHIELDS.

This Mr. Lincoln perused, and returned to General Whiteside, telling him verbally, that he did not think it consistent with his honor to negotiate for peace with Mr. Shields, unless Mr. Shields would withdraw his former offensive letter.

In a very short time General Whiteside called with a note from Mr. Shields, designating General Whiteside as his friend, to which Mr. Lincoln instantly replied designating me as his. On meeting General Whiteside, he proposed that we should pledge our honor to each other that we would endeavor to settle the matter amicably; to which I agreed, and stated to him the only conditions on which it could be settled ; viz., the withdrawal of Mr. Shields's first note, which he appeared to think reasonable, and regretted that the note had been written, saying however, that he had endeavored to prevail on Mr. Shields to write a milder one, but had not succeeded. He added, too, that I must promise not to mention it, as he would not dare to let Mr. Shields know that he was negotiating peace ; for, said he, " He would challenge me next, and as soon cut my throat as not." Not willing that he should suppose my principal less dangerous than his own, I promised not to mention our pacific intentions to Mr. Lincoln or any other person; and we started for Springfield forthwith.

We all, except Mr. Shields, arrived in Springfield late at night on Monday. We discovered that the affair had, somehow, got great publicity in Springfield, and that an arrest was probable. To prevent this, it was agreed by Mr. Lincoln and myself that he should leave early on Tuesday morning. Accordingly, he prepared the following instructions for my guide, on a suggestion from Mr. Butler that he had reason to believe that an attempt would be made by the opposite party to have the matter accommodated:

In case Whiteside shall signify a wish to adjust this affair without further difficulty, let him know that, if the present papers be withdrawn, and a note from Mr. Shields asking to know if I am the author of the articles of which he complains, and asking that I shall make him gentlemanly satisfaction if I am the author, and this without menace or dictation as to what that satisfaction shall be, a pledge is made that the following answer shall be given:

"I did write the 'Lost Township' letter which appeared in the *Journal* of the 2d inst., but had no participation in any form in any other article alluding to you. I wrote that wholly for political effect. I had no intention of injuring your personal or private character, or standing as a man or a gentleman; and I did not then think, and do not now think, that that article could produce, or has produced, that effect against you; and had I anticipated such an effect, I would have forborne to write it. And I will add, that your conduct towards me, so far as I knew, had always been gentlemanly, and that I had no personal pique against you, and no cause for any."

If this should be done, I leave it with you to manage what shall and what shall not be published.

If nothing like this is done, the preliminaries of the fight are to be :

1st. Weapons :—Cavalry broadswords of the largest size, precisely equal in all respects, and such as now used by the cavalry company at Jacksonville.

2d. Position :—A plank ten feet long, and from nine to twelve inches broad, to be firmly fixed on edge on the ground as the lines between us, which neither is to pass his foot over upon forfeit of his life. Next, a line drawn on the ground on either side of said plank and parallel with it, each at the distance of the whole length of the sword and three feet additional from the plank ; and the passing of his own such line by either party during the fight shall be deemed a surrender of the contest.

3d. Time :—On Thursday evening at five o'clock, if you can get it so ; but in no case to be at a greater distance of time than Friday evening at 5 o'clock.

4th. Place :—Within three miles of Alton, on the opposite side of the river, the particular spot to be agreed on by you.

Any preliminary details coming within the above rules, you are at liberty to make at your discretion ; but you are in no case to swerve from these rules, or to pass beyond their limits.

In the course of the forenoon I met General Whiteside, and he again intimated a wish to adjust the matter amicably. I then read to him Mr. Lincoln's instructions to an adjustment, and the terms of the hostile meeting, if there must be one, both at the same time.

He replied that it was useless to talk of an adjustment, if it could only be effected by the withdrawal of Mr. Shields's paper, for such withdrawal Mr. Shields would never consent to ; adding, that he would as soon think of asking Mr. Shields to "butt his brains out against a brick wall as to withdraw that paper." He proceeded : " I see but one course—that is a desperate remedy : 'tis to tell them, if they will not make the matter up, they must fight us." I replied, that, if he chose to fight Mr. Shields to compel him to do right, he might do so ; but as for Mr. Lincoln, he was on the defensive, and, I believe, in the right, and I should do nothing to compel him to do wrong. Such withdrawal having been made indispensable by Mr. Lincoln, I cut the matter short as to an adjustment, and I proposed to General Whiteside to accept the terms of the fight, which he refused to do until Mr. Shields' arrival in town, but agreed, verbally, that Mr. Lincoln's friends should procure the broadswords, and take them to the ground. In the afternoon he came to me, saying that some persons were swearing out affidavits to have us arrested, and that he intended to meet Mr. Shields immediately, and proceed to the place designated, lamenting, however, that I would not delay the time, that he might procure the interference of Governor Ford and General Ewing to mollify Mr. Shields. I told him that an accommodation, except upon the terms I mentioned, was out of question ; that to delay the meeting was to facilitate our arrest ; and, as I was determined not to be arrested, I should leave the town in fifteen minutes. I then pressed his acceptance of the preliminaries, which he disclaimed upon the ground that it would interfere with his oath of office as Fund Commissioner. I then, with two other friends, went to Jacksonville, where we joined Mr. Lincoln about 11 o'clock on Tuesday night. Wednesday morning we procured the broadswords, and proceeded to Alton, where we arrived about 11 o'clock A. M., on Thursday. The other party were in town before us. We crossed the river, and they soon followed. Shortly after, General Hardin and Dr. English presented to General Whiteside and myself the following note:

ALTON, September 22, 1842.

Messrs. WHITESIDE AND MERRYMAN : As the mutual personal friends of Messrs. Shields and Lincoln, but without authority from either, we earnestly desire to see a reconciliation of the misunderstanding which exists between them. Such difficulties should always be arranged amicably, if it is possible to do so with honor to both parties.

Believing, ourselves, that such an arrangement can possibly be effected, we respectfully but earnestly submit the following proposition for your consideration :

Let the whole difficulty be submitted to four or more gentlemen, to be selected by ourselves, who shall consider the affair, and report thereupon for your consideration.
JOHN J. HARDIN,
R. W. ENGLISH.

To this proposition General Whiteside agreed : I declined doing so without consulting Mr. Lincoln. Mr. Lincoln remarked that, as they had accepted the proposition, he would do so, but directed that his friends should make no terms except those first proposed. Whether the adjustment was finally made upon these very terms and no other, let the following documents attest :

MISSOURI, September 22, 1842.

GENTLEMEN :—All papers in relation to the matter in controversy between Mr. Shields and Mr. Lincoln having been withdrawn by the friends of the parties concerned, the friends of Mr. Shields ask the friends of Mr. Lincoln to explain all offensive matter in the articles which appeared in the *Sangamon Journal*, of the 2d, 9th, and 16th of September, under the signature of "Rebecca," and headed "Lost Townships."

It is due General Hardin and Mr. English to state that their interference was of the most courteous and gentlemanly character.

JOHN D. WHITESIDE.
WM. LEE D. EWING.
T. M. HOPE.

MISSOURI, September 22, 1842.

GENTLEMEN :—All papers in relation to the matter in controversy between Mr. Lincoln and Mr. Shields having been withdrawn by the friends of the parties concerned, we, the undersigned, friends of Mr. Lincoln, in accordance with your request that explanation of Mr. Lincoln's publication in relation to Mr. Shields in the *Sangamon Journal* of the 2d, 9th, and 16th of September be made, take pleasure in saying, that, although Mr. Lincoln was the writer of the article signed "Rebecca" in the *Journal* of the 2d, and that only, yet he had no intention of injuring the personal or private character or standing of Mr. Shields as a gentleman or a man, and that Mr. Lincoln did not think, nor does he now think, that said article could produce such an effect ; and, had Mr. Lincoln anticipated such an effect, he would have forborne to write it. We will state further, that said article was written solely for political effect, and not to gratify any personal pique against Mr. Shields, for he had none and knew of no cause for any. It is due to General Hardin and Mr. English to say that their interference was of the most courteous and gentlemanly character.

E. H. MERRYMAN.
A. T. BLEDSOE.
WM. BUTLER.

Let it be observed now, that Mr. Shields's friends, after agreeing to the arbitrament of four disinterested gentlemen, declined the contract, saying that Mr. Shields wished his own friends to act for him. They then proposed that we should explain without any withdrawal of papers. This was promptly and firmly refused, and General Whiteside himself pronounced the papers withdrawn. They then produced a note requesting us to " disavow " all offensive intentions in the publications, etc., etc. This we declined answering, and only responded to the above request for an explanation.

These are the material facts in relation to the matter, and I think present the case in a very different light from the garbled and curtailed statement of General Whiteside. Why he made that statement I know not, unless he wished to detract from the honor of Mr. Lincoln. This was ungenerous, more particularly as he on the ground requested us not to make in our explanation any quotations from the " Rebecca papers ; " also, not to make public the terms of reconciliation, and to unite with them in defending the honorable character of the adjustment.

General Whiteside, in his publication, says: " The friends of both parties agreed to withdraw the papers (temporarily) to give the friends of Mr. Lincoln an opportunity to explain." This I deny. I say the papers were withdrawn to enable Mr. Shields's friends to ask an explanation; and I appeal to the documents for proof of my position.

By looking over these documents, it will be seen that Mr. Shields had not before asked for an explanation, but had all the time been dictatorially insisting on a retraction.

General Whiteside, in his communication, brings to light much of Mr. Shields's manifestations of bravery behind the scenes. I can do nothing of the kind for Mr. Lincoln. He took his stand when I first met him at Tremont, and maintained it calmly to the last, without difficulty or difference between himself and his friends.

I cannot close this article, lengthy as it is, without testifying to the honorable and gentlemanly conduct of General Ewing and Dr. Hope, nor indeed can I say that I saw anything objectionable in the course of General Whiteside up to the time of his communication. This is so replete with prevarication and misrepresentation, that I cannot accord to the General that candor which I once supposed him to possess. He complains that I did not procrastinate time according to agreement. He forgets that by his own act he cut me off from that chance in inducing me, by promise, not to communicate our secret contract to Mr. Lincoln. Moreover, I could see no consistency in wishing for an extension of time at that stage of the affair, when in the outset they were in so precipitate a hurry that they could not wait three days for Mr. Lincoln to return from Tremont, but must hasten there, apparently with the intention of bringing the matter to a speedy issue. He complains, too, that, after inviting him to take a seat in the buggy I never broached the subject to him on our route here. But was I, the defendant in the case, with a challenge hanging over me, to make advances, and beg a reconciliation?

Absurd! Moreover, the valorous General forgets that he beguiled the tedium of the journey by recounting to me his exploits in many a well-fought battle,—dangers by " flood and field," in which I don't believe he ever participated,—doubtless with a view to produce a salutary effect on my nerves, and impress me with a proper notion of his fire-eating propensities.

One more main point of his argument and I have done. The General seems to be troubled with a convenient shortness of memory on some occasions. He does not remember that any explanations were offered at any time, unless it were a paper read when the "broadsword proposition" was tendered, when his mind was so confused by the anticipated clatter of broadswords, or something else, that he did "not know fully what it purported to be." The truth is, that, by unwisely refraining from mentioning it to his principal, he placed himself in a dilemma which he is now endeavoring to shuffle out of. By his inefficiency and want of knowledge of those laws which govern gentlemen in matters of this kind, he has done great injustice to his principal, a gentleman who, I believe, is ready at all times to vindicate his honor manfully, but who has been unfortunate in the selection of his friends, and this fault he is now trying to wipe out by doing an act of still greater injustice to Mr. Lincoln.

E. H. MERRYMAN.

---

* The following letter from Lincoln to his friend Speed furnishes the final outcome of the "duelling business."

SPRINGFIELD, October 5, 1842.

DEAR SPEED :—

You have heard of my duel with Shields, and I have now to inform you that the duelling business still rages in this city. Day before yesterday Shields challenged Butler, who accepted, proposed fighting next morning at sunrising in Bob Allen's meadow, one hundred yards distance, with rifles. To this Whiteside, Shields's second, said 'no' because of the law. Thus ended duel No. 2. Yesterday Whiteside chose to consider himself insulted by Dr. Merryman, so sent him a kind of quasi-challenge inviting him to meet him at the Planter's House in St. Louis, on the next Friday, to settle their difficulty. Merryman made me his friend, and sent Whiteside a note, inquiring to know if he meant his note as a challenge, and if so, that he would, according to the law in such case made and provided, prescribe the terms of the meeting. Whiteside returned for answer that if Merryman would meet him at the Planter's House as desired, he would challenge him. Merryman replied in a note, that he denied Whiteside's right to dictate time and place, but that he (Merryman) would waive the question of time, and meet him at Louisiana, Mo. Upon my presenting this note to Whiteside, and stating verbally its contents, he declined receiving it, saying he had business in St. Louis, and it was as near as Louisiana. Merryman then directed me to notify Whiteside that he should publish the correspondence between them, with such comments as he saw fit. This I did. Thus it stood at bed-time last night. This morning Whiteside, by his friend Shields, is praying for a new trial,

18

Dr. Merryman's elaborate and graphic account of the meeting at the duelling ground and all the preliminary proceedings is as full and complete a history of this serio-comic affair as any historian could give. Mr. Lincoln, as mentioned in the outset of this chapter, in the law office and elsewhere, as a rule, refrained from discussing it. I only remember of hearing him say this, in reference to the duel: "I did not intend to hurt Shields unless I did so clearly in self-defense. If it had been necessary I could have split him from the crown of his head to the end of his backbone;" and when one takes into into consideration the conditions of weapons and position required in his instructions to Dr. Merryman the boast does not seem impossible.

The marriage of Lincoln in no way diminished his love for politics; in fact, as we shall see later along, it served to stimulate his zeal in that direction. He embraced every opportunity that offered for a speech in public. Early in 1842 he entered into the Washingtonian movement organized to suppress the evils of intemperance. At the request of the society he delivered an admirable address, on Washington's birthday, in the Presbyterian Church, which, in keeping with former efforts, has been so often published that I need not quote it in full. I was then an ardent temperance reformer myself, and

---

on the ground that he was mistaken in Merryman's proposition to meet him at Louisiana, Mo., thinking it was the State of Louisiana. This Merryman hoots at, and is preparing his publication; while the town is in a ferment, and a street-fight somewhat anticipated. * *

Yours forever,

LINCOLN."

remember well how one paragraph of Lincoln's speech offended the church members who were present. Speaking of certain Christians who objected to the association of drunkards, even with the chance of reforming them, he said: " If they (the Christians) believe, as they profess, that Omnipotence condescended to take on himself the form of sinful man, and as such die an ignominious death, surely they will not refuse submission to the infinitely lesser condescension, for the temporal and perhaps eternal salvation of a large, erring, and unfortunate class of their fellow-creatures. Nor is the condescension very great. In my judgment such of us as have never fallen victims have been spared more from the absence of appetite than from any mental or moral superiority over those who have. Indeed, I believe, if we take habitual drunkards as a class, their heads and their hearts will bear an advantageous comparison with those of any other class." The avowal of these sentiments proved to be an unfortunate thing for Lincoln. The professing Christians regarded the suspicion suggested in the first sentence as a reflection on the sincerity of their belief, and the last one had no better effect in reconciling them to his views. I was at the door of the church as the people passed out, and heard them discussing the speech. Many of them were open in the expression of their displeasure. "It's a shame," I heard one man say, "that he should be permitted to abuse us so in the house of the Lord." The truth was the society was composed mainly of the roughs and drunkards of the town, who had evinced a desire to reform. Many of them were too fresh from the gutter to be taken at once into the society of such people as worshipped at the church where the speech was delivered. Neither was there that concert of effort so universal to-day between the churches and temperance societies to rescue the fallen. The whole thing, I repeat, was damaging to Lincoln, and gave rise to the opposition on the part of the churches which confronted him several years afterwards when he became a candidate against the noted Peter Cartwright for Congress. The charge, therefore, that in matters of religion he was a skeptic was not without its supporters, especially where his opponent was himself a preacher. But, nothing daunted, Lincoln kept on and labored zealously in the interest of the temperance movement. He spoke often again in Springfield, and also in other places over the country, displaying the same courage and adherence to principle that characterized his every undertaking.

Meanwhile, he had one eye open for politics as he moved along. He was growing more self-reliant in the practice of law every day, and felt amply able to take charge of and maintain himself in any case that happened to come into his hands. His propensity for the narration of an apt story was of immeasurable aid to him before a jury, and in cases where the law seemed to lean towards the other side won him many a case. In 1842, Martin Van Buren, who had just left the Presidential chair, made a journey through the West. He was accompanied by his former Secretary of the Navy, Mr. Paulding, and in June they reached the village of Rochester, distant from Springfield six miles. It was evening when they arrived, and on account of the muddy roads they decided to go no farther, but to rest there for the night. Word was sent into Springfield, and of course the leading Democrats of the capital hurried out to meet the distinguished visitor. Knowing the accommodations at Rochester were not intended for or suited to the entertainment of an ex-President, they took with them refreshments in quantity and variety, to make up for all deficiencies. Among others, they prevailed on Lincoln, although an ardent and pronounced Whig, to accompany them. They introduced him to the venerable statesman of Kinderhook as a representative lawyer, and a man whose wit was as ready as his store of anecdotes was exhaustless. How he succeeded in entertaining the visitor and the company, those who were present have often since testified. Van Buren himself entertained the crowd with reminiscences of politics in New York, going back to the days of Hamilton and Burr, and many of the crowd in turn interested him with graphic descriptions of early life on the western frontier. But they all yielded at last to the piquancy and force of Lincoln's queer stories. "Of these," relates one of the company,* "there was a constant supply, one following another in rapid succession, each more irresistible than its predecessor. The fun continued until after midnight, and until the distinguished traveller insisted that

---

* Jos. Gillespie, MS. letter, September 6, 1866.

his sides were sore from laughing." The yarns which Lincoln gravely spun out, Van Buren assured the crowd, he never would forget.

After April 14, 1841, when Lincoln retired from the partnership with Stuart, who had gone to Congress, he had been associated with Stephen T. Logan, a man who had, as he deserved, the reputation of being the best *nisi prius* lawyer in the State. Judge Logan was a very orderly but somewhat technical lawyer. He had some fondness for politics, and made one race for Congress, but he lacked the elements of a successful politician. He was defeated, and returned to the law. He was assiduous in study and tireless in search of legal principles. He was industrious and very thrifty, delighted to make and save money, and died a rich man. Lincoln had none of Logan's qualities. He was anything but studious, and had no money sense. He was five years younger, and yet his mind and make-up so impressed Logan that he was invited into the partnership with him. Logan's example had a good effect on Lincoln, and it stimulated him to unusual endeavors. For the first time he realized the effectiveness of order and method in work, but his old habits eventually overcame him. He permitted his partner to do all the studying in the preparation of cases, while he himself trusted to his general knowledge of the law and the inspiration of the surroundings to overcome the judge or the jury. Logan was scrupulously exact, and used extraordinary care in the preparation of papers. His words were well chosen, and his style of composition was stately and

U. S. COURT BUILDING, SPRINGFIELD, 1850–1860.

Lincoln and Logan's Office on Third Floor.

Photographed in 1886.

formal. This extended even to his letters. This Lincoln lacked in every particular. I have before me a letter written by Lincoln at this time to the proprietors of a wholesale store in Louisville, for whom suit had been brought, in which, after notifying the latter of the sale of certain real estate in satisfaction of their judgment, he adds: "As to the real estate we cannot attend to it. We are not real estate agents, we are lawyers. We recommend that you give the charge of it to Mr. Isaac S. Britton, a trustworthy man, and one whom the Lord made on purpose for such business." He gravely signs the firm name, Logan and Lincoln, to this unlawyerlike letter and sends it on its way. Logan never would have written such a letter. He had too much gravity and austere dignity to permit any such looseness of expression in letters to his clients or to anyone else.

In 1843, Logan and Lincoln both had their eyes set on the race for Congress. Logan's claim to the honor lay in his age and the services he had rendered the Whig party, while Lincoln, overflowing with ambition, lay great stress on his legislative achievements, and demanded it because he had been defeated in the nominating conventions by both Hardin and Baker in the order named. That two such aspiring politicians, each striving to obtain the same prize, should not dwell harmoniously together in the same office is not strange. Indeed, we may reasonably credit the story that they considered themselves rivals, and that numerous acrimonious passages took place between them. I was not surprised, therefore, one morning, to see Mr. Lincoln come rushing up into my quarters and with more or less agitation tell me he had determined to sever the partnership with Logan. I confess I was surprised when he invited me to become his partner. I was young in the practice and was painfully aware of my want of ability and experience ; but when he remarked in his earnest, honest way, " Billy, I can trust you, if you can trust me," I felt relieved, and accepted the generous proposal. It has always been a matter of pride with me that during our long partnership, continuing on until it was dissolved by the bullet of the assassin Booth, we never had any personal controversy or disagreement. I never stood in his way for political honors or office, and I believe we understood each other perfectly. In after years, when he became more prominent, and our practice grew to respectable proportions, other ambitious practitioners undertook to supplant me in the partnership. One of the latter, more zealous than wise, charged that I was in a certain way weakening the influence of the firm. I am flattered to know that Lincoln turned on this last named individual with the retort, " I know my own business, I reckon. I know Billy Herndon better than anybody, and even if what you say of him is true I intend to stick by him."

Lincoln's effort to obtain the Congressional nomination in 1843 brought out several unique and amusing incidents. He and Edward D. Baker were the two aspirants from Sangamon county, but Baker's long residence, extensive acquaintance, and general popularity were obstacles Lincoln could not overcome ; accordingly, at the last moment, Lincoln reluctantly withdrew from the field. In a letter to his friend Speed, dated March 24, 1843, he describes the situation as follows : " We had a meeting of the Whigs of the county here on last Monday, to appoint delegates to a district convention ; and Baker beat me, and got the delegation instructed to go for him. The meeting, in spite of my attempt to decline it, appointed me one of the delegates ; so that in getting Baker the nomination I shall be fixed a good deal like a fellow who is made groomsman to a man that has cut him out, and is marrying his own dear gal." Only a few days before this he had written a friend anent the Congressional matter, " Now if you should hear any one say that Lincoln don't want to go to Congress, I wish you, as a personal friend of mine, would tell him you have reason to believe he is mistaken. The truth is I would like to go very much. Still, circumstances may happen which may prevent my being a candidate. If there are any who be my friends in such an enterprise, what I now want is that they shall not throw me away just yet." * To another friend in the adjoining county of Menard a few days after the meeting of the Whigs in Sangamon, he explains how Baker defeated him.

The entire absence of any feeling of bitterness, or what the politicians call revenge, is the most striking feature of the letter. " It is truly gratify-

* Letter to R. S. Thomas, Virginia, Ill., Feb. 14, '43, MS.

ing," he says, "to me to learn that while the people of Sangamon have cast me off, my old friends of Menard, who have known me longest and best, stick to me. It would astonish if not amuse the older citizens to learn that I (a strange, friendless, uneducated, penniless boy, working on a flat-boat at ten dollars per month) have been put down here as the candidate of pride, wealth, and aristocratic family distinction. Yet so, chiefly, it was. There was, too, the strangest combination of church influence against me. Baker is a Campbellite, and therefore as I suppose, with few exceptions, got all that church. My wife has some relations in the Presbyterian churches and some with the Episcopalian churches, and therefore, wherever it would tell, I was set down as either the one or the other, while it was everywhere contended that no Christian ought to go for me, because I belonged to no church, was suspected of being a deist, and had talked about fighting a duel. With all these things Baker, of course, had nothing to do; nor do I complain of them. As to his own church going for him I think that was right enough ; and as to the influences I have spoken of in the other, though they were very strong, it would be grossly untrue and unjust to charge that they acted upon them in a body, or were very near so. I only mean that those influences levied a tax of considerable per cent. and throughout the religious controversy." To a proposition offering to instruct the Menard delegation for him he replies: "You say you shall instruct your delegates for me unless

I object. I certainly shall not object. That would be too pleasant a compliment for me to tread in the dust. And besides, if anything should happen (which, however, is not probable) by which Baker should be thrown out of the fight, I would be at liberty to accept the nomination if I could get it. I do, however, feel myself bound not to hinder him in any way from getting the nomination. I should despise myself were I to attempt it."

Baker's friends had used as an argument against Lincoln that he belonged to a proud and aristo-cratic family, referring doubtless to some of the distinguished relatives who were connected with him by marriage. The story reaching Lincoln's ears, he laughed heartily over it one day in a Springfield store and remarked :

" That sounds strange to me, for I do not remem-ber of but one who ever came to see me, and while he was in town he was accused of stealing a jew's-harp." * In the convention which was held shortly after at the town of Pekin neither Baker nor Lincoln obtained the coveted honor ; but John J. Hardin, of Morgan, destined to lose his life at the head of an Illinois regiment in the Mexican war, was nomi-nated, and in the following August, elected by a good majority. Lincoln bore his defeat manfully. He was no doubt greatly disappointed, but by no means soured. He conceived the strange notion that the publicity given his so-called " aristocratic family distinction " would cost him the friendship of his humbler constituents—his Clary's Grove

---

* Letter, A. Y. Ellis, July 16, '66, MS.

friends.　He took his friend James Matheney out into the woods with him one day and, calling up the bitter features of the canvass, protested " vehemently and with great emphasis " that he was anything but aristocratic and proud.　"Why, Jim," he said, " I am now and always shall be the same Abe Lincoln I was when you first saw me."

In the campaign of 1844 Lincoln filled the honorable post of Presidential Elector, and he extended the limits of his acquaintance by stumping the State.　This was the year the gallant and magnetic Clay went down in defeat.　Lincoln, in the latter end of the canvass, crossed over into Indiana and made several speeches.　He spoke at Rockport and also at Gentryville, where he met the Grigsbys, the Gentrys, and other friends of his boyhood.　The result of the election was a severe disappointment to Mr. Lincoln as well as to all other Whigs.　No election since the foundation of the Government created more widespread regret than the defeat of Clay by Polk.　Men were never before so enlisted in any man's cause, and when the great Whig chieftain went down his followers fled from the field in utter demoralization.　Some doubted the success of popular government, while others, more hopeful still in the face of the general disaster, vowed they would never shave their faces or cut their hair till Henry Clay became President.　As late as 1880 I saw one man who had lived up to his insane resolution. One political society organized to aid Clay's election sent the defeated candidate an address, in which they assured him that, after the smoke of battle

LINCOLN AND HERNDON'S LAW-OFFICE IN 1860.

had cleared away, he would ever be remembered as one "whose name honored defeat and gave it a glory which victory could not have brought." In Lincoln's case his disappointment was no greater than that of any other Whig. Many persons have yielded to the impression that Mr. Lincoln visited Clay at his home in Lexington and felt a personal loss in his defeat, but such is not the case. He took no more gloomy view of the situation than the rest of his party. He had been a leading figure himself in other campaigns, and was fully inured to the chilling blasts of defeat. They may have driven him in, but only for a short time, for he soon evinced a willingness to test the temper of the winds again.

No sooner had Baker been elected to Congress in August, 1844, than Lincoln began to manifest a longing for the tempting prize to be contended for in 1846. Hardin and Baker both having been required to content themselves with a single term each, the struggle among Whig aspirants narrowed down to Logan and Lincoln.* The latter's claim

---

* The Whig candidates for Congress in the Springfield district "rotated " in the following order : Baker succeeded Hardin in 1844, Lincoln was elected in 1846, and Logan was nominated but defeated in 1848. Lincoln publicly declined to contest the nomination with Baker in 1844; Hardin did the same for Lincoln in 1846—although both seem to have acted reluctantly; and Lincoln refused to run against Logan in 1848. Many persons insist that an agreement among these four conspicuous Whig leaders to content themselves with one term each actually existed. There is, however, no proof of any bargain, although there seems to have been a tacit understanding of the kind—maintained probably to keep other and less tractable candidates out of the field.

seemed to find such favorable lodgment with the party workers, and his popularity seemed so apparent, that Logan soon realized his own want of strength and abandoned the field to his late law partner. The convention which nominated Lincoln met at Petersburg May 1, 1846. Hardin, who, in violation of what was then regarded as precedent, had been seeking the nomination, had courteously withdrawn. Logan, ambitious to secure the honor next time for himself, with apparent generosity presented Lincoln's name to the convention, and there being no other candidate he was chosen unanimously. The reader need not be told whom the Democrats placed in the field against him. It was Peter Cartwright, the famous Methodist divine and circuit rider. An energetic canvass of three months followed, during which Lincoln kept his forces well in hand. He was active and alert, speaking everywhere, and abandoning his share of business in the law office entirely. He had a formidable competitor in Cartwright, who not only had an extensive following by reason of his church influence, but rallied many more supporters around his standard by his pronounced Jacksonian attitude. He had come into Illinois with the early immigrants from Kentucky and Tennessee, and had at one time or another preached to almost every Methodist congregation between Springfield and Cairo. He had extensive family connections all over the district, was almost twenty-five years older than Lincoln, and in every respect a dangerous antagonist. Another thing which operated much to Lincoln's

disadvantage was the report circulated by Cartwright's friends with respect to Lincoln's religious
views. He was charged with the grave offence of
infidelity, and sentiments which he was reported to
have expressed with reference to the inspiration of
the Bible were given the campaign varnish and
passed from hand to hand. His slighting allusion
expressed in the address at the Presbyterian Church
before the Washington Temperance Society, February 2d, four years before, to the insincerity of the
Christian people was not forgotten. It, too, played
its part; but all these opposing circumstances were
of no avail. Cartwright was personally very popular, but it was plain the people of the Springfield
district wanted no preacher to represent them in
Congress. They believed in an absolute separation
of Church and State. The election, therefore, of
such a man as Cartwright would not, to their way of
thinking, tend to promote such a result. I was
enthusiastic and active in Lincoln's interest myself.
The very thought of my associate's becoming a member of Congress was a great stimulus to my self-
importance. Many other friends in and around
Springfield were equally as vigilant, and, in the
language of another, "long before the contest closed
we snuffed approaching victory in the air." Our
laborious efforts met with a suitable reward. Lincoln was elected by a majority of 1511 in the district, a larger vote than Clay's two years before,
which was only 914. In Sangamon county his
majority was 690, and exceeded that of any of his
predecessors on the Whig ticket, commencing with

Stuart in 1834 and continuing on down to the days of Yates in 1852.

Before Lincoln's departure for Washington to enter on his duties as a member of Congress, the Mexican war had begun. The volunteers had gone forward, and at the head of the regiments from Illinois some of the bravest men and the best legal talent in Springfield had marched. Hardin, Baker, Bissell, and even the dramatic Shields had enlisted. The issues of the war and the manner of its prosecution were in every man's mouth. Naturally, therefore, a Congressman-elect would be expected to publish his views and define his position early in the day. Although, in common with the Whig party, opposing the declaration of war, Lincoln, now that hostilities had commenced, urged a vigorous prosecution. He admonished us all to permit our Government to suffer no dishonor, and to stand by the flag till peace came and came honorably to us. He declared these sentiments in a speech at a public meeting in Springfield, May 29, 1847. In the following December he took his seat in Congress. He was the only Whig from Illinois. His colleagues in the Illinois delegation were John A. McClernand, O. B. Ficklin, William A. Richardson, Thomas J. Turner, Robert Smith, and John Wentworth. In the Senate Douglas had made his appearance for the first time. The Little Giant is always in sight! Robert C. Winthrop, of Massachusetts, was chosen Speaker. John Quincy Adams, Horace Mann, Caleb Smith, Alexander H. Stephens, Robert Toombs, Howell Cobb, and

Andrew Johnson were important members of the House. With many of these the newly elected member from Illinois was destined to sustain another and far different relation.

On the 5th of December, the day before the House organized, Lincoln wrote me a letter about our fee in a law-suit, and reported the result of the Whig caucus the night before. On the 13th, he wrote again : " Dear William :—Your letter, advising me of the receipt of our fee in the bank case, is just received, and I don't expect to hear another as good a piece of news from Springfield while I am away." He then directed me from the proceeds of this fee to pay a debt at the bank, and out of the balance left to settle sundry dry-goods and grocery bills. The modest tone of the last paragraph is its most striking feature. "As you are all so anxious for me to distinguish myself," he said, " I have concluded to do so before long." January 8 he writes : "As to speech-making, by way of getting the hang of the House, I made a little speech two or three days ago on a post-office question of no general interest. I find speaking here and elsewhere about the same thing. I was about as badly scared, and no worse, as I am when I speak in court. I expect to make one within a week or two in which I hope to succeed well enough to wish you to see it." Meanwhile, in recognition of the assurances I had sent him from friends who desired to approve his course by a re-election, he says : " It is very pleasant to me to learn from you that there are some who desire that I should be re-elected. I most heartily thank them for the kind partiality, and I can say, as Mr. Clay said of the annexation of Texas, that, 'personally, I would not object' to a re-election, although I thought at the time, and still think, it would be quite as well for me to return to the law at the end of a single term. I made the declaration that I would not be a candidate again, more from a wish to deal fairly with others, to keep peace among our friends, and to keep the district from going to the enemy, than for any cause personal to myself, so that if it should happen that nobody else wishes to be elected I could not refuse the people the right of sending me again. But to enter myself as a competitor of others, or to authorize any one so to enter me, is what my word and honor forbid."

His announcement of a willingness to accept a re-election if tendered him by the people was altogether unnecessary, for within a few days after this letter was written his constituents began to manifest symptoms of grave disapproval of his course on the Mexican war question. His position on this subject was evidenced by certain resolutions offered by him in the House three weeks before. These latter were called the "Spot Resolutions," and they and the speech which followed on the 12th of January in support of them not only sealed Lincoln's doom as a Congressman, but in my opinion, lost the district to the Whigs in 1848, when Judge Logan had succeeded at last in obtaining the nomination.

Although differing with the President as to the

justice or even propriety of a war with Mexico, Lincoln was not unwilling to vote, and with the majority of his party did vote, the supplies necessary to carry it on. He did this, however, with great reluctance, protesting all the while that "the war was unnecessarily and unconstitutionally begun by the President." The "Spot Resolutions," which served as a text for his speech on the 12th of January, and which caused such unwonted annoyance in the ranks of his constituents, were a series following a preamble loaded with quotations from the President's messages. These resolutions requested the President to inform the House: "*First.* Whether the *spot* on which the blood of our citizens was shed as in his messages declared was or was not within the territory of Spain, at least after the treaty of 1819, until the Mexican revolution. *Second.* Whether that spot is or is not within the territory which was wrested from Spain by the revolutionary government of Mexico. *Third.* Whether that spot is or is not within a settlement of people, which settlement has existed ever since long before the Texas revolution, and until its inhabitants fled before the approach of the United States army." There were eight of these interrogatories, but it is only necessary to reproduce the three which foreshadow the position Lincoln was then intending to assume. On the 12th of January, as before stated, he followed them up with a carefully prepared and well-arranged speech, in which he made a severe arraignment of President Polk and justified the pertinence and propriety of the inquiries he had a few days before addressed to him. The speech is too long for insertion here. It was constructed much after the manner of a legal argument. Reviewing the evidence furnished by the President in his various messages, he undertook to "smoke him out" with this: "Let the President answer the interrogatories I proposed, as before mentioned, or other similar ones. Let him answer fully, fairly, candidly. Let him answer with facts, not with arguments. Let him remember, he sits where Washington sat; and so remembering, let him answer as Washington would answer. As a nation should not, and the Almighty will not, be evaded, so let him attempt no evasion, no equivocation. And if, so answering, he can show the soil was ours where the first blood of the war was shed; that it was not within an inhabited country, or if within such; that the inhabitants had submitted themselves to the civil authority of Texas or of the United States; and that the same is true of the site of Fort Brown, then I am with him for his justification. . . But if he cannot or will not do this—if, on any pretence, or no pretence, he shall refuse or omit it —then I shall be fully convinced of what I more than suspect already—that he is deeply conscious of being in the wrong; that he feels the blood of this war, like the blood of Abel, is crying to Heaven against him ; that he ordered General Taylor into the midst of a peaceful Mexican settlement purposely to bring on a war; that, originally having some strong motive—which I will not now stop to give my opinion concerning—to involve the countries in a war, and trusting to escape scrutiny by fixing the public gaze upon the exceeding brightness of military glory,—that attractive rainbow that rises in showers of blood, that serpent's eye that charms to destroy,—he plunged into it, and has swept on and on, till disappointed in his calculation of the ease with which Mexico might be subdued, he now finds himself he knows not where. He is a bewildered, confounded, and miserably perplexed man. God grant that he may be able to show that there is not something about his conscience more painful than all his mental perplexity." This speech, however clear may have been its reasoning, however rich in illustration, in restrained and burning earnestness, yet was unsuccessful in "smoking out" the President. He remained within the official seclusion his position gave him, and declined to answer. In fact it is doubtless true that Lincoln anticipated no response, but simply took that means of defining clearly his own position.

On the 19th inst., having occasion to write me with reference to a note with which one of our clients, one Louis Candler, had been "annoying" him, "not the least of which annoyance," he complains, "is his cursed unreadable and ungodly handwriting," he adds a line, in which with noticeable modesty he informs me : " I have made a speech, a copy of which I send you by mail." He doubtless felt he was taking rather advanced and perhaps questionable ground. And so he was, for very soon after, murmurs of dissatisfaction began to run through the Whig ranks. I did not, as some of Lincoln's biographers would have their readers believe, inaugurate this feeling of dissatisfaction. On the contrary, as the law partner of the Congressman, and as his ardent admirer, I discouraged the defection all I could. Still, when I listened to the comments of his friends everywhere after the delivery of his speech, I felt that he had made a mistake. I therefore wrote him to that effect, at the same time giving him my own views, which I knew were in full accord with the views of his Whig constituents. My argument in substance was : That the President of the United States is Commander-in-Chief of the Army and Navy ; that as such commander it was his duty, in the absence of Congress, if the country was about to be invaded and armies were organized in Mexico for that purpose, to go —if necessary—into the very heart of Mexico and prevent the invasion. I argued further that it would be a crime in the Executive to let the country be invaded in the least degree. The action of the President was a necessity, and under a similar necessity years afterward Mr. Lincoln himself emancipated the slaves, although he had no special power under the Constitution to do so. In later days, in what is called the Hodges letter, concerning the freedom of the slaves, he used this language :

" I felt that measures otherwise unconstitutional might become lawful by becoming indispensable."

Briefly stated, that was the strain of my argument. My judgment was formed on the law of nations and of war. If the facts were as I believed them, and my premises correct, then I assumed that the President's acts became lawful by becoming indispensable.

February 1 he wrote me, "Dear William : You fear that you and I disagree about the war. I regret this, not because of any fear we shall remain disagreed after you have read this letter, but because if you misunderstand I fear other good friends may also."

Speaking of his vote in favor of the amendment to the supply bill proposed by George Ashmun, of Massachusetts, he continues :

"That vote affirms that the war was unnecessarily and unconstitutionally commenced by the President ; and I will stake my life that if you had been in my place you would have voted just as I did. Would you have voted what you felt and knew to be a lie?   I know you would not.   Would you have gone out of the House,—skulked the vote ?   I expect not.   If you had skulked one vote you would have had to skulk many more before the close of the session.   Richardson's resolutions, introduced before I made any move or gave any vote upon the subject, make the direct question of the justice of the war ; so that no man can be silent if he would.   You are compelled to speak ; and your only alternative is to tell the truth or tell a lie. I cannot doubt which you would do. . .   I do not mean this letter for the public, but for you.   Before it reaches you you will have seen and read my pamphlet speech and perhaps have been scared anew by it. After you get over your scare read it over again, sentence by sentence, and tell me honestly what you think of it.   I condensed all I could for fear of being cut off by the hour rule ; and when I got through I had spoken but forty-five minutes.

"Yours forever,
"A. LINCOLN."

I digress from the Mexican war subject long
enough to insert, because in the order of time it
belongs here, a characteristic letter which he wrote
me regarding a man who was destined at a later
day to play a far different rôle in the national
drama. Here it is:

"WASHINGTON, Feb. 2, 1848.

"DEAR WILLIAM:

"I just take up my pen to say that Mr. Stephens,
of Georgia, a little, slim, pale-faced, consumptive man,
with a voice like Logan's, has just concluded the
very best speech of an hour's length I ever heard.
My old, withered, dry eyes are full of tears yet. If
he writes it out anything like he delivered it our people shall see a good many copies of it.

"Yours truly,

"A. LINCOLN."

To WM. H. HERNDON, ESQ.

February 15 he wrote me again in criticism of
the President's invasion of foreign soil. He still believed the Executive had exceeded the limit of his
authority. "The provision of the Constitution
giving the war-making power to Congress," he
insists, "was dictated, as I understand it, by the
following reasons: kings had always been involving
and impoverishing their people in wars, pretending
generally, if not always, that the good of the people was the object. This, our convention understood to be the most oppressive of all kingly
oppressions; and they resolved to so frame the
Constitution that no one man should hold the
power of bringing this oppression upon us. But

your view destroys the whole matter, and places our President where kings have always stood."

In June the Whigs met in national convention at Philadelphia to nominate a candidate for President. Lincoln attended as a delegate. He advocated the nomination of Taylor because of his belief that he could be elected, and was correspondingly averse to Clay because of the latter's signal defeat in 1844. In a letter from Washington a few days after the convention he predicts the election of "Old Rough." He says: "In my opinion we shall have a most overwhelming glorious triumph. One unmistakable sign is that all the odds and ends are with us—Barn-burners, Native Americans, Tyler-men, disappointed office-seeking Locofocos, and the Lord knows what not. . . . Taylor's nomination takes the Locos on the blind side. It turns the war thunder against them. The war is now to them the gallows of Haman, which they built for us and on which they are doomed to be hanged themselves."

Meanwhile, in spite of the hopeful view Lincoln seemed to take of the prospect, things in his own district were in exceedingly bad repair. I could not refrain from apprising him of the extensive defections from the party ranks, and the injury his course was doing him. My object in thus writing to him was not to threaten him. Lincoln was not a man who could be successfully threatened; one had to approach him from a different direction. I warned him of public disappointment over his course, and I earnestly desired to prevent him from

committing what I believed to be political suicide.
June 22d he answered a letter I had written him on
the 15th. He had just returned from a Whig caucus
held in relation to the coming Presidential election.
" The whole field of the nation was scanned ; all is
high hope and confidence," he said, exultingly.
" Illinois is expected to better her condition in this
race. Under these circumstances judge how heart-
rending it was to come to my room and find and
read your discouraging letter of the 15th." But
still he does not despair. " Now, as to the young
men," he says, "you must not wait to be brought
forward by the older men. For instance, do you
suppose that I should ever have got into notice if I
had waited to be hunted up and pushed forward
by older men? You young men get together
and form a Rough and Ready club, and have
regular meetings and speeches. Take in everybody
that you can get. . . . As you go along gather up
all the shrewd, wild boys about town, whether just
of age or a little under age. Let every one play
the part he can play best—some speak, some sing,
and all halloo. Your meetings will be of evenings ;
the older men and the women will go to hear you,
so that it will not only contribute to the election of
' Old Zack,' but will be an interesting pastime and
improving to the faculties of all engaged." He was
evidently endeavoring through me to rouse up all
the enthusiasm among the youth of Springfield possible under the circumstances. But I was disposed
to take a dispirited view of the situation, and therefore was not easily warmed up. I felt at this time,

MARY TODD LINCOLN.

Rev. PETER CARTWRIGHT.

STEPHEN T. LOGAN.

somewhat in advance of its occurrence, the death throes of the Whig party. I did not conceal my suspicions, and one of the Springfield papers gave my sentiments liberal quotation in its columns. I felt gloomy over the prospect, and cut out these newspaper slips and sent them to Lincoln. Accompanying these I wrote him a letter equally melancholy in tone, in which among other things I reflected severely on the stubbornness and bad judgment of the old fossils in the party, who were constantly holding the young men back. This brought from him a letter, July 10, 1848, which is so clearly Lincolnian and so full of plain philosophy, that I copy it in full. Not the least singular of all is his allusion to himself as an old man, although he had scarcely passed his thirty-ninth year.

"WASHINGTON, July 10, 1848.

" DEAR WILLIAM :
"Your letter covering the newspaper slips was received last night. The subject of that letter is exceedingly painful to me, and I cannot but think there is some mistake in your impression of the motives of the old men. I suppose I am now one of the old men ; and I declare on my veracity, which I think is good with you, that nothing could afford me more satisfaction than to learn that you and others of my young friends at home were doing battle in the contest and endearing themselves to the people and taking a stand far above any I have ever been able to reach in their admiration. I cannot conceive that other men feel differently. Of course I cannot demonstrate what I say ; but I was young once, and I am sure I was never ungenerously thrust back. I hardly know

what to say. The way for a young man to rise is to improve himself every way he can, never suspecting that anybody wishes to hinder him. Allow me to assure you that suspicion and jealousy never did help any man in any situation. There may sometimes be ungenerous attempts to keep a young man down; and they will succeed, too, if he allows his mind to be diverted from its true channel to brood over the attempted injury. Cast about and see if this feeling has not injured every person you have ever known to fall into it.

" Now, in what I have said I am sure you will suspect nothing but sincere friendship. I would save you from a fatal error. You have been a laborious, studious young man. You are far better informed on almost all subjects than I ever have been. You cannot fail in any laudable object unless you allow your mind to be improperly directed. I have some the advantage of you in the world's experience merely by being older; and it is this that induces me to advise.

" Your friend, as ever,

" A. LINCOLN."

Before the close of the Congressional session he made two more speeches. One of these, which he hastened to send home in pamphlet form, and which he supposes " nobody will read," was devoted to the familiar subject of internal improvements, and deserves only passing mention. The other, delivered on the 27th of July, was in its way a masterpiece; and it is no stretch of the truth to say that while intended simply as a campaign document and devoid of any effort at classic oratory, it was, perhaps, one of the best speeches of the session. It is too extended for insertion here without abridgment;

but one who reads it will lay it down convinced that Lincoln's ascendency for a quarter of a century among the political spirits in Illinois was by no means an accident; neither will the reader wonder that Douglas, with all his forensic ability, averted, as long as he could, a contest with a man whose plain, analytical reasoning was not less potent than his mingled drollery and caricature were effective. The speech in the main is an arraignment of General Cass, the Democratic candidate for President, who had already achieved great renown in the political world, principally on account of his career as a soldier in the war of 1812, and is a triumphant vindication of his Whig opponent, General Taylor, who seemed to have had a less extensive knowledge of civil than of military affairs, and was discreetly silent about both. Lincoln caricatured the military pretensions of the Democratic candidate in picturesque style. This latter section of the speech has heretofore been omitted by most of Mr. Lincoln's biographers because of its glaring inappropriateness as a Congressional effort. I have always failed to see wherein its comparison with scores of others delivered in the halls of Congress since that time could in any way detract from the fame of Mr. Lincoln, and I therefore reproduce it here :

" But the gentleman from Georgia [Mr. Iverson] further says, we have deserted all our principles, and taken shelter under General Taylor's military coat-tail ; and he seems to think this is exceedingly degrading. Well, as his faith is, so be it unto him. But can he remember no other military coat-tail, under which a certain other party have been sheltering for near a quarter of a century? Has he no acquaintance with the ample military coat-tail of General Jackson? Does he not know that his own party have run the last five Presidential races under that coat-tail? and that they are now running the sixth under the same cover? Yes, sir, that coat-tail was used not only for General Jackson himself, but has been clung to with the grip of death by every Democratic candidate since. You have never ventured, and dare not now venture from under it. Your campaign papers have constantly been ' Old Hickory's,' with rude likenesses of the old general upon them; hickory poles and hickory brooms your never-ending emblems. Mr. Polk himself was ' Young Hickory,' ' Little Hickory,' or something so; and even now your campaign paper here is proclaiming that Cass and Butler are of the ' Hickory stripe.' No, sir, you dare not give it up. Like a horde of hungry ticks, you have stuck to the tail of the Hermitage lion to the end of his life; and you are still sticking to it, and drawing a loathsome sustenance from it, after he is dead. A fellow once advertised that he had made a discovery by which he could make a new man out of an old one and have enough of the stuff left to make a little yellow dog. Just such a discovery has General Jackson's popularity been to you. You not only twice made Presidents of him out of it, but you have enough of the stuff left to make Presidents of several comparatively small men since; and it is your chief reliance now to make still another.

" Mr. Speaker, old horses and military coat-tails, or tails of any sort, are not figures of speech such as I would be the first to introduce into discussion here; but as the gentleman from Georgia has thought fit to introduce them, he and you are welcome to all you have made or can make by them.

If you have any more old horses, trot them out; any more tails, just cock them and come at us. I repeat, I would not introduce this mode of discussion here; but I wish gentlemen on the other side to understand that the use of degrading figures is a game at which they may find themselves unable to take all the winnings. [A voice ' No, we give it up.'] Aye! you give it up, and well you may; but for a very different reason from that which you would have us understand. The point—the power to hurt—of all figures consists in the truthfulness of their application; and, understanding this, you may well give it up. They are weapons which hit you, but miss us.

" But in my hurry I was very near closing on this subject of military tails before I was done with it. There is one entire article of the sort I have not discussed yet; I mean the military tail you Democrats are now engaged in dovetailing on to the great Michigander. Yes, sir, all his biographers (and they are legion) have him in hand, tying him to a military tail, like so many mischievous boys tying a dog to a bladder of beans. True, the material is very limited, but they are at it might and main. He invaded Canada without resistance, and he outvaded it without pursuit. As he did both under orders, I suppose there was to him neither credit nor discredit; but they are made to constitute a large part of the tail. He was not at Hull's surrender, but he was close by; he was volunteer aid to General Harrison on the day of the battle of the Thames; and as you said in 1840 Harrison was picking whortleberries two miles off while the battle was fought, I suppose it is a just conclusion with you to say Cass was aiding Harrison to pick whortleberries. This is about all, except the mooted question of the broken sword. Some authors say he broke it; some say he threw it away;

and some others, who ought to know, say nothing about it. Perhaps it would be a fair historical compromise to say if he did not break it, he did not do anything else with it.

" By the way, Mr. Speaker, did you know I am a military hero? Yes, sir, in the days of the Black Hawk war, I fought, bled, and came away. Speaking of General Cass's career, reminds me of my own. I was not at Stillman's defeat, but I was about as near it as Cass was to Hull's surrender; and, like him, I saw the place very soon afterward. It is quite certain I did not break my sword, for I had none to break, but I bent my musket pretty badly on one occasion. If Cass broke his sword, the idea is, he broke it in desperation; I bent the musket by accident. If General Cass went in advance of me picking whortleberries, I guess I surpassed him in charges upon the wild onions. If he saw any live fighting Indians, it was more than I did, but I had a good many bloody struggles with the mosquitos; and, although I never fainted from loss of blood, I can truly say I was often very hungry. Mr. Speaker, if ever I should conclude to doff whatever our Democratic friends may suppose there is of black-cockade Federalism about me, and, thereupon they shall take me up as their candidate for the Presidency, I protest that they shall not make fun of me as they have of General Cass by attempting to write me into a military hero."

After the adjournment of Congress on the 14th of August, Lincoln went through New York and some of the New England States making a number of speeches for Taylor, none of which, owing to the limited facilities attending newspaper reporting in that day, have been preserved. He returned to Illinois before the close of the canvass and continued his efforts on the stump till the election. At the second session of Congress, which began in December, he was less conspicuous than before. The few weeks spent with his constituents had perhaps taught him that in order to succeed as a Congressman it is not always the most politic thing to tell the truth because it is the truth, or do right because it is right. With the opening of Congress, by virtue of the election of Taylor, the Whigs obtained the ascendency in the control of governmental machinery. He attended to the duties of the Congressional office diligently and with becoming modesty. He answered the letters of his constituents, sent them their public documents, and looked after their pension claims. His only public act of any moment was a bill looking to the emancipation of the slaves in the District of Columbia. He interested Joshua R. Giddings and others of equally as pronounced anti-slavery views in the subject, but his bill eventually found a lodgment on " the table," where it was carefully but promptly laid by a vote of the House.

Meanwhile, being chargeable with the distribution of official patronage, he began to flounder about in explanation of his action in a sea of seemingly endless perplexities. His recommendation of the appointment of T. R. King to be Register or Receiver of the Land Office had produced no little discord among the other aspirants for the place. He wrote to a friend who endorsed and urged the appointment, " either to admit it is wrong, or come forward and sustain him." He then transmits to this same friend a scrap of paper—probably a few lines approving the selection of King—which is to be copied in the friend's own handwriting. "Get everybody," he insists, "(not three or four, but three or four hundred) to sign it, and then send to me. Also have six, eight, or ten of our best known Whig friends to write me additional letters, stating the truth in this matter as they understood it. Don't neglect or delay in the matter. I understand," he continues, "information of an indictment having been found against him three years ago for gaming or keeping a gaming house has been sent to the Department." He then closes with the comforting assurance: "I shall try to take care of it at the Department till your action can be had and forwarded on." And still people insist that Mr. Lincoln was such a guileless man and so free from the politician's sagacity!

In June I wrote him regarding the case of one Walter Davis, who was soured and disappointed because Lincoln had overlooked him in his recommendation for the Springfield post-office. "There must be some mistake," he responds on the 5th, "about Walter Davis saying I promised him the post-office. I did not so promise him. I did tell him that if the distribution of the offices should fall into my hands he should have something; and if I shall be convinced he has said any more than this I shall be disappointed. I said this much to him because, as I understand, he is of good character, is one of the young men, is of the mechanics, is always faithful and never troublesome, a Whig, and is poor, with the support of a widow-mother thrown almost exclusively on him by the death of his brother. If these are wrong reasons then I have been wrong; but I have certainly not been selfish in it, because in my greatest need of friends he was against me and for Baker."

Judge Logan's defeat in 1848 left Lincoln still in a measure in charge of the patronage in his district. After his term in Congress expired the "wriggle and struggle" for office continued; and he was often appealed to for his influence in obtaining, as he termed it, "a way to live without work." Occasionally, when hard pressed, he retorted with bitter sarcasm. I append a letter written in this vein to a gentleman still living in central Illinois, who, I suppose, would prefer that his name should be withheld:

"SPRINGFIELD, Dec. 15, 1849.

"――― Esq.

  "DEAR SIR :

"On my return from Kentucky I found your letter of the 7th of November, and have delayed answering it till now for the reason I now briefly state. From the beginning of our acquaintance I had felt the greatest kindness for you and had supposed it was reciprocated on your part. Last summer, under circumstances which I mentioned to you, I was painfully constrained to withhold a recommendation which you desired, and shortly afterwards I learned, in such a way as to believe it, that you were indulging in open abuse of me. Of course my feelings were wounded. On receiving your last letter the question occurred whether you were attempting to use me at the same time you would injure me, or whether you might not have been misrepresented to me. If the former, I ought not to answer you ; if the latter, I ought, and so I have remained in suspense. I now enclose you the letter, which you may use if you see fit.

" Yours, etc.

" A. LINCOLN."

No doubt the man, when Lincoln declined at first to recommend him, did resort to more or less abuse. That would have been natural, especially with an unsuccessful and disappointed office-seeker. I am inclined to the opinion, and a careful reading of the letter will warrant it, that Lincoln believed him guilty. If the recommendation which Lincoln, after so much reluctance, gave was ever used to further the applicant's cause I do not know it.

With the close of Lincoln's congressional career he drops out of sight as a political factor, and for the next few years we take him up in another capacity. He did not solicit or contend for a renomination to Congress, and such was the unfortunate result of his position on public questions that it is doubtful if he could have suceeeded had he done so.

CHAPTER X.

IMMEDIATELY following the adjournment of Congress in August, 1848, Mr. Lincoln set out for Massachusetts to take part in the presidential campaign. Being the only Whig in the delegation in Congress from Illinois, he was expected to do gallant work for his chief, General Taylor. As this chapter in his career seems to have escaped the notice of former biographers, the writers have thought best to insert here extracts from the various descriptions which they have been able to obtain of the tour and its incidents.

One of the most interesting accounts is from the pen of Hon. Edward L. Pierce, of Milton, Mass., whose memory is not less tenacious than is his style happy and entertaining. He says:

"It is not known at whose instance Mr. Lincoln made his visits to Massachusetts in 1848. The Whigs of the State were hard pressed at the time by a formidable secession growing out of General Taylor's nomination, and led by Henry Wilson, Charles Francis Adams, Charles Allen, Charles Sumner, Stephen C. Phillips, John G. Palfrey, E. Rockwood Hoar, Richard H. Dana, Jr., Anson Burlingame, John A. Andrew, and other leaders who had great weight with the people and were all effective public speakers. Generally the State had had a sufficient supply of orators of its own, but in that emergency some outside aid was sought. Gen. Leslie Coombs was invited from Kentucky, and Mr. Lincoln was induced to come also, on his way home from Washington at the end of the session.

"The Whig State Convention met at Worcester, September 13th. The Free-Soil secession was greater here than in any part of the State. It was led by Judge Charles Allen, who was elected to Congress from the district. There was a meeting of the Whigs at the City Hall on the evening before the convention. Ensign Kellogg presided and except his introductory remarks, Mr. Lincoln's speech, which lasted one and a half or two hours, was the only one. The Boston *Advertiser's* report was nearly a column in length. It said: 'Mr. Lincoln has a very tall and thin figure, with an intellectual face, showing a searching mind and a cool judgment. He spoke in a clear and cool and very eloquent manner, carrying the audience with him in his able arguments and brilliant illustrations, only interrupted by warm and frequent applause. He began by expressing a real feeling of modesty in addressing an audience "this side of the mountains," a part of the country where, in the opinion of the people of his section, everybody was supposed to be instructed and wise. But he had devoted his attention to the question of the coming presidential election, and was not unwilling to exchange with all whom he might meet the ideas to which he had arrived.' . This passage gives some reason to suppose that, conscious of his powers, he was disposed to try them before audiences somewhat different from those to which he had been accustomed, and therefore he had come to New England. The first part of his speech was a reply, at some length, to the charge that General Taylor had no political principles; and he maintained that the General stood on the true Whig principle, that the will of the people should prevail against executive influence or the veto power of the President. He justified the Whigs for omitting to put a national platform before the people, and, according to a Free-Soil report, said that a political platform should be frowned down whenever and wherever presented. But the stress of his speech was against the Free-Soilers, whose position as to the exclusion of slavery from the territories, he claimed, to be that of the Whigs; while the former were subject to the further criticism that they had but one principle, reminding him of the Yankee peddler, who, in offering for sale a pair of pantaloons, described them as 'large enough for any man, and small enough for any boy.' He condemned the Free-Soilers as helping to elect Cass, who was less likely to promote freedom in the territories than Taylor and passed judgment on them as having less principle than any party. To their defence of their right and duty to act independently, 'leaving consequences to God,' he replied, that 'when divine or human law does not clearly point out what is our duty, it must be found out by an intelligent judgment, which takes in the results of action.' The Free-Soilers were much offended by a passage which does not appear in the Whig report. Referring to the anti-slavery men, he said they were better treated ' in Massachusetts than in the West, and, turning to William S. Lincoln, of Worcester, who had lived in Illinois, he remarked that in that State they had recently killed one of them. This allusion to Lovejoy's murder at Alton, was thought by the Free-Soilers to be heartless, and it was noted that Mr. Lincoln did not repeat it in other speeches. It was probably a casual remark, which came into his mind at the moment, and meant but little, if anything. Cheers were given at the end of the speech for the eloquent Whig member from Illinois. The Whig reports spoke of the speech as 'masterly and convincing' and 'one of the best ever made in Worcester;' while the Free-Soil report describes it as 'a pretty tedious affair.' The next morning he spoke at an open-air meeting, following Benjamin F. Thomas and Ex-Governor Levi Lincoln, but his speech was cut short by the arrival by train of the delegates from Boston, who, with the speakers, proceeded at once to the hall. The convention listened to a long address to the people, reported by a committee, and then to a brilliant speech from Rufus Choate, followed by others from Robert C. Winthrop, the Whig Speaker of the House of Representatives, Charles Hudson, M. C., and Benjamin F. Thomas. Mr. Lincoln listened to these, but was not himself called out.

Mr. Lincoln spoke at Washingtonian Hall, Bromfield street, Boston, on the 15th, his address lasting an hour and a half, and, according to the report, 'seldom equaled for sound reasoning, cogent argument and keen satire.' Three cheers were given for 'the Lone Star of Illinois,' on account of his being the only Whig member from the State. He spoke at Lowell the 16th, and at the Lower Mills, Dorchester, now a part of Boston, on Monday, the 18th. At this last place the meeting was held in Richmond Hall, and the chairman was N. F. Safford, living till 1891, who introduced him as one of the Lincolns of Hingham, and a descendant of Gen. Benjamin Lincoln. Mr. Lincoln, as he began, disclaimed descent from the Revolutionary officer, but said, playfully, that he had endeavored in Illinois to introduce the principles of the Lincolns of Massachusetts. A few of his audience are still living. They were struck with his height, as he arose in the low-studded hall. He spoke at Chelsea on the 19th, and a report states that his speech 'for aptness of illustration, solidity of argument, and genuine eloquence, was hard to beat.' Charles Sumner had defended the Free-Soil cause at the same place the evening before. Mr. Lincoln spoke at Dedham, in Temperance Hall, on the 20th, in the daytime. Two Whig nominating conventions met there the same day, at one of which Horace Mann was nominated for a second term in Congress. A report states that he 'spoke in an agreeable and entertaining way.' He left abruptly to take a train in order to meet another engagement, and was escorted to the station by the Dorchester band. The same evening he spoke at Cambridge. The report describes him as 'a capital specimen of a Sucker Whig, six feet at least in his stockings.' Of his speech, it was said that 'it was plain, direct and to the point, powerful and convincing, and telling with capital effect upon the immense audience. It was a

model speech for the campaign.' His last speech
was on the 22d, at Tremont Temple, with George
Lunt presiding, in company with William H. Seward,
whom he followed, ending at 10.30 P. M. The Whig
newspaper, the *Atlas*, the next morning gave more
than a column to Mr. Seward's speech, but stated
that it had no room for the notes which had been
taken of Mr. Lincoln's, describing it, however, as
' powerful and convincing, and cheered to the echo.'
The Free-Soil paper (Henry Wilson's) refers to the
meeting, mentioning Mr. Seward, but not Mr. Lincoln. The next day Mr. Lincoln left Boston for
Illinois. The *Atlas* on Monday contained this paragraph : ' In answer to the many applications which
we daily receive from different parts of the State for
this gentleman to speak, we have to say that he left
Boston on Saturday morning on his way home to
Illinois.'

It is evident from all the contemporaneous reports,
that Mr. Lincoln made a marked impression on all his
audiences. Their attention was drawn at once to his
striking figure ; they enjoyed his quaintness and
humor ; and they recognized his logical power and
his novel way of putting things. Still, so far as his
points are given in the public journals, he did not
rise at any time above partisanship, and he gave
no sign of the great future which awaited him as a
political antagonist, a master of language, and a leader
of men. But it should be noted, in connection with
this estimate, that the Whig case, as put in that
campaign, was chiefly one of personalities, and was
limited to the qualities and career of Taylor as a

soldier, and to ridicule of his opponent, General Cass. Mr. Lincoln, like the other Whig speakers, labored to prove that Taylor was a Whig.

Seward's speech at Tremont Temple, to which Lincoln listened, seems to have started a more serious vein of thought on slavery in the mind of the future President. That evening, when they were together as fellow-lodgers at a hotel, Lincoln said : " Governor Seward, I have been thinking about what you said in your speech. I reckon you are right. We have got to deal with this slavery question, and got to give much more attention to it hereafter than we have been doing." *

It is curious now to recall how little support, in the grave moments of his national career which came twelve years later, Mr. Lincoln received from the Whigs of Massachusetts, then conspicuous in public life, whom he met on his visit. Mr. Lunt, who presided at Faneuil Hall, was to the end of his life a pro-slavery conservative. Judge Thomas, in Congress, during the early part of the civil war, was obstructive to the President's policy. Mr. Winthrop voted against Lincoln in 1860 and 1864. Mr. Choate died in 1859, but, judged by his latest utterances, his marvelous eloquence would have been no patriotic inspiration if he had outlived the national struggle. On the other hand, the Free-Soilers of Massachusetts, whom Mr. Lincoln came here to discredit, became, to a man, his supporters ; and on many of their leaders he relied as his support in the great conflict. Sumner

* Seward's Life, vol. ii, p. 80.

was chairman of the Senate Committee on Foreign Affairs during the war; Wilson was chairman of the Committee on Military Affairs; Adams was Minister to England; and Andrew War-Governor of the State. These, as well as Palfrey, Burlingame and Dana, who, in 1848, almost every evening addressed audiences against both Taylor and Cass, while Mr. Lincoln was here, were earnest and steadfast in their devotion to the Government during the civil war; and the last three received important appointments from him. How the press treated Mr. Lincoln may be learned from the following editorial in the Lowell *Journal and Courier*, in its issue of September 18, 1848:

WHIG MEETING.

The sterling Whigs of Lowell came together last Saturday evening, at the City Hall. The meeting was called to order by the Chairman of the Whig Central Committee, Hon. Linus Child. Homer Bartlett, Esq., was chosen chairman, and A. Gilman, secretary. After a few animating remarks from the Chairman, he introduced George Woodman, Esq., of Boston, who made a very pertinent and witty off-hand speech, which was frequently interrupted by the spontaneous plaudits of the audience. At the close of his speech Mr. Woodman introduced the Hon. Abraham Lincoln, of Illinois. It would be doing injustice to his speech to endeavor to give a sketch of it. It was replete with good sense, sound reasoning, and irresistible argument, and spoken with that perfect command of manner and matter which so eminently distinguishes the Western orators. He disabused the public of the erroneous suppositions that Taylor was not a Whig; that Van Buren was anything more than a thorough Loco-foco on all subjects other than Free Territory, and hardly safe on that ; and showed up, in a masterly manner, the inconsistency and folly of those Whigs, who, being drawn off from the true and oldest free-soil organization known among the parties of the Union, would now lend their influence and votes to help Mr. Van Buren into the presidential chair. His speech was interrupted by frequent cheers of the audience. At the close the secretary, by request, read the letter of General Taylor to Captain Alison, which had just been received, in which he says: " From the beginning till now, I have declared myself to be a Whig, on all proper occasions."

Ex-Governor Gardner, after a brief history of the Whig Convention at Worcester, Mass., contributes this pleasing reminiscence :

"Gov. Levi Lincoln, the oldest living Ex-Governor of Massachusetts, resided in Worcester. He was a man of culture and wealth ; lived in one of the finest houses in that town, and was a fine specimen of a gentleman of the old school. It was his custom to give a dinner party when any distinguished assemblage took place in Worcester, and to invite its prominent participants. He invited to dine, on this occasion, a company of gentlemen, among them myself, who was a delegate from Boston. The dining-room and table arrangements were superb, the dinner exquisite, the wines abundant, rare, and of the first quality.

"I well remember the jokes between Governor Lincoln and Abraham Lincoln as to their presumed relationship. At last the latter said : 'I *hope* we both belong, as the Scotch say, to the same clan ;

but I *know* one thing, and that is, that we are both good Whigs.'

"That evening there was held in Mechanics' Hall (an immense building) a mass-meeting of delegates and others, and Lincoln was announced to speak. No one there had ever heard him on the stump, and in fact knew anything about him. When he was announced, his tall, angular, bent form, and his manifest awkwardness and low tone of voice, promised nothing interesting. But he soon warmed to his work. His style and manner of speaking were novelties in the East. He repeated anecdotes, told stories admirable in humor and in point, interspersed with bursts of true eloquence, which constantly brought down the house. His sarcasm of Cass, Van Buren and the Democratic party was inimitable, and whenever he attempted to stop, the shouts of 'Go on! go on!' were deafening. He probably spoke over an hour, but so great was the enthusiasm time could not be measured. It was doubtless one of the best efforts of his life. He spoke a day or two afterward in Faneuil Hall, with William H. Seward, but I did not hear him.

"In 1861 business called me to Washington, and I paid my respects to the President at the White House. He came forward smiling and with extended hand, saying: 'You and I are no strangers; we dined together at Governor Lincoln's in 1848.' When one remembers the increased burden on the President's mind at this trying time, the anxieties of the war, the army, the currency, and the rehabilitating the civil officers of the country, it seemed astonishing to me to hear him continue : ' Sit down. Yes, I had been chosen to Congress then from the wild West, and with hayseed in my hair I went to Massachusetts, the most cultured State in the Union, to take a few lessons in deportment. That was a grand dinner—a superb dinner; by far the finest I ever saw in my life. And the great men who were there, too ! Why, I can tell you just how they were arranged at table.' He began at one end, and mentioned the names in order, and, I verily believe, without the omission of a single one."

This chapter would be incomplete without the account of Mr. George H. Monroe, a young man living in Dedham, Mass., in 1848, who, forty years later, wrote out his recollections of Mr. Lincoln's visit to that town. Mr. Monroe has a vivid and retentive memory, and has since been identified with the public life and journalism of Massachusetts : " Massachusetts, on account of the great defection of Whigs to the Free-Soilers, and Daniel Webster's sudden and damaging attitude toward General Taylor's nomination to the presidency, began to be considered rather doubtful ground for the Whigs. The national committee sent Mr. Lincoln to the State, after Congress had adjourned, to make some speeches. Our people knew very little about him then. I lived in Dedham, the shire town of Norfolk county, and was secretary of a Whig club there. One of the county courts was in session, and it was determined to have a meeting in the daytime, before it adjourned. I was commissioned to go to Boston to engage the speaker. I went at once to see my friend, Colonel Schouler, of the Boston *Atlas*.　He told me that a new man had just come into the State from Washington, who, he thought, would answer our purpose exactly, and said he would get him for me if possible.　That man was Abraham Lincoln.　When the day for the meeting came I went to 'the Tremont House and found Mr. Lincoln there.　I remember well how tall, awkward and ungainly he was in appearance.　I remember how reticent he was, too, but I attributed this to my own youth, for I was only just past twenty-one years of age.　He was as sober a man in point of expression as ever I saw.　There were others in the party later, but in the journey out in the cars he scarcely said a word to one of us.　I did not see him smile on any part of the journey.　He seemed uneasy and out of sympathy with his surroundings, as it were.　I should say that the atmosphere of Boston was not congenial to him.　We took him to one of the most elegant houses in the town of Dedham, and here he seemed still less, if possible, at home.　The thing began to look rather blue for us. When we went over to the hall it was not much better. It was a small hall, and it was only about half full ; for Mr. Lincoln had not spoken in Boston yet, and there was nothing in his name particularly to attract. But at last he arose to speak, and almost instantly there was a change.　His indifferent manner vanished as soon as he opened his mouth.　He went right to his work.　He wore a black alpaca sack, and he turned up the sleeves of this, and then the cuffs of his shirt.　Next he loosened his necktie, and soon after he took it off altogether.　All the time he was

gaining upon his audience.   He soon had it as by a
spell.   I never saw men more delighted.   His style
was the most familiar and off-hand possible.   His eye
had lighted up and changed the whole expression of
his countenance.   He began to bubble out with humor.
But the chief charm of the address lay in the homely
way he made his points.   There was no attempt at
eloquence or finish of style.   But, for plain pungency
of humor, it would have been difficult to surpass his
speech.   In this making of points which come home
to the general mind, I don't think Lincoln was ever
surpassed by any American orator.   I often thought
of it afterward, when he was exhibiting this faculty in
a more ambitious way on a broader field.   The speech
which I am trying to describe was not a long one.
It abruptly ended in a half-hour's time.   The bell that
called to the steam cars sounded.   Mr. Lincoln instantly stopped.   ' I am engaged to speak at Cambridge to-night,' said he, ' and I must leave.'   The
whole audience seemed to rise in protest.   ' Oh, no !
go on ! finish it ! ' was heard on every hand.   One gentleman arose and pledged himself to take his horse
and carry him across the country.   But Mr. Lincoln
was inexorable.   ' I can't take any risks,' said he.
' I have engaged to go to Cambridge, and I must be
there.   I came here as I agreed, and I am going there
in the same way.'   A more disappointed audience
was never seen ; but Mr. Lincoln had fairly wakened
it up, and it stayed through the afternoon and into
the evening to listen to other speakers.   We tried to
get him to come again, but it was impossible.   I
heard the speech finished afterward in Tremont

21

Temple, Boston; and it is a notable fact that on the same evening, and from the same platform, William H. Seward also spoke, and made the only political speech he ever delivered in Boston. Who could have dreamed then that in Lincoln we were listening to the man who was to be the future president of the United States, and to leave a reputation second only to that of Washington! Mr. Lincoln moved his Boston audience in much the same way I have described, but Mr. Seward made the first speech, and was looked upon as the chief star, of course. Seward's speech was much more ambitious and comprehensive than that of Lincoln. The latter had not begun to treat broad principles in the 1848 campaign. Mr. Seward's argument was a triumph of intellect, after the most careful preparation. I don't think Mr. Lincoln had ever written his speech at all. He aimed at not much more than to be bright, effective and taking with his audience, and his success was perfect here."

THE GLOBE TAVERN, SPRINGFIELD.

Photographed in 1886.

CHAPTER XI.

AFTER the wedding of Lincoln and Miss Todd at the Edwards mansion we hear but little of them as a married couple till the spring of 1843, when the husband writes to his friend Speed, who had been joined to his "black-eyed Fanny" a little over a year, with regard to his life as a married man. "Are you possessing houses and lands," he writes, "and oxen and asses and men-servants and maid-servants, and begetting sons and daughters? We are not keeping house, but boarding at the Globe Tavern, which is very well kept now by a widow lady of the name of Beck. Our room (the same Dr. Wallace occupied there) and boarding only costs us four dollars a week." Gaining a livelihood was slow and discouraging business with him, for we find him in another letter apologizing for his failure to visit Kentucky, "because," he says, "I am so poor and make so little headway in the world that I drop back in a month of idleness as much as I gain in a year's sowing." But by dint of untiring efforts and the recognition of influential friends he managed through rare frugality to move along. In his struggles, both in the law and for political advancement, his wife shared in his sacrifices. She was a plucky little woman, and in fact endowed with a more restless ambition than he. She was gifted with a rare insight into the motives that actuate mankind, and there is no doubt that much of Lincoln's success was in a measure attributable to her acuteness and the stimulus of her influence. His election to Congress within four years after their marriage afforded her extreme gratification. She loved power and prominence, and when occasionally she came down to our office, it seemed to me then that she was inordinately proud of her tall and ungainly husband. She saw in him bright prospects ahead, and his every move was watched by her with the closest interest. If to other persons he seemed homely, to her he was the embodiment of noble manhood, and each succeeding day impressed upon her the wisdom of her choice of Lincoln over Douglas—if in reality she ever seriously accepted the latter's attentions. "Mr. Lincoln may not be as handsome a figure," she said one day in the office during her husband's absence, when the conversation turned on Douglas, "but the people are perhaps not aware that his heart is as large as his arms are long."

Mrs. Lincoln accompanied her husband to Washington and remained during one session of Congress. While there they boarded at the same house with Joshua R. Giddings, and when in 1856 the valiant old Abolitionist came to take part in the canvass in Illinois, he early sought out Lincoln, with whom he had been so favorably impressed several years before. On his way home from Congress Lincoln came by way of Niagara Falls and down Lake Erie to Toledo or Detroit. It happened that, some time after, I went to New York and also returned by way of Niagara Falls. In the office, a few days after my return, I was endeavoring to entertain my partner with an account of my trip, and among other things described the Falls. In the attempt I indulged in a good deal of imagery. As I warmed up with the subject my descriptive powers expanded accordingly. The mad rush of water, the roar, the rapids, and the rainbow furnished me with an abundance of material for a stirring and impressive picture. The recollection of the gigantic and awe-inspiring scene stimulated my exuberant powers to the highest pitch. After well-nigh exhausting myself in the effort I turned to Lincoln for his opinion. "What," I inquired, "made the deepest impression on you when you stood in the presence of the great natural wonder?" I shall never forget his answer, because it in a very characteristic way illustrates how he looked at everything. "The thing that struck me most forcibly when I saw the Falls," he responded, "was, where in the world did all that water come from?" He had no eye for the magnificence and grandeur of the scene, for the rapids, the mist, the angry waters, and the roar of the whirlpool, but his mind, working in its accustomed channel, heedless of beauty or awe, followed irresistibly back to the first cause. It was in this light he viewed every question. However great the verbal foliage that concealed the nakedness of a good idea Lincoln stripped it all down till he could see clear the way between cause and effect. If there was any secret in his power this surely was it.

After seeing Niagara Falls he continued his journey homeward. At some point on the way, the vessel on which he had taken passage stranded on a sand bar. The captain ordered the hands to collect all the loose planks, empty barrels and boxes and force them under the sides of the boat. These empty casks were used to buoy it up. After forcing enough of them under the vessel she lifted gradually and at last swung clear of the opposing sand bar. Lincoln had watched this operation very intently. It no doubt carried him back to the days of his navigation on the turbulent Sangamon, when he and John Hanks had rendered similar service at New Salem dam to their employer, the volatile Offut. Continual thinking on the subject of lifting vessels over sand bars and other obstructions in the water suggested to him the idea of inventing an apparatus for that purpose. Using the principle involved in the operation he had just witnessed, his plan was to attach a kind of bellows on each side of the hull of the craft just below the water line, and, by an odd system of ropes and pulleys, whenever the keel grated on the sand these bellows were to be filled with air, and thus buoyed up, the vessel was expected to float clear of the shoal. On reaching home he at once set to work to demonstrate the feasibility of his plan. Walter Davis, a mechanic having a shop near our office, granted him the use of his tools, and likewise assisted him in making the model of a miniature vessel with the arrangement as above described. Lincoln manifested ardent interest in it. Occasionally he would bring the model in the office, and while whittling on it would descant on its merits and the revolution it was destined to work in steamboat navigation. Although I regarded the thing as impracticable I said nothing, probably out of respect for Lincoln's well-known reputation as a boatman. The model was sent or taken by him to Washington, where a patent was issued, but the invention was never applied to any vessel, so far as I ever learned, and the threatened revolution in steamboat architecture and navigation never came to pass. The model still reposes in undisturbed slumber on the shelves in the Patent Office, and is the only evidence now existing of Lincoln's success as an inventor.*

Shortly before the close of his term in Congress he appears in a new rôle. Having failed of a re-election he became an applicant for the office of Commissioner of the General Land Office. He had been urged to this step by many of his Whig friends in Illinois, but he was so hedged about with other

---

* Following is a copy of Lincoln's application for the patent on his "Improved Method of Lifting Vessels Over Shoals" : " What I claim as my invention, and desire to secure by letters patent, is the combination of expansible buoyant chambers placed at the sides of a vessel with the main shaft or shafts by means of the sliding spars, which pass down through the buoyant chambers and are made fast to their bottoms and the series of ropes and pulleys or their equivalents in such a manner that by turning the main shaft or shafts in one direction the buoyant chambers will be forced downwards into the water, and at the same time expanded and filled with air for buoying up the vessel by the displacement of water, and by turning the shafts in an opposite direction the buoyant chambers will be contracted into a small space and secured against injury.

"A. LINCOLN."

aspirants from his own State that he soon lost all heart in the contest. He was too scrupulous, and lacked too much the essentials of self-confidence and persistence, to be a successful suitor for office. In a letter to Joshua Speed, who had written him of a favorable reference to him by Mr. Crittenden, of Kentucky,* he says, February 20, 1849, "I am flattered to learn that Mr. Crittenden has any recollection of me which is not unfavorable ; and for the manifestation of your kindness towards me I sincerely thank you. Still, there is nothing about me to authorize me to think of a first-class office, and a second-class one would not compensate me for being sneered at by others who want it for themselves. I believe that, so far as the Whigs in Congress are concerned, I could have the General Land Office almost by common consent ; but then Sweet and Dav. Morrison and Browning and Cyrus Edwards all want it, and what is worse, while I think I could easily take it myself I fear I shall have trouble to get it for any other man in Illinois. The reason is that McGaughey, an Indiana ex-member of Congress, is here after it, and being personally known he will be hard to beat by any one who is not." But, as the sequel proved, there was no need to fear the

---

* Lincoln had asked Speed to see Crittenden (then Governor of Kentucky) and secure from the latter a recommendation for Baker, who wanted a first-class foreign mission. Crittenden did not approve of Baker, but suggested that he would favor Lincoln, whom he regarded as a rising man. Speed suggested to Lincoln to apply for the place himself. "I have pledged myself to Baker," he answered, "and cannot under any circumstances consent to the use of my name so long as he is urged for the same place."

Hoosier statesman, for although he had the endorsement of General Scott and others of equal influence, yet he was left far behind in the race, and along with him Lincoln, Morrison, Browning, and Edwards. A dark horse in the person of Justin Butterfield, sprang into view, and with surprising facility captured the tempting prize. This latter and successful aspirant was a lawyer of rather extensive practice and reputation in Chicago. He was shrewd, adroit, and gifted with a knowledge of what politicians would call good management—a quality or characteristic in which Lincoln was strikingly deficient. He had endorsed the Mexican war, but, strangely enough, had lost none of his prestige with the Whigs on that account.*

The close of Congress and the inauguration of Taylor were the signal for Lincoln's departure from Washington. He left with the comforting assur-

---

* The following letter by Butterfield's daughter is not without interest :

"CHICAGO, Oct. 12th, 1888.
"MR. JESSE W. WEIK.
   "*Dear Sir:*
"My father was born in Keene, N. H., in 1790, entered Williams College, 1807, and removed to Chicago in 1835. After the re-accession of the Whigs to power he was on the 21st of June in 1849 appointed Commissioner of the Land Office by President Taylor. A competitor for the position at that time was Abraham Lincoln, who was beaten, it was said, by ' the superior dispatch of Butterfield in reaching Washington by the Northern route,' but more correctly by the paramount influence of his friend Daniel Webster.
"He held the position of Land Commissioner until disabled by paralysis in 1852. After lingering for three years in a disabled and enfeebled condition, he died at his home in Chicago, October 23d, 1855, in his sixty-third year.

"Very respectfully,
"ELIZABETH SAWYER."

ance that as an office-seeker he was by no means a success. Besides his lack of persistence, he had an unconscious feeling of superiority and pride that admitted of no such flexibility of opinion as the professional suitor for office must have, in order to succeed. He remained but a few days at his home in Illinois, however, before he again set out for Washington. The administration of President Taylor feeling that some reward was due Lincoln for his heroic efforts on the stump and elsewhere in behalf of the Whig party and its measures, had offered him the office of either Governor or Secretary of Oregon, and with the view of considering this and other offers he returned to Washington. Lincoln used to relate of this last-named journey an amusing incident illustrating Kentucky hospitality. He set out from Ransdell's tavern in Springfield, early in the morning. The only other passenger in the stage for a good portion of the distance was a Kentuckian, on his way home from Missouri. The latter, painfully impressed no doubt with Lincoln's gravity and melancholy, undertook to relieve the general monotony of the ride by offering him a chew of tobacco. With a plain "No, sir, thank you; I never chew," Lincoln declined, and a long period of silence followed. Later in the day the stranger, pulling from his pocket a leather-covered case, offered Lincoln a cigar, which he also politely declined on the ground that he never smoked. Finally, as they neared the station where horses were to be changed, the Kentuckian, pouring out a cup of brandy from a flask which had lain concealed in his satchel, offered it to Lincoln with the remark, " Well, stranger, seeing you don't smoke or chew, perhaps you'll take a little of this French brandy. It's a prime article and a good appetizer besides." His tall and uncommunicative companion declined this last and best evidence of Kentucky hospitality on the same ground as the tobacco. When they separated that afternoon, the Kentuckian, transferring to another stage, bound for Louisville, shook Lincoln warmly by the hand. "See here, stranger," he said, good-humoredly, "you're a clever, but strange companion. I may never see you again, and I don't want to offend you, but I want to say this : my experience has taught me that a man who has no vices has d——d few virtues. Good-day." Lincoln enjoyed this reminiscence of the journey, and took great pleasure in relating it. During this same journey occurred an incident for which Thomas H. Nelson, of Terre Haute, Indiana, who was appointed Minister to Chili by Lincoln, when he was President, is authority. "In the spring of 1849," relates Nelson, "Judge Abram Hammond, who was afterwards Governor of Indiana, and I arranged to go from Terre Haute to Indianapolis in the stage coach. An entire day was usually consumed in the journey. By daybreak the stage had arrived from the West, and as we stepped in we discovered that the entire back seat was occupied by a long, lank individual, whose head seemed to protrude from one end of the coach and his feet from the other. He was the sole occupant, and was sleeping

soundly. Hammond slapped him familiarly on the
shoulder, and asked him if he had chartered the
stage for the day. The stranger, now wide awake,
responded, 'Certainly not,' and at once took the
front seat, politely surrendering to us the place of
honor and comfort. We took in our travelling
companion at a glance. A queer, odd-looking fellow he was, dressed in a well-worn and ill-fitting
suit of bombazine, without vest or cravat, and a
twenty-five-cent palm hat on the back of his head.
His very prominent features in repose seemed dull
and expressionless. Regarding him as a good subject for merriment we perpetrated several jokes.
He took them all with the utmost innocence and
good-nature, and joined in the laugh, although at
his own expense. At noon we stopped at a wayside hostelry for dinner. We invited him to eat
with us, and he approached the table as if he considered it a great honor. He sat with about half
his person on a small chair, and held his hat under
his arm during the meal. Resuming our journey
after dinner, conversation drifted into a discussion
of the comet, a subject that was then agitating
the scientific world, in which the stranger took
the deepest interest. He made many startling
suggestions and asked many questions. We
amazed him with words of learned length and
thundering sound. After an astounding display of
wordy pyrotechnics the dazed and bewildered
stranger asked: 'What is going to be the up-
shot of this comet business?' I replied that I
was not certain, in fact I differed from most scien-

tists and philosophers, and was inclined to the opinion that the world would follow the darned thing off! Late in the evening we reached Indianapolis, and hurried to Browning's hotel, losing sight of the stranger altogether. We retired to our room to brush and wash away the dust of the journey. In a few minutes I descended to the portico, and there descried our long, gloomy fellow-traveller in the center of an admiring group of lawyers, among whom were Judges McLean and Huntington, Edward Hannigan, Albert S. White, and Richard W. Thompson, who seemed to be amused and interested in a story he was telling. I enquired of Browning, the landlord, who he was. "Abraham Lincoln, of Illinois, a member of Congress," was the response. I was thunderstruck at the announcement. I hastened upstairs and told Hammond the startling news, and together we emerged from the hotel by a back door and went down an alley to another house, thus avoiding further contact with our now distinguished fellow-traveller. Curiously enough, years after this, Hammond had vacated the office of Governor of Indiana a few days before Lincoln arrived in Indianapolis, on his way to Washington to be inaugurated President. I had many opportunities after the stage ride to cultivate Mr. Lincoln's acquaintance, and was a zealous advocate of his nomination and election to the Presidency. Before leaving his home for Washington, Mr. Lincoln caused John P. Usher and myself to be invited to accompany him. We agreed to join him in Indianapolis. On reaching that city the Presidential party had already arrived, and upon inquiry we were informed that the President-elect was in the dining-room of the hotel, at supper. Passing through, we saw that every seat at the numerous tables was occupied, but failed to find Mr. Lincoln. As we were nearing the door to the office of the hotel, a long arm reached to my shoulder and a shrill voice exclaimed, ' Hello, Nelson ! do you think, after all, the world is going to follow the darned thing off ? ' It was Mr. Lincoln."

The benefits and advantages of the territorial posts offered by President Taylor to Lincoln were freely discussed by the latter's friends. Some urged his acceptance on the usual ground that when Oregon was admitted as a State, he might be its first Senator. Lincoln himself had some inclination to accept. He told me himself that he felt by his course in Congress he had committed political suicide, and wanted to try a change of locality—hence the temptation to go to Oregon. But when he brought the proposition home to his fireside, his wife put her foot squarely down on it with a firm and emphatic No. That always ended it with Lincoln. The result of the whole thing proved a fortunate deliverance for him, the propriety of which became more apparent as the years rolled by.*

---

* About this time Grant Goodrich, a lawyer in Chicago, proposed to take Lincoln into partnership with him. Goodrich had an extensive and paying practice there, but Lincoln refused the offer, giving as a reason that he tended to consumption, and if he removed to a

While a member of Congress and otherwise immersed in politics Lincoln seemed to lose all interest in the law. Of course, what practice he himself controlled passed into other hands. I retained all the business I could, and worked steadily on until, when he returned, our practice was as extensive as that of any other firm at the bar. Lincoln realized that much of this was due to my efforts, and on his return he therefore suggested that he had no right to share in the business and profits which I had made. I responded that, as he had aided me and given me prominence when I was young and needed it, I could afford now to be grateful if not generous. I therefore recommended a continuation of the partnership, and we went on as before. I could notice a difference in Lincoln's movement as a lawyer from this time forward. He had begun to realize a certain lack of discipline—a want of mental training and method. Ten years had wrought some change in the law, and more in the lawyers, of Illinois. The conviction had settled in the minds of the people that the pyrotechnics of court room and stump oratory did not necessarily imply extensive or profound ability in the lawyer who resorted to it. The courts were becoming graver and more learned, and the lawyer was learning as a preliminary and indispensable condition to

---

city like Chicago, he would have to sit down and study harder than ever. The close application required of him and the confinement in the office, he contended, would soon kill him. He preferred going around on the circuit, and even if he earned smaller fees he felt much happier.

success that he must be a close reasoner, besides having at command a broad knowledge of the principles on which the statutory law is constructed. There was of course the same riding on circuit as before, but the courts had improved in tone and morals, and there was less laxity—at least it appeared so to Lincoln. Political defeat had wrought a marked effect on him. It went below the skin and made a changed man of him. He was not soured at his seeming political decline, but still he determined to eschew politics from that time forward and devote himself entirely to the law. And now he began to make up for time lost in politics by studying the law in earnest. No man had greater power of application than he. Once fixing his mind on any subject, nothing could interfere with or disturb him. Frequently I would go out on the circuit with him. We, usually, at the little country inns occupied the same bed. In most cases the beds were too short for him, and his feet would hang over the foot-board, thus exposing a limited expanse of shin bone. Placing a candle on a chair at the head of the bed, he would read and study for hours. I have known him to study in this position till two o'clock in the morning. Meanwhile, I and others who chanced to occupy the same room would be safely and soundly asleep. On the circuit in this way he studied Euclid until he could with ease demonstrate all the propositions in the six books. How he could maintain his mental equilibrium or concentrate his thoughts on an abstract mathematical proposition,

while Davis, Logan, Swett, Edwards, and I so in-
dustriously and volubly filled the air with our
interminable snoring was a problem none of us
could ever solve. I was on the circuit with Lincoln probably one-fourth of the time. The remainder of my time was spent in Springfield looking
after the business there, but I know that life on the
circuit was a gay one. It was rich with incidents,
and afforded the nomadic lawyers ample relaxation
from all the irksome toil that fell to their lot.
Lincoln loved it. I suppose it would be a fair
estimate to state that he spent over half the year
following Judges Treat and Davis around on the
circuit. On Saturdays the court and attorneys, if
within a reasonable distance, would usually start
for their homes. Some went for a fresh supply of
clothing, but the greater number went simply to
spend a day of rest with their families. The only
exception was Lincoln, who usually spent his Sun-
days with the loungers at the country tavern, and
only went home at the end of the circuit or term of
court. "At first," * relates one of his colleagues
on the circuit, "we wondered at it, but soon learned
to account for his strange disinclination to go
home. Lincoln himself never had much to say
about home, and we never felt free to comment on
it. Most of us had pleasant, inviting homes, and as
we struck out for them I'm sure each one of us down
in our hearts had a mingled feeling of pity and sympathy for him." If the day was long and he was

---

* David Davis, MS.

22

oppressed, the feeling was soon relieved by the narration of a story. The tavern loungers enjoyed it, and his melancholy, taking to itself wings, seemed to fly away. In the role of a story-teller I am prone to regard Mr. Lincoln as without an equal. I have seen him surrounded by a crowd numbering as many as two and in some cases three hundred persons, all deeply interested in the outcome of a story which, when he had finished it, speedily found repetition in every grocery and lounging place within reach. His power of mimicry, as I have before noted, and his manner of recital, were in many respects unique, if not remarkable. His countenance and all his features seemed to take part in the performance. As he neared the pith or point of the joke or story every vestige of seriousness disappeared from his face. His little gray eyes sparkled; a smile seemed to gather up, curtain like, the corners of his mouth; his frame quivered with suppressed excitement; and when the point—or " nub " of the story, as he called it—came, no one's laugh was heartier than his. These backwoods allegories are out of date now, and any lawyer, ambitious to gain prominence, would hardly dare thus to entertain a crowd, except at the risk of his reputation; but with Lincoln it gave him, in some mysterious way, a singularly firm hold on the people.

Lincoln was particularly strong in Menard county, and while on the circuit there he met with William Engle and James Murray, two men who were noted also for their story-telling proclivities. I am not now asserting for the country and the period what would at a later day be considered a very high standard of taste. Art had not such patrons as to-day, but the people loved the beautiful as Nature furnished it, and the good as they found it, with as much devotion as the more refined classes now are joined to their idols. Newspapers were scarce, and the court-house, with its cluster of itinerant lawyers, disseminated much of the information that was afterwards broken up into smaller bits at the pioneer's fireside. A curious civilization indeed, but one through which every Western State distant from the great arterial river or seaboard has had to pass.

When Lincoln, Murray, and Engle met, there was sure to be a crowd. All were more or less masters in their art. I have seen the little country tavern where these three were wont to meet after an adjournment of court, crowded almost to suffocation with an audience of men who had gathered to witness the contest among the members of the strange triumvirate. The physician of the town, all the lawyers, and not unfrequently a preacher could be found in the crowd that filled the doors and windows. The yarns they spun and the stories they told would not bear repetition here, but many of them had morals which, while exposing the weaknesses of mankind, stung like a whip-lash. Some were no doubt a thousand years old, with just enough " verbal varnish " and alterations of names and dates to make them new and crisp. By virtue of the last-named application, Lincoln was enabled to draw from Balzac a "droll story," and locating it in "Egypt"* or in Indiana, pass it off for a purely original conception. Every recital was followed by its "storm of laughter and chorus of cheers." After this had all died down, some unfortunate creature, through whose thickened skull the point had just penetrated, would break out in a guffaw, starting another wave of laughter which, growing to the proportions of a billow, would come rolling in like a veritable breaker. I have known these story-telling jousts to continue long after midnight—in some cases till the very small hours of the morning. I have seen Judge Treat, who was the very impersonation of gravity itself, sit up till the last and laugh until, as he often expressed it, "he almost shook his ribs loose." The next day he would ascend the bench and listen to Lincoln in a murder trial, with all the seeming severity of an English judge in wig and gown. Amid such surroundings, a leading figure in such society, alternately reciting the latest effusion of the bar-room or mimicking the clownish antics of the negro minstrel, he who was destined to be an immortal emancipator, was steadily and unconsciously nearing the great trial of his life. We shall see further on how this rude civilization crystallized both his logic and his wit for use in another day.

Reverting again to Mr. Lincoln as a lawyer, it is proper to add that he detested the mechanical work of the office. He wrote few papers—less perhaps than any other man at the bar. Such work was

---

* The word Egypt, so frequently used in this book, refers to that portion of Illinois which lies south of the famous National Road.

usually left to me for the first few years we were together. Afterwards we made good use of students who came to learn the law in our office. A Chicago lawyer,* in a letter to me about Mr. Lincoln, in 1866, says : "Lincoln once told me that he had taken you in as a partner, supposing you had system and would keep things in order, but that he found out you had no more system than he had, but that you were in reality a good lawyer, so that he was doubly disappointed." Lincoln knew no such thing as order or method in his law practice. He made no preparation in advance, but trusted to the hour for its inspiration and to Providence for his supplies. In the matter of letter-writing † he made no distinction between one of a business nature or any other kind. If a happy thought or expression struck him he was by no means reluctant to use it. As early as 1839 he wrote to a gentle-

---

* W. C. Whitney, MS.

† " I wish you would learn of Everett what he would take, over and above a discharge, for all trouble we have been at to take his business out of our hands and give it to somebody else. It is impossible to collect money on that or any other claim here, now, and although you know I am not a very petulant man, I declare that I am almost out of patience with Mr. Everett's endless importunities. It seems like he not only writes all the letters he can himself, but he gets everybody else in Louisville and vicinity to be constantly writing to us about his claim. I have always said that Mr. Everett is a very clever fellow, and I am very sorry he cannot be obliged ; but it does seem to me he ought to know we are interested to collect his claim, and therefore would do it if we could. I am neither joking nor in a pet when I say we would thank him to transfer his business to some other, without any compensation for what we have done, provided he will see the court costs paid for which we are security."—MS. letter to Joshua F. Speed, March 27, 1842.

man about a matter of business, observing crustily that " a d——d hawk-billed Yankee is here besetting me at every turn I take, saying that Robert Kenzie never received the $80 to which he was entitled." In July, 1851, he wrote a facetious message to one of his clients, saying: " I have news from Ottawa that we win our case. As the Dutch justice said when he married folks, ' Now where ish my hundred tollars.' " * He was proverbially careless as to habits. In a letter to a fellow-lawyer in another town, apologizing for failure to answer sooner, he explains: " First, I have been very busy in the United States Court ; second, when I received the letter I put it in my old hat and buying a new one the next day the old one was set aside, and so the letter was lost sight of for a time." This hat of Lincoln's—a silk plug—was an extraordinary receptacle. It was his desk and his memorandum-book. In it he carried

---

* The following unpublished letter in possession of C. F. Gunther, Esq., Chicago, Ills., shows how he proposed to fill a vacancy in the office of Clerk of the United States Court. It reads like the letter of a politician in the midst of a canvass for office:

"SPRINGFIELD, ILL., December 6, 1854.
"Hon. JUSTICE McLEAN.

" SIR: I understand it is in contemplation to displace the present Clerk and appoint a new one for the Circuit and District Courts of Illinois. I am very friendly to the present incumbent, and both for his own sake and that of his family, I wish him to be retained so long as it is possible for the Court to do so.

" In the contingency of his removal, however, I have recommended William Butler as his successor, and I do not wish what I write now to be taken as any abatement of that recommendation.

" William J. Black is also an applicant for the appointment, and I write this at the solicitation of his friends to say that he is every way worthy of the office, and that I doubt not the conferring it upon him will give great satisfaction.

"Your ob't servant,
"A. LINCOLN."

his bank-book and the bulk of his letters. Whenever in his reading or researches he wished to preserve an idea, he jotted it down on an envelope or stray piece of paper and placed it inside the lining. Afterwards when the memorandum was needed there was only one place to look for it.*

How Lincoln appeared and acted in the law office has been graphically and, I must confess, truthfully told by a gentleman now in New York, who was for several years a student in our office. I beg to quote a few lines from him: " My brother met Mr. Lincoln in Ottawa, Ill.,† one day, and said to him : ' I have a brother whom I would very much like to have enter your office as a student.' 'All right !' was his reply ; 'send him down and we will take a look at him.' I was then studying law at Grand Rapids, Mich., and on hearing from my brother I immediately packed up and started for Springfield. I arrived there on Saturday night. On Sunday Mr. Lincoln was pointed out to me. I well remember this first sight of him. He was striding along, holding little Tad, then about six years old, by the hand, who could with the greatest difficulty keep up with his father. In the morning I applied at the office of

---

* Lincoln had always on the top of our desk a bundle of papers into which he slipped anything he wished to keep and afterwards refer to. It was a receptacle of general information. Some years ago, on removing the furniture from the office, I took down the bundle and blew from the top the liberal coat of dust that had accumulated thereon. Immediately uuderneath the string was a slip bearing this endorsement, in his hand: " When you can't find it anywhere else, look in this."

† John H. Littlefield, *Brooklyn Eagle*, October 16, 1887.

Lincoln and Herndon for admission as a student. The office was on the second floor of a brick building on the public square, opposite the court-house. You went up one flight of stairs and then passed along a hallway to the rear office, which was a medium-sized room. There was one long table in the center of the room, and a shorter one running in the opposite direction, forming a T, and both were covered with green baize. There were two windows which looked into the back yard. In one corner was an old-fashioned secretary with pigeon-holes and a drawer, and here Mr. Lincoln and his partner kept their law papers. There was also a book-case containing about 200 volumes of law as well as miscellaneous books. The morning I entered the office Mr. Lincoln and his partner, Mr. Herndon, were both present. Mr. Lincoln addressed his partner thus: 'Billy, this is the young man of whom I spoke to you. Whatever arrangement you make with him will be satisfactory to me.' Then, turning to me, he said, 'I hope you will not become so enthusiastic in your studies of Blackstone and Kent as did two young men whom we had here. Do you see that spot over there?' pointing to a large ink stain on the wall. 'Well, one of these young men got so enthusiastic in his pursuit of legal lore that he fired an inkstand at the other one's head, and that is the mark he made.' I immediately began to clean up about the office a little. Mr. Lincoln had been in Congress and had the usual amount of seeds to distribute to the farmers. These were sent out with Free Soil and Republican documents. In my efforts to clean up, I found that some of the seeds had sprouted in the dirt that had collected in the office. Judge Logan and Milton Hay occupied the front offices on the same floor with Lincoln and Herndon, and one day Mr. Hay came in and said with apparent astonishment: 'What's happened here?' 'Oh, nothing,' replied Lincoln, pointing to me, 'only this young man has been cleaning up a little.' One of Lincoln's striking characteristics was his simplicity, and nowhere was this trait more strikingly exhibited than in his willingness to receive instruction from anybody and everybody. One day he came into the office and addressing his partner, said: 'Billy, what's the meaning of antithesis?' Mr. Herndon gave him the definition of the word, and I said: 'Mr. Lincoln, if you will allow me, I will give you an example.' 'All right, John, go ahead,' said Mr. Lincoln in his hearty manner. 'Phillips says, in his essay on Napoleon, "A pretended patriot, he impoverished the country; a professed Catholic, he imprisoned the Pope,"' etc. Mr. Lincoln thanked me and seemed very much pleased. Returning from off the circuit once he said to Mr. Herndon: 'Billy, I heard a good story while I was up in the country. Judge D—— was complimenting the landlord on the excellence of his beef. "I am surprised," he said, "that you have such good beef. You must have to kill a whole critter when you want any." "Yes," said the landlord, "we never kill less than a whole critter."

"Lincoln's favorite position when unravelling some knotty law point was to stretch both of his legs at full length upon a chair in front of him. In this position, with books on the table near by and in his lap, he worked up his case. No matter how deeply interested in his work, if any one came in he had something humorous and pleasant to say, and usually wound up by telling a joke or an anecdote. I have heard him relate the same story three times within as many hours to persons who came in at different periods, and every time he laughed as heartily and enjoyed it as if it were a new story. His humor was infectious. I had to laugh because I thought it funny that Mr. Lincoln enjoyed a story so repeatedly told.

"There was no order in the office at all. The firm of Lincoln and Herndon kept no books. They divided their fees without taking any receipts or making any entries on books. One day Mr. Lincoln received $5000 as a fee in a railroad case. He came in and said: ' Well, Billy,' addressing his partner, Mr. Herndon, ' here is our fee; sit down and let me divide.' He counted out $2,500 to his partner, and gave it to him with as much nonchalance as he would have given a few cents for a paper. Cupidity had no abiding place in his nature.

"I took a good deal of pains in getting up a speech which I wanted to deliver during a political campaign. I told Mr. Lincoln that I would like to read it to him. He sat down in one chair, put his feet into another one, and said: ' John, you can fire away with that speech; I guess I can stand it.' I unrolled the manuscript, and proceeded with some trepidation. ' That's a good point, John,' he would say, at certain places, and at others: ' That's good —very good indeed,' until I felt very much elated over my effort. I delivered the speech over fifty times during the campaign. Elmer E. Ellsworth, afterwards colonel of the famous Zouaves, who was killed in Alexandria, early in the war, was nominally a student in Lincoln's office. His head was so full of military matters, however, that he thought little of law. Of Ellsworth, Lincoln said: ' That young man has a real genius for war ! ' "

During the six years following his retirement from Congress, Lincoln, realizing in a marked degree his want of literary knowledge, extended somewhat his research in that direction. He was naturally indisposed to undertake anything that savored of exertion, but his brief public career had exposed the limited area of his literary attainments. Along with his Euclid therefore he carried a well-worn copy of Shakespeare, in which he read no little in his leisure moments. " In travelling on the circuit," relates one of his associates at the bar, * " he was in the habit of rising earlier than his brothers of the bar. On such occasions he was wont to sit by the fire, having uncovered the coals, and muse, and ponder, and soliloquize, inspired, no doubt, by that strange psychological influence which is so poetically described by Poe in ' The Raven.' On one of these occasions, at the town of Lincoln, sitting in the position described, he quoted aloud and at length the poem called ' Immortality.' When he

---

* Lawrence Weldon, letter, Feb. 10, 1866, MS.

had finished he was questioned as to the authorship and where it could be found. He had forgotten the author, but said that to him it sounded as much like true poetry as anything he had ever heard. He was particularly pleased with the last two stanzas."

Beyond a limited acquaintance with Shakespeare, Byron, and Burns, Mr. Lincoln, comparatively speaking, had no knowledge of literature. He was familiar with the Bible, and now and then evinced a fancy for some poem or short sketch to which his attention was called by some one else, or which he happened to run across in his cursory reading of books or newspapers. He never in his life sat down and read a book through, and yet he could readily quote any number of passages from the few volumes whose pages he had hastily scanned. In addition to his well-known love for the poem " Immortality " or " Why should the Spirit of Mortal be Proud," he always had a great fondness for Oliver Wendell Holmes' " Last Leaf," the fourth stanza of which, beginning with the verse, " The mossy marbles rest," I have often heard him repeat. He once told me of a song a young lady had sung in his hearing at a time when he was laboring under some dejection of spirits. The lines struck his fancy, and although he did not know the singer— having heard her from the sidewalk as he passed her house—he sent her a request to write the lines out for him. Within a day or two he came into the office, carrying in his hand a delicately perfumed envelope which bore the address, " Mr. Lincoln—

Present," in an unmistakable female hand. In it, written on gilt-edged paper, were the lines of the song. The plaintive strain of the piece and its melancholy sentiment struck a responsive chord in a heart already filled with gloom and sorrow. Though ill-adapted to dissipate one's depression, something about it charmed Lincoln, and he read and re-read it with increasing relish. I had forgotten the circumstance until recently, when, in going over some old papers and letters turned over to me by Mr. Lincoln, I ran across the manuscript, and the incident was brought vividly to my mind. The envelope, still retaining a faint reminder of the perfumed scent given it thirty years before, bore the laconic endorsement, "Poem—I like this," in the handwriting of Mr. Lincoln. Unfortunately no name accompanied the manuscript, and unless the lady on seeing this chooses to make herself known, we shall probably not learn who the singer was. The composition is headed, "The Enquiry." I leave it to my musical friends to render it into song. Following are the lines:

"Tell me, ye winged winds
  That round my pathway roar,
  Do ye not know some spot
  Where mortals weep no more?
  Some lone and pleasant vale
  Some valley in the West,
  Where, free from toil and pain,
  The weary soul may rest?
  The loud wind dwindled to a whisper low,
  And sighed for pity as it answered, No.

"Tell me, thou mighty deep,
  Whose billows round me play,
  Knows't thou some favored spot,
  Some island far away,
  Where weary man may find
  The bliss for which he sighs;
  Where sorrow never lives
  And friendship never dies?
  The loud waves rolling in perpetual flow
  Stopped for awhile and sighed to answer, No.

"And thou, serenest moon,
  That with such holy face
  Dost look upon the Earth
  Asleep in Night's embrace—
  Tell me, in all thy round
  Hast thou not seen some spot
  Where miserable man
  Might find a happier lot?
  Behind a cloud the moon withdrew in woe,
  And a voice sweet but sad responded, No.

"Tell me, my secret soul,
  Oh, tell me, Hope and Faith,
  Is there no resting-place
  From sorrow, sin, and death?
  Is there no happy spot
  Where mortals may be blessed,
  Where grief may find a balm
  And weariness a rest?
  Faith, Hope, and Love, best boon to mortals given,
  Waved their bright wings and whispered, Yes, in Heaven."*

Judge S. H. Treat, recently deceased, thus

---

* Persons familiar with literature will recognize this as a poem written by Charles Mackay, an English writer who represented a London newspaper in the United States during the Rebellion as its war correspondent. It was set to music as a chant, and as such was frequently rendered in public by the famous Hutchinson family of singers. I doubt if Mr. Lincoln ever knew who wrote it.

describes Lincoln's first appearance in the Supreme Court of Illinois. "A case being called for hearing, Mr. Lincoln stated that he appeared for the appellant and was ready to proceed with the argument. He then said: 'This is the first case I have ever had in this court, and I have therefore examined it with great care. As the Court will perceive by looking at the abstract of the record, the only question in the case is one of authority. I have not been able to find any authority to sustain my side of the case, but I have found several cases directly in point on the other side. I will now give these authorities to the court, and then submit the case."

A lawyer in Beardstown relates this: * "Lincoln came into my office one day with the remark: 'I see you've been suing some of my clients, and I've come down to see about it.' He had reference to a suit I had brought to enforce the specific performance of a contract. I explained the case to him, and showed my proofs. He seemed surprised that I should deal so frankly with him, and said he would be as frank with me; that my client was justly entitled to a decree, and he should so represent it to the court; and that it was against his principles to contest a clear matter of right. So my client got a deed for a farm which, had another lawyer been in Mr. Lincoln's place, would have been consumed by the costs of litigation for years, with the result probably the same in the end." A

* J. Henry Shaw, letter, June 13, 1866, MS.

young man once wrote to Lincoln, enquiring for the best mode of obtaining a thorough knowledge of the law. " The mode is very simple," he responded, "though laborious and tedious. It is only to get books and read and study them carefully. Begin with Blackstone's Commentaries, and after reading carefully through, say twice, take up Chitty's Pleadings, Greenleaf's Evidence, and Story's Equity in succession. Work, work, work, is the main thing."*

Lincoln never believed in suing for a fee. If a client would not pay on request he never sought to enforce collection. I remember once a man who had been indicted for forgery or fraud employed us to defend him. The illness of the prosecuting attorney caused some delay in the case, and our client, becoming dissatisfied at our conduct of the case, hired some one else, who superseded us most effectually. The defendant declining to pay us the fee demanded, on the ground that we had not represented him at the trial of the cause, I brought suit against him in Lincoln's absence and obtained judgment for our fee. After Lincoln's return from the circuit the fellow hunted him up and by means of a carefully constructed tale prevailed on him to release the judgment without receiving a cent of pay. The man's unkind treatment of us deserved no such mark of generosity from Lincoln, and yet he could not resist the appeal of any one in

---

* Letter to J. M. Brockman, Sept. 25, 1859, MS.

poverty and want. He could never turn from a woman in tears. It was no surprise to me or any of his intimate friends that so many designing women with the conventional widows' weeds and easy-flowing tears overcame him in Washington. It was difficult for him to detect an impostor, and hence it is not to be marvelled at that he cautioned his secretaries : "Keep them away—I cannot stand it."

On many questions I used to grow somewhat enthusiastic, adopting sometimes a lofty metaphor by way of embellishment. Lincoln once warned me : "Billy, don't shoot too high—aim lower and the common people will understand you. They are the ones you want to reach—at least they are the ones you ought to reach. The educated and refined people will understand you any way. If you aim too high your ideas will go over the heads of the masses, and only hit those who need no hitting." While it is true that from his peculiar construction Lincoln dwelt entirely in the head and in the land of thought, and while he was physically a lazy man, yet he was intellectually energetic ; he was not only energetic, but industrious ; not only industrious, but tireless ; not only tireless, but indefatigable. Therefore if in debate with him a man stood on a questionable foundation he might well watch whereon he stood. Lincoln could look a long distance ahead and calculate the triumph of right. With him justice and truth were paramount. If to him a thing seemed untrue he could not in his nature

23

simulate truth. His retention by a man to defend a lawsuit did not prevent him from throwing it up in its most critical stage if he believed he was espousing an unjust cause. This extreme conscientiousness and disregard of the alleged sacredness of the professional cloak robbed him of much so-called success at the bar. He once wrote to one of our clients: "I do not think there is the least use of doing anything more with your lawsuit. I not only do not think you are sure to gain it, but I do think you are sure to lose it. Therefore the sooner it ends the better."* Messrs. Stuart and Edwards once brought a suit against a client of ours which involved the title to considerable property. At that time we had only two or three terms of court, and the docket was somewhat crowded. The plaintiff's attorneys were pressing us for a trial, and we were equally as anxious to ward it off. What we wanted were time and a continuance to the next term. We dared not make an affidavit for continuance, founded on facts, because no such pertinent and material facts as the law contemplated existed. Our case for the time seemed hopeless. One morning, however, I accidentally overheard a remark from Stuart indicating his fear lest a certain fact should happen to come into our possession. I felt some relief, and at once drew up a fictitious plea, averring as best I could the substance of the doubts I knew existed in Stuart's mind. The

---

* Letter to H. Keeling, Esq., March 3, 1858, MS.

plea was as skilfully drawn as I knew how, and was framed as if we had the evidence to sustain it. The whole thing was a sham, but so constructed as to work the desired continuance, because I knew that Stuart and Edwards believed the facts were as I pleaded them. This was done in the absence and without the knowledge of Lincoln. The plea could not be demurred to, and the opposing counsel dared not take the issue on it. It perplexed them sorely. At length, before further steps were taken, Lincoln came into court. He looked carefully over all the papers in the case, as was his custom, and seeing my ingenious subterfuge, asked, " Is this seventh plea a good one? " Proud of the exhibition of my skill, I answered that it was. " But," he inquired, incredulously, " is it founded on fact? " I was obliged to respond in the negative, at the same time following up my answer with an explanation of what I had overheard Stuart intimate, and of how these alleged facts could be called facts if a certain construction were put upon them. I insisted that our position was justifiable, and that our client must have time or be ruined. I could see at once it failed to strike Lincoln as just right. He scratched his head thoughtfully and asked, " Hadn't we better withdraw that plea? You know it's a sham, and a sham is very often but another name for a lie. Don't let it go on record. The cursed thing may come staring us in the face long after this suit has been forgotten." The plea was withdrawn. By some agency—not our own—the case was continued and our client's interests were saved.

I only relate this incident to illustrate Lincoln's far-seeing capacity; it serves to show how over-cautious he seemed to be with regard to how his record might look in the future. I venture the assertion that he was the only member of the bar in Springfield who would have taken such a conscientious view of the matter.

One phase of Lincoln's character, almost lost sight of in the commonly accepted belief in his humility and kindly feeling under all circumstances, was his righteous indignation when aroused. In such cases he was the most fearless man I ever knew. I remember a murder case in which we appeared for the defence, and during the trial of which the judge—a man of ability far inferior to Lincoln's—kept ruling against us. Finally, a very material question, in fact one around which the entire case seemed to revolve, came up, and again the Court ruled adversely. The prosecution was jubilant, and Lincoln, seeing defeat certain unless he recovered his ground, grew very despondent. The notion crept into his head that the Court's rulings, which were absurd and almost spiteful, were aimed at him, and this angered him beyond reason. He told me of his feelings at dinner, and said: " I have determined to crowd the Court to the wall and regain my position before night." From that time forward it was interesting to watch him. At the reassembling of court he arose to read a few authorities in support of his position. In his comments he kept within the bounds of propriety just far enough to avoid a reprimand for contempt of court.

He characterized the continued rulings against him as not only unjust but foolish ; and, figuratively speaking, he pealed the Court from head to foot. I shall never forget the scene. Lincoln had the crowd, a portion of the bar, and the jury with him. He knew that fact, and it, together with the belief that injustice had been done him, nerved him to a feeling of desperation. He was wrought up to the point of madness. When a man of large heart and head is wrought up and mad, as the old adage runs, " he's mad all over." Lincoln had studied up the points involved, but knowing full well the calibre of the judge, relied mostly on the moral effect of his personal bearing and influence. He was alternately furious and eloquent, pursuing the Court with broad facts and pointed inquiries in marked and rapid succession. I remember he made use of this homely incident in illustration of some point: " In early days a party of men went out hunting for a wild boar. But the game came upon them unawares, and scampering away they all climbed the trees save one, who, seizing the animal by the ears, undertook to hold him, but despairing of success cried out to his companions in the trees, ' For God's sake, boys, come down and help me let go.' " The prosecution endeavored to break him down or even " head him off," but all to no pur- pose. His masterly arraignment of law and facts had so effectually badgered the judge that, strange as it may seem, he pretended to see the error in his former position, and finally reversed his decision in Lincoln's favor. The latter saw his triumph, and surveyed a situation of which he was the master. His client was acquitted, and he had swept the field.

In the case of Parker *vs.* Hoyt, tried in the United States Court in Chicago, Lincoln was one of the counsel for the defendant. The suit was on the merits of an infringement of a patent water wheel. The trial lasted several days and Lincoln manifested great interest in the case. In his earlier days he had run, or aided in running, a saw-mill, and explained in his argument the action of the water on the wheel in a manner so clear and intelligible that the jury were enabled to comprehend the points and line of defence without the least difficulty. It was evident he had carried the jury with him in a most masterly argument, the force of which could not be broken by the reply of the opposing counsel. After the jury retired he became very anxious and uneasy. The jury were in another building, the windows of which opened on the street, and had been out for some two hours. " In passing along the street, one of the jurors on whom we very much relied," relates Lincoln's associate in the case,* " he being a very intelligent man and firm in his convictions, held up to him one finger. Mr. Lincoln became very much excited, fearing it indicated that eleven of the jury were against him. He knew if this man was for him he would never yield his opinion. He added, if he was like a juryman he had in Tazewell county, the defendant was safe. He was there employed, he said, to prosecute a suit for

---

* Grant Goodrich, letter, Nov. 9, 1866, MS.

divorce. His client was a pretty, refined, and interesting little woman, and in court. The defendant, her husband, was a gross, morose, querulous, faultfinding, and uncomfortable man, and entirely unfitted for the husband of such a woman ; but although he was able to prove the use of very offensive and vulgar epithets applied by the husband to his wife, and all sorts of annoyances, yet there were no such acts of personal violence as were required by the statute to justify a divorce. Lincoln did the best he could, and appealed to the jury to have compassion on the woman, and not to bind her to such a man and such a life as awaited her if required to live longer with him. The jury took about the same view of it in their deliberations. They desired to find for his fair client, but could discover no evidence which would really justify a verdict for her. At last they drew up a verdict for the defendant, and all signed but one fellow, who on being approached with the verdict said, coolly : ' Gentlemen, I am going to lie down to sleep, and when you get ready to give a verdict for that little woman, then wake me and not until then ; for before I will give a verdict against her I will lie here till I rot and the pismires carry me out through the key-hole.' ' Now,' observed Lincoln, ' if that juryman will stick like the man in Tazewell county we are safe.' Strange to relate, the jury did come in, and with a verdict for the defendant. Lincoln always regarded this as one of the gratifying triumphs of his professional life."